Journey to the Holocaust
Anti-Semitism, the Bible and History

SUSANNA KOKKONEN

DEDICATED TO HOLOCAUST SURVIVORS

First published in 2014 in Finland, Matka holokaustiin, by Aikamedia.

Second edition published in 2017 in Finland by B&C Handling.

Third edition published in 2019 in Finland by B&C Handling.

Swedish edition published in 2018 in Finland, Vägen till Förintelsen, by B&C Handling.

Second edition published in 2019 in Finland by B&C Handling.

This edition published in 2020.

Journey to the Holocaust, Anti-Semitism, the Bible and History.

2020 Susanna Kokkonen. All rights reserved.

ISBN 9789529431540

1.Anti-Semitism 2.The Bible 3.Holocaust 4. Judaism 5. Christianity

Translation from the original Finnish: Mirkka Jantunen; Susanna Kokkonen
English language editing: Kathryn W. Zachem

All rights reserved.

Table of Contents

Foreword

1. In the Beginning God Created – God's Plan for Mankind   7
2. The History of a People – The Fathers and Mothers of a Nation   23
3. From Galilee to Rome – From a Persecuted Faith to a Religion   43
4. Persecution of the Jews in the Middle Ages – From Crusades to Black Death   65
5. From Enlightenment to World War – Impact of the Enlightenment Era on the Jewish History of Europe   79
6. The Nazi Final Solution – Steps on the Path of Genocide   109
7. Contemporaries of Genocide – How Did People React?   141
8. Of Faith and Knowledge After the Holocaust – Lessons   183
9. Dead Bones Live – The Return   205
10. Holocaust Denial   219
11. Nuclear Weapon Threat   231
12. Jerusalem – The Glory Is Revealed   241

Endnotes

Dear Reader,

We live in a time of upheaval. This is both a result of history and, in part, of the choices the generations before us have made. This book in your hands touches the course of history. It is neither strictly academic nor ideological-religious, but rather includes both Biblical material and pure world history, as the title suggests. My purpose is to point out clearly the connection between the study of history we deem scientific and the eternal revelation of the Bible. God is infinite, almighty, omnipotent and omnipresent, yet He cares enough for man to intervene in the course of history. If this care can be seen in the past, it means that the future is known to Him as well. If the God of history has used individuals to fulfill His plans in the past, so will He do in our time. The significance of one single human life can be immeasurable.

The connection between the Bible and history is seen most brightly and clearly in the people of Israel. From the beginning – ever since God called Abraham – persecutors have followed right at the heels of this people. In a negatively peculiar way, the very survival of anti-Semitism up until our times proves their selection by God. Anti-Semitism is essentially rebellion toward the selection of God, in whatever form it may manifest itself. Despite the bloody persecutions fueled by hatred, the Jewish people still live on. In the history of mankind, many people groups have been born and have died. Many languages have become silent, and many cultures have been destroyed. But one people has, despite persecution, continued its journey through history, following the laws and statutes of God. Even more significant is the fact that these people – the people of Israel – live today in the very land from which they were driven into exile thousands of years ago.

Jerusalem is the eternal city of God's holiness. It is the most disputed city in the world, and in the future, it will hold an even more central position in world events. How nations relate to Jerusalem will be a critical factor in what God decrees for these nations. In the case of Christianity, as the churches distance themselves from the Word of God in general, so will their stance on Israel change to accommodate the common way of thinking. This is exactly what happened in Nazi Germany. So, the question remains: is history repeating itself once more?

In recent years, we have heard news of civil wars, international conflicts, violent storms, earthquakes and famine. We have also seen the growth and manifestation of anti-Semitism in many forms around the world. It is the Middle East that has experienced armed and violent political conflict the most, but in almost the entire Western world, this decade has seen changes on both the political and societal fronts. While some of the changes in the Western world are only rhetorical, this book points out that great changes always begin specifically from speeches. The only way we can stand firm is to stand on the rock set by the Bible. I hope this book will demonstrate clearly how reliable the Word of God is as it unites with history.

On a final note, this book has been translated and edited by a team. Any mistakes are mine and for those I do apologize. Let us hope that the message -even imperfectly expressed- is clear.

With Great Expectation,
Susanna

1 In the Beginning God Created – God's Plan for Mankind

"Then God said, 'Let Us make man in Our image, according to Our likeness…' So God created man in His own image; in the image of God He created him; male and female He created them."[1]

Jerusalem remains behind me as I start my journey to the Dead Sea. All of a sudden, with no warning, the golden city changes into hills, sand and desert. The vast desert space is both comforting and frightening. It is strange to think that the story of mankind started in this harsh environment with its simple rugged life. Abraham, the father of many nations, wandered to the Promised Land through this route. I realize that he lived thousands of years ago, but something happens to me today: as soon as Jerusalem is behind me, I am in Abraham's world. His world is before me, just as he saw it when he was here.

Every so often, I see shepherd boys with their sheep. In the distance, I see those tiny white spots following their shepherd. He does not drive them; rather, the sheep follow him. Suddenly, I realize that everything I learned from the Bible is right here, before my eyes. As the car gets closer to the Dead Sea, I see the high hills and caves of the sand dunes on both sides. Many strongholds and hiding places are available here. I know that God is a fortress to His people; He is a hiding place and a stronghold. King David hid from Saul right here in Ein Gedi. It is impossible to think about another book at this point – only the Bible exists for me. Here the Bible is more real to me than my own life.

I see a gazelle before he sees me. It would be impossible for an artist to *re-create his gracefulness and gentle eyes. In the Bible, the gazelle is an example of speed. "Gazelle" is also one of the names for the Messiah, as in the Song of Solomon, where the beauty of the gazelle is recognized. The Messiah Himself will come leaping upon the mountains like this beautiful, graceful animal. Yet a gazelle is also completely defenseless in the face of its enemies – all it can do is rely on its speed and run away. As if understanding my thoughts from afar, the gazelle runs away. I remember that my feet can become like his feet, fast and sure on this unstable ground of life.*

Time stops here. Only the gazelles, caves and hills are real to me. They are real to me because here in this place, the Bible is so real. I am where the Bible was brought forth, and I am where the Scriptures were found. The Scriptures were found in the place where they were supposed to be, exactly at the right time. The caves of Qumran are a part of this place. The scrolls found in Qumran are a thousand years older than the versions used in the first Bible translations.

I look around me in wonder. This is the place where the Scriptures were found.

Man could never have planned this. In this place, the Word is alive.

The Bible, God's Word to mankind at all times and in all places, contains in itself the history of mankind. While the Bible begins from Creation, the very beginning of man's story, even man's end is visible right at the beginning. For this is the question: if God had not known from the beginning how man would act, would He have called him *Adam*? Like all Hebrew words, the word Adam contains several different meanings. First is the word *adama*, which means "earth" and refers to the way a man was created from the earth. The whole concept refers to man's fragile nature, the way he came and the way he will go. But there is an additional meaning contained in man's name: it comes from the Hebrew word *dam*, which means "blood." According to Leviticus 17, we understand that there is no life without blood. But it goes even deeper than this, for there is also no eternity without the shedding of blood. So here, at the beginning of Genesis, we have man's fate written down: created from the earth with all his weaknesses, but also liberated through the shedding of blood. If we read the Bible in this manner, we realize that in the very first chapters of Scripture, we have everything we need to know.

God had just created man when the first seed of doubt was sown in man's mind. It was doubt that changed the relationship between the Creator and his creation. It could be argued that everything that has happened in history since then started in the Garden of Eden. Man's doubt concerned the only boundary God had set for his autonomy, but on a deeper level, it really concerned the validity of God's word. Had God set boundaries man should follow? Is what God has spoken to be followed to the letter? Is it possible to subtract something from God's word? Can we decide to change what God has said? Finally, is it possible to misunderstand what God has said?

From that first doubt, it was easy to go in the wrong direction. In order to understand history in light of the Bible, it is absolutely vital for us to understand the nature of doubt and our fall into sin. History in general, as well as the persecution of the Jews more specifically, is all related to this. Doubt and the fall into sin are two things that characterize man's relationship to God and His word. When we want to understand World War II and its tragic events, one of the questions we need to ask ourselves concerns the Christian reaction to what happened. What we are really discussing is the authority and reliability of God's word.

The very first question of the Bible was asked by the serpent, and it related to the authority of God's word: *"And he said to the woman, 'Has God indeed said, "You shall not eat of every tree of the garden?"'"*[2] Eve replied by saying that there was one tree from which they were not allowed to eat. That tree was the tree of the knowledge of good and evil: in Hebrew, *Etz Ha-Dat Tov ve Ra*. Many rabbinic authorities have subsequently discussed the nature of this tree and its meaning in human history.

One of the best-known rabbinic authorities was – and still is – the rabbi known simply as *Rashi, Rabbi Shlomo Yitzhaki*, whose writings are studied by every student of Rabbinic commentary. Rashi is generally believed to have descended from King David. He lived during the Crusades, about 1040-1104 AD, and it may well be that this difficult period had an impact on his commentary; he is thought to have died of sorrow in seeing what was happening around him. Rashi naturally commented on the story of man's fall into sin. According to him, the first sin was not the act of eating the forbidden fruit, but rather Eve's reply to the serpent, as she did not accurately repeat what God had said. God said not to eat from the fruit of the tree.[3] In Eve's reply, however, there is a claim that God had forbidden them to touch the fruit.[4]

In Judaism, there is a clear understanding that God's word cannot be changed. Therefore, it follows that evil came into the world because of insufficient respect for God's word. It is true that God had given man free will from the beginning, but according to this interpretation, it was only after the fall that man started choosing evil as a kind of automatic reflex. This tendency is directly related to the authority of God's word: if we have free will, we must have statutes that govern our behavior, and the Bible is such a guideline.

Otherwise, without guidelines, we will not have an accurate way to choose right from wrong.

From doubting God's word, the distance to sinning was very short. Once Eve had started a conversation with the serpent, it was easy for the treacherous serpent to charm and convince Eve that *"the tree was good for food, that it was pleasant to the eyes, and a tree desirable to make one wise…"*[5] It is true that the Bible does not use the word "sin" here, but regardless, many rabbis have thought that it was at this moment that man's tendency to choose evil over good was born. It might be more accurate to speak about man's tendency to go astray, as the Hebrew word *chet*, which is commonly used for sin, refers to being lost or, for instance, shooting a ball just past the goal or missing the mark. In other words, it means losing the absolute best. It is interesting that, following the fall into sin, God did not ask Adam what he had done.

The Bible says: *"Then the Lord God called to Adam and said to him, 'Where are you?'"*[6] The Lord knew where Adam was and what he had done, so why did He ask? The point, I believe, is whether Adam knew where he was – not just in the physical sense, but metaphorically. From this fateful moment, the consequences of their action became real to Adam and Eve.

Since that moment in the Garden of Eden, we all have carried the consequences of their choice. With our free will, we are nevertheless weak and often make wrong choices. Judaism teaches that each person, without exception, sins, but that God is well aware of man's weakness and treats him with mercy and justice. In the encounter between man and God, perfect justice meets perfect grace. Repenting is a choice that is always available, but it must involve action in addition to man's words.

In an article by *Rabbi Yaakov Meir*, the rabbi says that repentance is possible not just because man can change his mind, but because God in His mercy responds to repentance. After the encounter between man and God, it is God who says that man regrets his actions and will not repeat them again.[7] A well-known rabbi from the Middle Ages is the doctor and philosopher *Rabbi Moshe ben Maimon,* also known as *Maimonides*, who lived in Spain and Egypt from 1135 to 1204 AD. Maimonides defined repentance as man rejecting his former behavior and committing himself not to repeat it. Following that decision, God can agree with him; man has repented not only in his own eyes, but also in God's eyes, as expressed by the prophet Isaiah: *"Let the wicked forsake his way, And the unrighteous man his thoughts; Let him return to the Lord, And He will have mercy on him…"*[8] Repentance is complete only at that moment of mutual recognition.

From doubt and the subsequent fall, the way to the first murder was painfully short. It is here that the word "sin" is mentioned for the first time, as God warns man of sin crouching at the door.[9] God was trying to stop *Cain* from committing sin. It is worthwhile to remember that the next time word "sin" is mentioned in the book of Genesis – this time as an active verb – it is again in that same context: *"For I also withheld you from sinning against Me…"*[10] In the case of Cain, God's words were not enough to stop him from committing sin, and the consequences were immediate and terrifying: a murder was committed between brothers. Following this, God again asked a question, but this time it was related to the relationship between men: *"Then the Lord said to Cain, 'Where is Abel your brother?'"*[11] Cain's reply was blood-curdling: *"I do not know. Am I my brother's keeper?"*[12] Had Cain been able to see farther into the future, one wonders if he would have replied this way. How many murderers have spoken these words in a court of law? How have they replied on their death beds when faced with eternity? Why, then, are there always some who would answer this question in a completely different way? After all, God created man in His image – this is the worth that comes to every man from the very act of Creation.

It is important to see the parallels between the events of the first pages of the Bible and modern history. In the 1930s, German churches, individuals and governments had to reply to these very same questions with regard to the increasing persecution and murder of their Jewish brethren. Entire nations now had to decide if they believed in God's word as the ultimate moral authority. If there was indeed such an authority, the nations had to find a moral compass in its light and come to an understanding of the meaning of being "my brother's keeper." In practice, it became clear that centuries of Christian tradition had not taught anything of real meaning in a moment of crisis. Societies, churches and individuals were clueless when faced with evil; some even made their choice to serve the evil. It can easily be seen that entire nations were unknowledgeable about God's word regarding these three questions: Has God really spoken? Where am I? Where is my brother? It could be further argued that just like Cain, churches argued back to God: *Am I my brother's keeper?*

If it is true that our future is clearly revealed to us in the first pages of the Bible, including the way men behave in moments of crisis, this can only mean that the Bible is both infallible and trustworthy, and that the Word is given by God Himself. If it is true that the Bible includes the past, the present and the future, we can clearly conclude that God is a God of history who acts not just outside the reality of men, but also through men. Even, at the moment of creation, God gave us signs of the future, yet in His love and grace, He allowed us to choose our own direction.

This freedom of choice was extended to nations and governments in addition to individuals. Modern history gives us countless examples of how statesmen acted either for or against God and His will. Both in the Bible and in our modern history, the consequences were often dramatic and immediate. This means that the history we study is only partly the history of mankind. The other part is about God using men and their circumstances. I believe that God's presence in a nation has always given it a measure of security. On the other hand, if God is pushed away, chaos and disorder reign in the absence of His hand of protection.

The Bible is also a love story from the very beginning of the book until its last pages. It is God's love letter to the world He created. This is true in a very practical way because the word "love" is first mentioned in the Bible in a remarkably prophetic context. Although human relationships are talked about from the Creation, the word "love," in any way or form, appears for the first time when God tests Abraham: *"Then He said, 'Take now your son, your only son Isaac, whom you love…'"*[13] Love in its first mention is the love between a father and a son in the context of sacrifice. We tend to think about this very strange tale primarily as the willingness of Abraham to sacrifice his son. Isaac, however, was not a small boy, but a thirty-year-old man who also had to be willing to be sacrificed. Therefore, both men were ready to sacrifice and to be sacrificed. These events of the first pages are a key to everything that follows.

The Bible, God's Word, was copied faithfully word to word. In 1947, as if by chance, copies were found by shepherd boys in the caves of Qumran. Subsequently, copies that were a thousand years older than the oldest ones that had been used for Bible translations were discovered in the same area. Qumran was a settlement of the sect of *Essenes,* a kind of Jewish monastic order. Roman troops arrived there in 68 AD and destroyed the settlement. Essenes lived in isolation, using their time for studying and faithfully copying the Bible. It is indeed possible that *John the Baptist* belonged to this group. It is obvious that the Essenes hid their Bible copies in jars of clay from the Roman army; as we know, the Romans were out to put an end to the Judean rebellions. The lone men of Qumran must have known that the enemy troops were getting closer.

Standing in the harsh sunlight of Qumran today, one wonders about the Essenes and their attempts to hide the scrolls. The truth is that they succeeded in hiding this treasure until 1947, thousands of years later, when the shepherd's stone hit the jar of clay. Many books of the Bible have been found in one cave, including a full copy of the book of Isaiah. This is a unique story, and my recommendation to you is that the caves must be seen for yourself.

Essenes of Qumran, thousands of years later, I am here. Please hear me. I want you to know how important your work was to all the world.

God of History

Evidence of God's acting in history is easily found in the Biblical period, as well as in modern times. Examples include significant historic personalities and their actions toward God's people. In the Bible, God influences kings and nations. Their thoughts and actions help God to fulfill His purposes through other persons of influence. One such story is that of *Balak,* Prince of Moab, who lived around 1400 BC. The Prince heard of the Israelites coming through his kingdom on their way from Egypt to the Promised Land. In this situation, he was faced with different options – one of which might have been a war, of course. But Balak did something else altogether: he invited a known seer, a prophet, to come and curse the Israelites.

God intervened in a supernatural manner by using a donkey to speak to the prophet. In the end, from whatever way the prophet looked at the Israelites, he was only able to bless and not curse them.[14] *"How shall I curse whom God has not cursed? And how shall I denounce whom the Lord has not denounced?... Behold, I have received a command to bless; He has blessed, and I cannot reverse it."*[15]

The Prophet *Jeremiah's* name in Hebrew, *Yirmiyahu*, means *God will raise*. The prophet was active between the years 627-586 BC, and he increasingly spoke about *King Nebuchadnezzar,* using the title *"king of Babylon, My servant."*[16] In other words, the king, otherwise known as a cruel and merciless figure, was God's servant in fulfilling His purposes. King Nebuchadnezzar governed from 605-562 BC, and indeed, it was this king who destroyed Jerusalem completely. When he visited Jerusalem for the first time, he merely set the king of Judah, *Jehoiakim*, as a servant king who paid tribute to the king of Babylon. It is therefore interesting that the Hebrew name of this king really has the same meaning as the prophet Jeremiah's name: *God will raise*. The prophet had warned King Jehoiakim repeatedly. It was the secular lifestyle of the king and his court that endangered the kingdom and brought on a catastrophe that could have been avoided. Indeed, Jeremiah's words were fulfilled, for King Nebuchadnezzar returned to put down the Judean rebellion, also taking with him a sizeable group of exiles. Despite this, Nebuchadnezzar was God's servant. Other Jewish sources likewise speak about him in the same manner, as a weapon of God. It is clear, then, that God used the king in a way that was understandable to his contemporaries.

Exactly as Jeremiah had prophesied, the Jewish exiles eventually received permission to return to Judah. The set time was seventy years later, and the purpose was to rebuild the temple. Prophets *Ezekiel* and *Daniel*, who themselves went into exile, understood this. The names of these prophets also describe their specific tasks. The Hebrew name *Yehezkel* means *God strengthens*, and *Daniel* means *God is my judge*. In the book of *Ezra,* we see how God raised up *King Cyrus* to come to the aid of the exiles, and he thus became a builder of the temple as well. Cyrus governed from 559-530 BC. When he won a war against Babylon, the Jewish exiles fell under his authority. This is what Cyrus announced throughout his kingdom: *"All the kingdoms of the earth the Lord God of heaven has given me. And He has commanded me to build Him a house at Jerusalem which is in Judah."*[17] Because of this proclamation by the king, Jewish exiles were allowed to return to Judah. As they left Babylon, they were able to bring with them Jewish ritual objects and gifts from the royal warehouse, which had been taken from the temple when it was destroyed.

Ezra arrived in Jerusalem in 458 BC, and the story of *Nehemiah* is from the same period. In fact, the books of Ezra and Nehemiah were originally one story in the Bible. The books describe the same period, and the names of the two men even mean essentially the same thing: *Ezra* means *aid* and *Nehemiah* means *consolation*. The royal cup-bearer Nehemiah received permission to travel to Judah: *"And the king granted them to me according to the good hand of my God upon me."*[18]

In the book of *Esther*, the name of God is not mentioned, but the whole book is an example of God bringing a person into a position for a purpose. Esther's destiny was to change history by saving her people from complete annihilation. The story begins like a fairytale. A wealthy and powerful king was looking for a wife; of all the women in Shushan, Esther was chosen. And so it was, as if by chance, that the Jewish Esther, an orphan, was chosen from among all the beautiful women to become the queen. She did not tell him of her origins. At the same time, an enemy of the Jews, *Haman*, a powerful official in the king's court, plotted against the Jewish people. Esther, along with her wise uncle, managed to advise the king of Haman's evil plot, and the Jews were allowed to defend themselves. Once a year, the entire Jewish world celebrates Purim, a festival to recall this story and its implications for the future of the Jewish people. The name *Purim* comes from the word *pur*, "lot," in remembrance of how Haman cast lots to destroy the Jews.

What makes this story so interesting are two historic facts.

First of all, the identity of the enemy is very important. Haman was a descendant of *Agag*; he came from an enemy nation, Amalek, that is always mentioned in a negative context in the Bible.[19] As we recall, God had told Israel's first king, *Saul*, to destroy the Amalekites, but Saul lost his kingship because he disobeyed God's command.[20] *Mordechai*, Esther's uncle, was a Benjamite from the house of Saul. In this way, the Bible shows us the consequences of Saul's disobedience. Centuries after Saul's disobedience, Mordechai faced the same enemy, and the Jewish people were at the brink of destruction once more. In the end, however, it was Haman who was hanged on the gallows, which he had built for the Jewish Mordechai.

Let us go forward for a moment to the immediate post-war period in Europe, in 1947, where we meet a man by the name of *Rudolf Hoess*. Hoess was born in Baden-Baden, Germany, in 1900. He eventually joined the SS and became the infamous commandant of the *Auschwitz-Birkenau* concentration camp, where among other cruelties, he built a gallows for the miserable, wretched inmates of the camp. The same Rudolf Hoess, as ordered by the post-war Polish government, was hanged in Auschwitz-Birkenau on April 16, 1947. This was not the first hanging of Nazi war criminals – as a result of the *Nuremberg* war trials in 1946, the court designated twelve Nazi war criminals to be hanged. One escaped and another one committed suicide, but the other ten Nazi leaders were all hanged. It is – mysteriously- as if history repeats itself, for in the case of Esther, too, not only Haman was hanged, but also his ten sons.[21]

Modern history gives countless examples of how God's favor or disappointment reflected on the fates of nations and peoples. It could be argued that the Golden Age of Spain began to wane following its expulsion of the Jews in 1492. Eventually, Spain as a nation state came to complete bankruptcy. This can be contrasted with the Turkish sultan: he received many of those same exiles, and consequently, a Turkish rise to prominence began. In France, the Catholic discrimination of its *Protestant Christians*, the *Huguenots*, culminated in their mass murder in 1572, resulting in a decline in France's flourishing trade, whereas the Netherlands received the Huguenot refugees and started to build a commercial empire. Large parts of Eastern Europe, where Jews were persecuted and murdered for centuries, became Communist territory, a development that some might consider a penalty. The British Mandate closed the gates to Jewish immigrants during World War II, and immediately at the war's end, Great Britain lost its global leadership position.

This is all admittedly a matter of speculation, for history is not exact science, and in many ways, it is hard to analyze causes and actions where human factors are concerned. There is, however, one more case – not from history, but something that happens in front of our own eyes. The United States of America has been a world leader for centuries, militarily, economically and in countless other ways. This nation was born as a safe haven for the persecuted, and it has consistently and constantly stood with Israel in all the international forums. God has blessed the United States as long as the nation has stood for Israel.

God acts in history. This, to me, is a fact, and nowhere is it more evident than in Jewish history. God is not as interested in property as He is in human souls. He does guide people and events; He is interested in the fates of the nations. Perhaps that is why God, in revealing Himself through the Ten Commandments, said, first of all: *"I am the Lord your God, who brought you out of the land of Egypt…"[22]* In other words, God revealed Himself as a God who had already acted for His people. In a painful and horrifying manner, it can be argued that the constant, vociferous and continuous presence of anti-Semitism in Europe, as well as in the Middle East, is proof of Divine choice. This anti-Semitism is global, and today, it is present in the very nations that once fought the Nazis – including the United States of America. Anti-Semitism has changed its garments, but not its content, and it is never far away. The oldest hatred has survived until our day, in all social classes and nations. So, just as God chose the Jewish people for an eternal covenant, so have its persecutors chosen this people as their eternal object of hatred. The Holocaust, like other Jewish persecution, is not only an assault against the Jews, but must also be seen as an assault against the God of the Jews. The intent was to destroy the name of God, since the Jews are evidence of God's existence.

Well-known Holocaust survivors and authors *Elie Wiesel* and *Primo Levi* spoke about this aspect. Elie Wiesel was born in Romania in 1928. He and his family were deported to Auschwitz-Birkenau where his parents and his sister perished; Wiesel himself survived, later receiving the Nobel Peace Prize in recognition of his work as an author, human rights activist and journalist. Primo Levi was a chemist, born in Italy in 1919, who was also taken to Auschwitz-Birkenau. As he returned and started writing, he could not find a publisher for his story. Both authors are considered best-selling eyewitnesses, but at the time, no one was interested in the horrors of the Holocaust.

Both of these survivors considered the Holocaust an attack against God Himself: an assault against the Jews and against God's *Name*.[23] What is the meaning of "God's Name" here? In Judaism, it is absolutely forbidden to take the name of God in vain. Therefore, the word *Ha-Shem*, meaning "the Name," is commonly used to refer to God. In the Holocaust, Jews lost their names as soon as they arrived at a camp, instead becoming mere numbers. Their names were taken from them as a way to insult the God who had revealed His name through this nation.

Naturally, our names are important to God, too, as He declares: *"Fear not, for I have redeemed you; I have called you by your name…"*[24]

In the Bible, God changed a person's name as their destiny became evident. The names of the prophets are an expression of their mission. Therefore, it can be argued that when the Nazis took away the names of their victims, it was not merely an administrative procedure. It was an act of spiritual violence against the expressed will of God.

In order for us to understand and discern the times we are living in, we need to understand the past. Past and future are like two sides of a coin: as I stand in a place connected to history, I am living both the past and the present. I am part of a chain that includes the past, but at the same time, I can see the present and the possibilities of the future.

Even though the future is unknown, some knowledge of it has been revealed through prophecy. From the Biblical period through the Diaspora and on to the modern State of Israel, much prophecy has been fulfilled. Even today, in a mysterious way, the Scriptures become reality in front of our eyes.

That is why we will go on a journey. We start from the beginning and journey toward the future.

2 The History of a People - The Fathers and Mothers of a Nation

"Then they journeyed from Bethel. And when there was but a little distance to go to Ephrath, Rachel labored in childbirth, and she had hard labor. Now it came to pass, when she was in hard labor, that the midwife said to her, 'Do not fear; you will have this son also.' And so it was, as her soul was departing (for she died), that she called his name Ben-Oni; but his father called him Benjamin. So Rachel died and was buried on the way to Ephrath (that is, Bethlehem)."[25]

In December 2012, I am at home in Jerusalem when a strange longing to visit Rachel's tomb rises up in me. I long to go by the Bethlehem road to Rachel's tomb. I am not sure I will succeed, for I know that according to the strict security orders, I cannot just take my car and drive there. But in this case, the thought comes clearly from God, for He prepares a way unexpectedly. Only a few days later, I am in Bethlehem with a group led by an evangelist. The entire day, I have a yearning to go to Rachel's tomb, situated between Bethlehem and Jerusalem. I wait, that I might pray exactly in that place.

It is already dark and late in the evening when our tourist bus veers onto the road leading to the tomb. Young soldiers stop us for a security check, and then it is immediately time to get off the bus. I am overwhelmed by a mysterious sensation. Throughout the ages, Jewish women have come to pray in this exact place. I feel like I am becoming part of a chain to which so many women before me have belonged. Even now, despite being late in the evening, *the graveside is full of praying women. We are surrounded by innumerable stars too many to count, just as the Word says.*

And Naava is here.

Naava Appelbaum was a young Israeli girl who, on the eve of her wedding day in September 2003, went to a cafe with her father. The place was Hillel Cafe on Emek Refaim Street in Jerusalem. Her father had just arrived from the United States and wanted to spend that special day together with his daughter. But a suicide bomber arrived just at that moment, killing both father and daughter in an instant. Nothing could be done – the bomb was lethal. What was supposed to be the happiest day of Naava's life became the day of her death. But Naava lives on forever at Rachel's grave. To what place would Naava's wedding dress belong after her death? Where could an unused bridal dress be taken after her death as a result of an evil act? Here, to Rachel's tomb, nowhere else.

Naava's wedding dress is on the wall behind us. We pray standing before the grave. I think about Rachel. You, Rachel, beloved woman, died on the way. Thousands of years later, I stand before your grave and pray. I am a part of your daughters' chain. Jewish women come here to weep. Just as you cried with the words of the prophet for your children who were driven into exile or killed, your tomb is a home for desperate prayer. It is here where many bring their hopes, disappointments and prayers. I watch them, the women young and old, and begin to weep as well. I pray and weep the same way as so many women before me.

Rachel, oh, how I would like to speak to you! Do not cry. We remember you. All your daughters are here.

The history of the Jewish people began with its patriarchs and matriarchs, the fathers and mothers of the nation. It began with a choice that God Himself made thousands of years ago. If we think about the Bible profoundly, it is a book with two major themes: *choices* and *covenants*. God called a man named *Abram* whose special trait was his faith. About four thousand years ago, Abram left his own land and family to wander to an unknown land, which God would show him. Abram, later *Abraham*, began his journey from the present Iraqi region toward the area of present-day Israel. He lived in the city of *Ur* on the west bank of the *River Euphrates* in what is now southern Iraq. This is interesting, for the ruins of the city of Ur today are on the opposite side of the river from the city of *Nasiriyah,* where the American and British troops defeated Saddam Hussein in 2003. That is where Abram began his journey. God changed his destiny, and for that reason He gave Abram, *the honored father,* the new name of Abraham, *the father of nations*. Abraham's wife *Sarai* became *Sarah*, which means *princess*. The people who came forth from this man and his wife are the people God calls His wife. He swore an oath to His wife, which has never been revoked. *"I will make you a great nation; I will bless you and make your name great; and you shall be a blessing. I will bless those who bless you, and I will curse him who curses you; and in you all the families of the earth shall be blessed."*[26] This is how the descendants of Abraham became the very instrument with which God can bring mankind to Himself. But this would not have happened, had one man not been obedient. He left everything he was familiar with and journeyed into an unknown destiny.

In Abraham's story, there are prophetic details that I believe have to do with what the Jewish people experience today, thousands of years later. One of these is a battle that was fought when the allied enemy kings attacked the kings of *Sodom* and *Gomorrah*. The story began earlier when *Lot*, Abraham's nephew, followed Abraham from their country of origin. After arriving in the land of Canaan, Lot chose the better area for himself. And so it happened that after this first wrong choice, he chose to live in sinful Sodom, which in the end was destroyed. Our story refers to an incident where the kings' alliance attacked the two cities, Sodom and Gomorrah, and captured Lot as a prisoner of war as well. Hearing that Lot had been captured, Abraham went to defend his nephew and succeeded in reclaiming all the possessions and hostages the two cities had lost. The king of Sodom would have wanted to compensate Abraham for his help, but Abraham, the faithful servant of God, refused everything. At the same time, a strange and mysterious meeting took place between Abraham and *Melchizedek,* the king of *Salem*. The name unites two Hebrew words, *melech* and *tzedek*, which mean *king* and *righteousness*. The word "Salem," meaning Jerusalem, comes, of course, from the word *shalom*, meaning "peace," but it also means *perfection* and *wholeness*. Abraham paid his tithes to this King of Righteousness, called also the Priest of the Most High God, and the king in turn blessed Abraham.[27] We read of two kings, very different from one another, to whom Abraham related in very different ways. But who was this mysterious Melchizedek? The Psalmist stated that the Messiah would be *"a priest forever according to the order of Melchizedek."*[28] During Abraham's encounter with Melchizedek, bread and wine were blessed. This act of *kidush,* sanctification, took place in Salem. Thus, the city of Jerusalem is mentioned in the Bible for the first time in the context of holiness.

The Lord counted it as righteousness to Abraham that he believed. Once more God appeared to Abraham: when Abraham started to prepare an offering to the Lord, a peculiar sight appeared before him. *"And when the vultures came down on the carcasses, Abram drove them away. Now when the sun was going down, a deep sleep fell upon Abram; and behold, horror and great darkness fell upon him."*[29] Many rabbis have said that the vultures symbolize nations, which are described as vultures in various prophecies. These nations now came to take away Abraham's offering even before the Covenant was consummated, which is prophetic of the ages to come. As Abraham was sleeping, God passed through the pieces for the offering. *"And it came to pass, when the sun went down and it was dark, that behold, there appeared a smoking oven and a burning torch that passed between those pieces."*[30] God established the Covenant and continues to uphold it even if the Jewish people are sleeping.

Abraham saw into the future. When his wife Sarah died, Abraham wanted to bury her in *Hebron*, where they were staying. His purpose was to buy the cave of *Machpelah*. The Hittites, who lived in Hebron, offered the burial place to Abraham for free, but he refused. Abraham instead paid *Ephron* the Hittite for the cave, and in this way, the cave became Abraham's heritage tomb.[31] Thus, Hebron is the first area that the Jews purchased in the land of Israel. In addition, it was a place where Abraham had earlier built an altar to the Lord[32] and where the Lord's messengers told him that he would eventually have heirs.[33] How far-sighted Abraham was in paying for the tomb, because today, this very city of the forefathers and foremothers is the most disputed area in the Middle East. In some sense, it might be even more disputed than Jerusalem, and it is quite interesting that *King David* ruled in Hebron for seven and a half years before ruling in Jerusalem. The word *Machpelah* in Hebrew refers to *pairs* or *doubles*; therefore, the meaning of the word is fulfilled when both the patriarchs and matriarchs are buried there in pairs: Abraham and Sarah; *Isaac* and *Rebecca* (1900 BC) and *Jacob* and *Leah* (1800 BC). The word "Hebron" has many meanings in Hebrew: its basic meaning is *unity* or *unification*, and it also means *friend*. This is extraordinary because Abraham, who established the presence of the Jews in Hebron exactly, was the only man in the Bible God called His friend.[34] The entire history of the people of Israel began from Hebron "as a place," the same way it began with Abraham "as a man."

After Abraham's death, God appeared again and confirmed His eternal covenant with both Isaac and Jacob. One night, He appeared to Isaac in Bersheba: *"And the Lord appeared to him the same night and said, 'I am the God of your father Abraham; do not fear, for I am with you. I will bless you and multiply your descendants for My servant Abraham's sake.' So he built an altar there..."*[35] God appeared also to Isaac's son Jacob between Bersheba and Harran, in a dream in which Jacob saw a ladder reaching up to heaven: *"And behold, the Lord stood above it and said: 'I am the Lord God of Abraham your father and the God of Isaac; the land on which you lie I will give to you and your descendants... and in you and in your seed all the families of the earth shall be blessed."*[36] Jacob's story is peculiar. He deceived and was himself deceived. His name means *he grasps the heel* but also *he deceives*. Later God gave him a new name, *Israel*, which means *the one who struggled with God* and *Prince of God*. Even though Jacob had been given a new name, the God of the Bible still refers to Himself as the God of Jacob, as a reminder that God was Jacob's God even when he did wrong.

Jacob's story, with all its lies and struggles, materializes in his son *Joseph*. One of the strangest events in Jacob's life is the fate of his young son

Joseph, who was sold as a slave to Egyptians by his envious brothers. This very event would later be of great significance in the forming of the Jewish identity. About 1700 BC in the land of Canaan and the surrounding communities, there was a great famine. Jacob had to send his sons to Egypt, where grain was available. At this point, Jacob's other sons did not know the fate of their brother Joseph, who had become a mighty man and ruler in Egypt. Joseph immediately recognized his brothers even though they did not recognize him. With Joseph's forgiveness of his brothers, the entire household of Jacob moved to Egypt.[37] Joseph said to his brothers: *"God sent me before you to preserve life."*[38] Joseph's name literally means *addition*, which is very symbolic, since God added spiritual and material possessions to Joseph. In Judaism, Joseph is seen as a type of Messiah.

Interestingly, *Angelo Roncalli*, a Catholic priest who helped the Jews during World War II, took this verse by Joseph and made it his own. He later became *Pope John XXIII,* whose term from 1958 to 1963 was very significant as the turmoil of the war was in fresh memory. When meeting a Jewish delegation for the first time as Pope, Roncalli, stepping into the room, said to their astonishment: *"I am Joseph, your brother."* In the year 2000, this encounter was turned into a movie named after the same verse.

After Joseph's death, it is possible that it was Pharaoh *Ramses II* who forced the Jews into slave labor. He ruled from 1290-1224 BC[39] and was known for his building projects. The Bible, though it does not mention the Pharaoh's name, says that the enslaved Jews built a city called Rameses in Egypt. Jews were treated as slave labor, and in their agony, they cried out to God. The Biblical description of their slavery does not differ from descriptions of forced labor by slaves or prisoners of other periods. It is extremely interesting that at the very time that their conditions of slavery worsened, God had already chosen a savior for the people, a savior who would lead them back home. This was also the moment of desperation. God heard their cry and remembered His covenant with His people. *"So God heard their groaning, and God remembered His covenant with Abraham, with Isaac, and with Jacob. And God looked upon the children of Israel, and God acknowledged them."*[40] Moses was born in about 1300 BC, around 350 years after Jacob arrived in Egypt with his family. Moses first became the Prince of Egypt and later God's chosen vessel to lead the Jewish people out of slavery.

The story of slavery eventually turned into a journey of freedom. Like so many stories, this one began with one person's obedience. When Moses was born, Pharaoh had just decreed that all Jewish baby boys were to be killed. According to the decree, even Moses should have died, but his mother hid him in a reed basket and sent it floating on the River Nile. The story culminated when the basket suddenly floated before Pharaoh's daughter. *"Then the daughter of Pharaoh came down to bathe at the river. And her maidens walked along the riverside; and when she saw the ark among the reeds, she sent her maid to get it. And when she opened it, she saw the child, and behold, the baby wept. So she had compassion on him, and said, 'This is one of the Hebrews' children.'"*[41] Because of the brave act by Pharaoh's daughter, this good deed by one woman brought freedom to the Jewish people. There might not have been any other person in all of Egypt that could have defied Pharaoh's order, but God had seen this in advance too.

Why did the liberator of the Jewish people need to learn Egyptian wisdom? This is an interesting aspect. But God prepared Moses for his task in various ways, and this preparation and the intervention of Pharaoh's daughter are remembered in the book of Acts, where *Stephen* mentions them in his plea to the *Sanhendrin*.[42] Interesting, the former Israeli Chief Rabbi

Israel Meir Lau survived the Holocaust as a child, which was extremely rare. He survived because of the help of a Russian prisoner of war at the concentration camp. On Holocaust Remembrance Day (*Yom HaShoah*) in 2009, this esteemed rabbi spoke of Pharaoh's daughter as the first *Righteous Among the Nations* in history, a title *Yad Vashem* awards to non-Jews who took great risks to save Jews during the Holocaust.

During the Jewish *Pesach* or Passover, celebrated in remembrance of the exile from Egypt, God's four promises as told in the Bible are remembered.[43] When the people left Egypt, God fulfilled His promises: to take His people out of Egypt's suffering, to save them from slavery, to deliver them and to be their God. At the pinnacle of their suffering, God had already prepared Moses as their deliverer. The people had almost lost their faith at a time when deliverance was already so close. Freedom came through God's miracles, and through His servant Moses, who led the Jewish people through the wilderness to the Promised Land. Their journey took place in about 1280-1260 BC. During this journey, they went from being a people to becoming a nation, marked by slavery but also by the wilderness journey in which they experienced God's guidance and provision. When God gave His people the Torah at Mount Sinai, the people became a nation with a King and a Law: the Lord Himself is the King of Israel, and the Lord Himself gave them the Law. These laws given by God have been a unifying factor among the Jewish people as well as the foundation for the Western judicial system. As long as God's law is the foundation of a society, it will have order and stability, but if it is removed, the consequences will be terrifying and unpredictable.

At the end of the wilderness journey, *Jericho* was finally conquered when its walls came down. To Christians everywhere, the conquest of Jericho exemplifies the courage and faith of *Joshua* and *Caleb*. Forty years earlier, as the people were first approaching the Promised Land, God had advised Moses to send twelve spies, one representing each of the twelve tribes, to explore the land. The spies returned with a bad report: surely, the land was fertile and beautiful, but the Israelites would never be able to conquer it. Only Joshua and Caleb believed that it could be done; Caleb said: *"Let us go up at once and take possession, for we are well able to overcome it."*[44] Because of their unbelief, the people did not enter the Promised Land at that time. Instead, the journey continued in vain for forty years until the conquering of Jericho around 1240-1220 BC. The Jewish nation then settled in various parts of the land according to the borders of their tribes. Out of the generation that left from Egypt, only the faithful and brave Caleb and Joshua were among those who entered the Promised Land. God said of His servant: *"But My servant Caleb, because he has a different spirit in him and has followed Me fully, I will bring into the land where he went, and his descendants shall inherit it."*[45]

But why was Jericho the first city the Israelites conquered? It was because Jericho was located about ten kilometers from the Jordan River, along an established route, so conquering the city meant controlling the entrance to the entire nation. This is the strategic explanation; however, it is also interesting that Jericho was, and still remains, the oldest discovered settlement on the entire planet. It existed about 7000 years before Joshua. It is as if God wanted to show that all land belongs to Him. Even the world's oldest human settlement belongs under His power. Joshua's Hebrew name, *Yehoshua*, means *God is salvation*. Joshua honored God's principle of ownership by not taking anything from the conquered Jericho. Therefore, archaeologists have found even grain in the ruins of Jericho, which is usually not found in conquered cities that were already looted. As proof of the Bible's reliability, another city conquered by Joshua, *Tel Hazor*, was recently discovered.[46]

Kingdom in the Promised Land

"It happened after this that David inquired of the Lord, saying: 'Shall I go up to any of the cities of Judah?' And the Lord said to him, 'Go up.' David said, 'Where shall I go up?' And He said, 'To Hebron.' ...David was thirty years old when he began to reign, and he reigned forty years. In Hebron he reigned over Judah seven years and six months, and in Jerusalem he reigned thirty-three years over all Israel and Judah. And the king and his men went to Jerusalem against the Jebusites, the inhabitants of the land... Nevertheless David took the stronghold of Zion (that is, the City of David)...So David went on and became great, and the Lord God of hosts was with him."[47]

Even though I lived in Jerusalem for years, I had never visited the City of David. You might ask, is Jerusalem not the City of David as a whole? Yes it is. Even the name "Jerusalem" contains deeper meanings, because "Yerushalayim" does not only mean "the city of peace." It also means "perfect and whole," and even "heritage" or "legacy," since Jerusalem is God's perfect heritage and also the legacy left by David. The original settlement of David is now an archaeological excavation revealing the lives he and the kings after him led. I send all the visitors there, yet I do not know what I am missing myself.

In January 2013, a rabbi asks me to meet some visiting pastors in the City of David. I have a feeling of anticipation. On a beautiful winter morning as the sun is shining, we step into the city of a harpist, a warrior and a poet. Wondrous tunes seem to play in the air as we begin our tour. Most likely not coming from a radio, these tunes penetrate our heart because we know the significance of this place. It is as if we feel a presence: the presence of a king *who asked God where to go and what to do, and who always received an answer. We see ruins of palaces, residences, engravings of names and royal seals. We are in the past.*

I think of King David.

I am at the place where you, the king, lived. My brother David, what made you a warrior after God's heart? Was it your humility? You always repented. My brother David, do you know that we are here? Do you know how God speaks to us through you, thousands of years after your death? My brother David, it has been 3000 years since you came here, but your city is still proof that your God exists.

My brother David, do you know that your city is the city of the Great King?

Just as the Bible describes, the tribes in the land of Israel became a kingdom in about 1040 BC. More than a century before, in about 1200-1020 BC, *Naomi, Boaz* and *Ruth* encountered one another in the town of Bethlehem. The Jewish Naomi and her family had fled from the famine to neighboring Moab, but after losing her family, Naomi returned to Bethlehem with only her daughter-in-law, the loyal Moabite Ruth. Ruth's exemplary loyalty was rewarded. After marrying Boaz, she entered into the lineage of King David and therefore the lineage of the Messiah Himself. The book of Ruth uses the words *redeemer* and *redemption* more than any other book of the Bible. Bethlehem, the city from where the Messiah was to come, staged the events preceding His coming. The vocabulary of the book of Ruth refers to a distant future. For example, when the local women blessed Ruth, they wished for her to be *"like Rachel and Leah."*[48] Why them and not Sarah and Rebekah, who preceded Rachel and Leah as mothers? The explanation has to do with Ruth's special role in the history of salvation and how Judaism interprets the coming of the Messiah. Rachel was the mother of Joseph, and in Judaism, Joseph is an example of the Messiah because of his righteous nature. Leah, in turn, was the mother of Judah, and the Messiah had to come from the tribe of Judah, *the Lion of Judah*. Ruth's contemporaries did not live to see what we now know: King David, from whose family and house the Messiah would be born, was descended from Ruth.

The books of Joshua and Judges mention *Shiloh*, which was the religious capital of the Israelites three hundred years before Jerusalem. It was a place where they gathered to celebrate the Biblical feasts. The Hebrew word *Shiloh* is one of the names of the Messiah, and therefore it is a prophetic name. It comes from the word *shalva*, meaning *peace*. The Messiah will be the Prince of Peace. The Prophet *Samuel*, whose name means *God hears* (for it was difficult for his mother to become pregnant, so God heard her prayers and gave her Samuel), was born in about 1110 BC and grew up in the Tabernacle of Shiloh in the care of the high priest *Eli*.

The name of King David is also prophetic, for the Hebrew *David* means *beloved*. David ruled from about 1010 to 970 BC. He was the most significant ruler in the history of the people of Israel, for he was able to unite the tribes into a kingdom governing a vast area from Syria to Egypt and all the way into Jordan. Archaeological proof of the kingdom and government of David began to be found in the 1990s in the areas of modern Israel and Jordan. His name has been found etched on rocks, where he is referred to as a king and the head of a family dynasty. In 1993, archaeologists made a discovery in the ruins of

Dan in Northern Israel: a victory statue engraved about a century after David's death. Similar engravings were found in Moab (in what is now Jordan), and a third one was found in the hieroglyphs of Egypt.[49]

The City of David in Jerusalem dates to the times of Abraham, who was blessed by Melchizedek, the king of Salem. The city is located south of the Temple Mount, right outside the walls of the Old City in current Jerusalem. In the Bible, the word Zion (*Tzion* in Hebrew) is a synonym for Jerusalem, even though it is later used to refer to the entire land of Israel. Tzion means *marking/sign,* so in this case, Jerusalem was marked by God to be a place for Himself. Jerusalem is also called *Ariel* in the Bible, meaning *lion*, which in turn refers to *the Messiah*, who is *the Lion of Judah.* Most likely, one very important practical issue for David was the location of a water supply that could be secured during enemy attack. The City of David is an unbelievable experience, as the archaeological discoveries speak of the history and reality of the Bible. The spiritual meaning of the place is apparent too, for we are where everything began. On *Mount Moriah*, Abraham was ready to sacrifice his only son, and centuries later, Jesus died nearby. David lived all his life near God, and out of all the cities, he came to Jerusalem. Jerusalem was in God's plans from the beginning of time. Even when the nation was split in two, Jerusalem remained the capital of Judah, and we know that *"David rested with his fathers and was buried in the City of David."*[50]

David was succeeded by his son *Solomon* in 970 BC, who reigned for the next forty years. The Bible tells us that there was peace during Solomon's time, which is quite fitting, since his name, *Shlomo*, comes from the word *shalom,* meaning peace. After Solomon, the northern tribes detached from the kingdom, splitting the nation into two kingdoms: Israel in the north and Judah in the south, made up of two tribes, Judah and Benjamin. (These names have a great significance: *Judah* means *praise*, and *Benyamin* means *the son of my right hand*, therefore *the son of God's right hand*.) The Bible tells in detail the history of these two kingdoms. They were ruled by kings, some of whom are referred to as those who *"did what was right in the eyes of the Lord,"*[51] whereas others *"did evil in the eyes of the Lord."*[52] Despite this very sad story, God showed His faithfulness to His covenants. Even though He saw all the atrocities being done in the land, He was very patient. Very often, the Bible explains that the reason for His patience had to do with the previous promises God had given to David: *"Nevertheless for David's sake the Lord his God gave him a lamp in Jerusalem... because David did what was right in the eyes of the Lord..."*[53]

However, there were serious consequences for breaking the statutes given by God. In His mercy, God sent prophets to warn the kings of Israel and Judah about the very serious results their lifestyles would bring about, consequences that would touch not only the kings but also their subjects. The name of the Prophet *Elijah* means *my God is the Lord.* Elijah operated in proximity to the corrupt King *Ahab* and Queen *Jezebel*, who ruled in about 875-854 BC. He warned them that not a drop of water would fall because of their sins. He even had to call down fire from heaven to destroy the prophets of *Baal,* a Canaanite idol, in order to receive rain for the land. After the entire incident, he still had to return to the palace with his warnings.[54] Because these warnings were not taken seriously enough, the Bible tells us: *"In those days the Lord began to cut off parts of Israel; and Hazael conquered them in all the territory of Israel."*[55]

The prophets understood with clarity that God used the armies of foreign nations to back up their words. Already around 722 BC, Assyrians destroyed Israel, and the ten tribes of Israel disappeared into the nations.[56]

Jeremiah was especially outspoken, speaking the word of the Lord that had come to him: *"...if that nation against whom I have spoken turns from its evil, I will relent of the disaster that I thought to bring upon it."*[57] The prophets never came to proclaim only an upcoming judgment but always brought a message from God of an opportunity to repent. They asked the people to abandon their idols, dispense justice and help the poor. They referred to a distant future and the last days that were to take place centuries later. Dispersion occurred because the message of the prophets was not heeded. Many of the prophets operated during the years 700-400 BC; the siege of Jerusalem occurred in about 710 BC and the first deportations about 600 BC. Even today, there is a concept in Judaism called *churban*, which means *destruction* or *catastrophe*. The destruction of the First Temple was *the first churban*.

As evidence that God's covenant with His people was always valid, an entirely new period began when the Jews returned from exile, just as the prophecies stated: *"In the first year of Darius the son of Ahasuerus ... in the first year of his reign I, Daniel, understood by the books the number of the years specified by the word of the Lord through Jeremiah the prophet, that He would accomplish seventy years in the desolations of Jerusalem."*[58] Cyrus, the next king of Persia, then proclaimed: *"Who is among you of all His people? May his God be with him, and let him go up to Jerusalem which is in Judah, and build the house of the Lord God of Israel (He is God), which is in Jerusalem."*[59] The rebuilding of the temple is described in detail in the books of Ezra and Nehemiah. It happened under threats of their enemies, so some stood watch on the walls while others built. The modern state of Israel was built exactly in the same manner Nehemiah described: *"So it was, from that time on, that half of my servants worked at construction, while the other half held the spears, the shields, the bows, and wore armor; and the leaders were behind all the house of Judah. Those who built on the wall, and those who carried burdens, loaded themselves so that with one hand they worked at construction, and with the other held a weapon."*[60] Despite these dangerous conditions, reconstruction was completed in about 515 BC. The Jewish people once again lived in their own land.

A new empire then arose again – this time, Greece. *Alexander the Great* spread the Greek language and culture all around the Middle East in the fourth century BC. Along with the Greek culture, he spread its religious belief in multiple deities, which conflicted with the doctrine of Judaism, with the belief in one God who did not allow idol worship. The situation became extremely tense in 167 BC when the Temple of Jerusalem was disgraced. Alexander the Great had died, leaving no clear heir, as a result of which his kingdom was divided into three areas. One of them was the area of the Seleucids.[61] They were the conquerors of the time who came from the nations of Greek origin. Many have believed that the Seleucid ruler *Antiochus Epiphanes* (ca. 215-164 BC), who desecrated the Temple, was the antichrist to whom Daniel referred in his prophecy.[62] He appealed to the Greek-minded Jews who no longer wanted to follow the God-given laws. So, in many ways, he acted just as the prophet had predicted. It is apparent, however, that Daniel saw the end of time, and just as *John* stated: *"...even now many antichrists have come, by which we know that it is the last hour."*[63] In a sense, Antiochus was a representative of the "upcoming antichrists" who have contempt for Judaism's one God. He succeeded in seducing the Greek-minded Jews but failed to persuade all Jews to reject their faith. Desecration of the Temple was the last straw to the faithful Jews, followed by a rebellion led by *Judas Maccabeus* in about 167-160 BC. The rebellion is thought to have been as much a war between secularized Jews and their religion-abiding brothers as a war against foreign rulers. In any case, its end result was the re-dedication of the Temple of Jerusalem in 165 BC. The Jews were now independent in their own land.

However, a new world ruler was ready to take the stage; therefore, it was only a matter of time before independence would end. Rome was established in a strategically significant place along the Tiber River in about 750 BC. In the century before Jesus was born, Rome already governed an ever-growing empire. Even though the Maccabees ruled independently in Jerusalem after defeating Antiochus Epiphanes, disputes and quarrels soon began to arise among them. It was actually because of these internal wars that *Pompey (the Great)* conquered Jerusalem in 63 BC. Once again, the Jews lived under foreign rule, and it was in this situation that Jesus was born in 6 BC, during the time of *Emperor Augustus,* who ruled in about 27 BC – 14 AD.

"And a certain man lame from his mother's womb ... seeing Peter and John about to go into the temple, asked for alms. And fixing his eyes on him, with John, Peter said, 'Look at us.' So he gave them his attention, expecting to receive something from them. Then Peter said, 'Silver and gold I do not have, but what I do have I give you: In the name of Jesus Christ of Nazareth, rise up and walk.'"[64]

My sister from Finland comes to visit me in Israel in the summer of 2011. Although I have lived in the country for years, I have not felt such intense presence of God in a long time. Not even at the holy sites. We drive around Lake Gennesaret. I am constantly on the verge of tears. I feel the *closeness of Jesus everywhere. In the Galilee everything reminds of Jesus and the disciples.*

A few weeks earlier God said clearly that I must be baptized in the Jordan River. I, who have always chuckled at this practice, decided to obey. The miracle of all miracles! I have no idea who would baptize me, but God sends His servant Carrie from the United States for the task. It is absolutely silent at the waterside in the morning, with no one else on the beach. I cry when Carrie immerses me in the water, in the manner of the Jewish mikveh bath. Was this how John the Baptist did it, too?

I try to pull myself together as we walk the short distance from Capernaum, the city of Jesus, to the other side of the road.

We come to the place where it is believed Jesus met his disciples for the first time after his death and resurrection. It was morning then, and the disciples had been fishing all night, in vain. Peter, after having denied Jesus, had returned to his old profession as a fisherman. How appropriate was that! Peter thought he had to return to his old way of life. He did not yet know that the Lord was waiting for them on the other shore. Peter's life was about to change forever, which in turn would change the entire world.

There are heart-shaped stones on the beach. They remind me of love and of the grace that changed Peter. I cry and cannot believe such great love is true. It is so true that Peter, who had denied Jesus, soon walked in Jerusalem, and people hoped his shadow would fall on them so they would be healed.

The heart-shaped stones really exist.

Later, in the spring of 2013, I return to Galilee. I want to see the Jesus boat whose ancient nails bear witness that it comes from Jesus' time. Was this the very boat that carried the disciples and Jesus? How amazing that it has stood the test of time. What a wonderful thought that a boat from Jesus' time was found. I think about the fishermen Jesus chose to share his life with. How these unlearned men became men of God. How they spread the Message throughout the world.

I feel such a deep connection that it brings tears to my eyes. I am here, and here is where they were.

3 From Galilee to Rome – From a Persecuted Faith to a Religion

"All the saints greet you, but especially those who are of Caesar's household."[65]

Rome is an eternal city, but it can never be Jerusalem. How often have I wandered in Rome, surrounded by its magnificent art, style and immense history. It is a strange feeling to traverse the streets of Rome, in the middle of evidence from the past. It is almost like walking through a great museum or an archaeological excavation. I love the enchantment of Rome, yet it does not represent the heavenly.

Rome tells us about the power of earthly rulers. The Arch of Titus recounts a destroyed Jewish temple, but in reality, the Jews have returned to their land of origin, whereas the Rome of Titus no longer exists. Rome and its ruins tell of tyranny, flaring fires, underground tombs and persecuted Christians. Rome tells of an empire destroyed by its own vice. Nations flooded over its inertia. Rome is not an eternal city but a human work destroyed by its own impossibility. Nevertheless, there are reminders of the Bible. I walk on Via Appia, the very road that Paul took to Rome. The road still exists.

I am moved the most by a small road on the hills of Rome. There is a spot called Quo Vadis, which is a question: "Where are you going?" It is told that during the time of persecution, Christians were burned as torches, and on one of the nights of the burning torches, Peter turned around and started walking away from Rome, afraid, with his back toward the flames. It is told that at that exact moment, Jesus was walking toward Rome and happened to meet Peter on the way. "Quo Vadis Domine?" "Where are you going, Lord?" asked Peter after recognizing Jesus. "I will go to Rome to be crucified again for you." After hearing Jesus' answer, Peter turned around and went back. He was crucified on a cross upside-down, because he did not see himself worthy of being crucified in the same manner as Jesus.

It is a hot, sunny Roman day, but the spirit of death hovers over the Colosseum, which is always in the shadows. Blood has stained this place. Away from this place of terrors! Away from the shadows! I love you, beautiful Rome, but at the same time, you make me mourn. In a strange, terrifying way, Rome has become a part of the Bible.

In about 66 AD, Jews succeeded in conquering Jerusalem back from Rome. But by 70 AD, the Romans had regained control over it, and this time, they destroyed the Second Temple. All the treasures of the temple were taken away, and they have not yet been found. The fortification of *Masada,* high above the Dead Sea, was the last fort the Jewish fighters were able to hold, thanks to its difficult location – a fact every visitor to Masada encounters. The Romans could not allow the rebels to win, so they conquered the fort. After climbing to the top of the mountain, they were greeted by a dreadful silence: all they found were the dead bodies of close to a thousand people. The people chose freedom rather than surrendering to the Romans. All of this was a part of the destruction of the Second Temple, *the second churban* or destruction of Judaism. After this, Judaism had to change. Since there was no temple, sacrifices could not be made. According to the Talmud, they were now replaced by the sacrifice of the heart, through prayer.[66] Between 132and 135 AD, *Simon Bar Kochba* rebelled against the Romans. But in the year 135 AD, the Romans made Jerusalem a proper Roman city and renamed Judea

Palestine. Let us be reminded that God has never called the Land by any name other than Israel and Judea. Quite fed up with the Israelites' stubborn resistance, the Romans deliberately named the area after the Jews' historic enemy, the Philistines.

The Jewish *Diaspora*, which means *dispersion*, began when they were forcibly scattered all around the world. Most were taken as slaves to Rome and the surrounding areas, which might make Rome the oldest remaining Jewish community in Europe. This is really true: Roman Jews are still in Rome, but the Romans have perished. We know from history that during similar dispersions, the people have usually assimilated into surrounding nations in such a way that they no longer exist as a distinct people. But this has never happened to the Jews, despite continuous attempts to obliterate them. The Romans were long ago swept away into the swirls of migrations and their own depravity, but even persecutions could not annihilate a people whose Covenant with God was still valid.

Since that time, Jewish history has been preserved for us, along with the Bible, in such sources as the *Talmud* and *Midrash.* The word "Talmud" comes from Hebrew and means *learning*. The Talmud is a rabbinic commentary on various aspects and applications of Jewish law to different situations. It includes the *Mishna*, a collection from the second century AD, which in turn incorporates the oral Torah. The Talmud also includes *Gemara*, which comes from the fifth century and is connected to the Mishna and the Bible. The word "Midrash" comes from Hebrew, meaning searching or examining, and it contains more detailed interpretations of selected Bible stories.

One thing we need to make immediately clear is that as Christianity developed, it became the leading actor in the drama. After Jesus and the original apostles died, one of the main intents of the church seems to have been the abandonment of its Jewish roots. If we were to isolate only one historical development that had the most profound effect on the hatred and persecution of Jews, above all else, we would have to choose Christianity. This protagonist hated the Jews, while at the same time professing to believe in the Jewish God. That mighty testimony, which began as a proclamation about sin, repentance and forgiveness, a message to be taken to all the world, turned into a doctrine about religion. Walking through the Colosseum, one cannot help but think about martyrdom. The blood of martyrs in the Roman arena was not shed because of a new religion. Even the very thought of this is horrifying. Their sacrifice was too great to birth dead cathedrals and new doctrines. And yet, this is exactly what happened: very soon, Christianity was unrecognizable if viewed in light of the book of Acts. Christianity grew during persecution and spread in different directions throughout the world. Yet even so, the persecuted turned into persecutors, much too soon.

The persecution of Christians in Rome took place during the reign of different rulers, and the severity of persecution depended upon the ruler. The worship of Emperor Augustus as a deity began only after his death, but it then became a tradition, and, as far as we know, all emperors succeeding him were worshipped. Christians were not then -really- persecuted because of whom they believed in, but because of whom they did not agree to worship. This new monotheistic religion, which shunned compromise, did not fit with the tradition of emperor worship and a polytheistic society. As examples, we can mention persecutions of Christians at the following times under multiple emperors: in 64, *Nero*; 113, *Trajan*; 160-170, *Marcus Aurelius*; 202-203, *Septimius Severus*; 235-236, *Maximianus*; 250-251, *Decius;* 253-260, *Valerian*; 274-287, *Aurelian*; 303-312, *Diocletian.*[67] Despite persecutions – or perhaps it would be more fitting to say *because* of them – Christianity spread throughout all the Roman Empire. After about three hundred years of hostilities, persecutions ended when Christianity was legalized in Rome. *Emperor Constantine the Great*, who ruled from 306 to 337, implemented the legalization of Christianity, and for political reasons, set himself up as the head and ruler of the church. In 380, *Flavius Theodosius* made Christianity the official religion of Rome, making other religions illegal at the same time. By the turn of the fourth century, most Roman citizens had converted to Christianity.[68] The persecutions seemed to be easily forgotten, even though one would think they would have left a deep, gaping wound in the soul of Christianity.

When Christianity became an official religion, persecutions changed. The formerly persecuted were now a mighty presence in the land, and the door to abuse was flung wide open. This was the time when the basic principles and practices of Christianity were formed. Modesty gave way to titles and positions. The early church fathers began to modify and change Biblical principles into a system that despised Judaism and denied its own roots. It changed into a new system at the same time that Europe fell deep into the insecure and very dark Middle Ages. The impact of the church fathers was so profound and enduring that even today, we cannot consider the state of Christianity in the world without starting with them. We, too, are prisoners of their thinking.

How, then, did this development begin? Jesus and the disciples celebrated Biblical feasts and God's ordained day of rest, the Sabbath. We know that during the revolt of *Bar Kochba*, *Emperor Hadrian* outlawed the study of the Bible, circumcision and the keeping of the Sabbath. The early church continued all these practices anyway. If we consider the *Council of Nicaea*, the first Council convened by Emperor Constantine the Great in 325, we see how purposefully they started to distance the faith from Judaism. Even though Constantine was a leading politician who summoned the Council for his own political aspirations, the Nicaean Creed, introduced by the Council, is used by almost all denominations even today. Above all, Constantine was a Roman who despised Judaism, like all Romans did.

The Emperor was the product of his time and, as such, was also ensnared by Greek philosophy. The Greek way of thinking quickly began to affect the church, even though it was completely opposed to the Jewish way of thinking and thus the opposite of the way Jesus and the apostles thought. As a matter of fact, Constantine was the first emperor who started to limit the rights of the Jews.[69] It was decided that Easter would be celebrated on the first Sunday following a full moon. This meant that it was no longer during the Jewish time of Passover, which was when Jesus Himself celebrated the feast. Constantine the Great stated that the hands of the Jews were stained by blood, so it was out of the question for a Christian feast to overlap their feast. It can be rightly said that paganism entered into Christianity during the time of Constantine, with the support of the church fathers. Also, the Cross became the symbol of Christianity after the first Council. To us, it became a symbol of love, but to many millions of others, it symbolized hatred and violence. For centuries after the first Council, Jews were murdered in the very shadow of the cross. The Laodicean Council, in 364 AD, accepted a law under which the so-called Jewish Christians – those who, for instance, observed the Sabbath – should be punished.[70]

At the same time that Christianity began to distance itself from its roots, the Roman Empire was being constricted all the more, under the pressure of foreign nations. Change took place so slowly that the dots cannot always be connected, but I firmly believe that from a wider perspective, the end of Rome had already begun in 70 AD, when they destroyed the Second Temple. Many immoral practices weakened the empire internally. For example, when families wanted only one female child, baby girls were thrown into the streets right after birth, where they were arbitrarily at the mercy of either good or bad people. Naturally, they often perished. Comparison with the abortion policy of the Western World in our time is not far-fetched. The weakened Roman Empire, at the end of the 300s, no longer posed a military threat to the barbaric nations banging at its gates. Also, Emperor Constantine moved his capital to Constantinople in the Byzantine region (now known as Istanbul), rightly understanding that Rome had strength only in the East at that time.

The destruction of the Roman Empire was followed by the end of the entire classical civilization. Suddenly, an insecure medieval era took place, in which the Church was one of the few forces uniting people. Only *Charlemagne* was the kind of mighty ruler the Roman emperors had once been. So, in 800, he was crowned by the Pope as the ruler of the Roman Empire. Charlemagne took his oath in the name of Christianity, for which purpose he started great military operations and mass executions, thinking that in this way, pagans would best understand the message of Christianity – an example we see played out through the ages. This Holy Roman Empire, which started with Charlemagne, remained a political force throughout the Middle Ages, but it was unable to create real stability in times of turbulence.

Church Foundation

"This is the message which we have heard from Him and declare to you, that God is light and in Him is no darkness at all."[71]

Early Christianity, which the church fathers developed, began to consider Jews as less worthy, damned and undeserving of mercy – both by God and by men. The concept "church fathers" referred to theologians and teachers, who formulated dogmas until 700. In their thinking, the Jews were considered worse than pagans, for the simple reason that they had faced the truth and yet rejected it. This theology is called *Theology of Contempt,* which stands in complete opposition to the *Theology of The Cross.* As a matter of fact, the concept of teaching contempt was identified by Jewish French historian *Jules Isaac* (1877-1963).[72] Theology of Contempt still exists and affects many theological faculties and churches. One part of this was "making the Bible Greek," which meant not merely a language but rather the loss and belittling of the Bible's authenticity and Hebrew roots. This was the beginning of a path that is still seen in Bible translations today, since one translation goal, perhaps unspoken, is often to erase Judaism from the Scriptures. A great Bible teacher of our time, *Derek Prince* (1915-2003), said that many of the translators, whose translations are still in use today, had to deviate from normal translating principles in order to make the Bible fit the accepted theology (instead of fitting theology to the Bible).[73]

The entire doctrine of Christianity is founded on the belief of Jesus' death, for which the Jews were deemed responsible. This understanding was preached in Europe in the Middle Ages, and at the turn of the 17th century, it was called *Deicide,* the *murder of God,* taken from medieval Latin. Let us take a look at what Jesus Himself said of His death as he spoke to the disciples: *"How then could the Scriptures be fulfilled, that it must happen thus? ... But all this was done that the Scriptures of the prophets might be fulfilled."*[74] Present at Jesus' death were both the Jews and the Gentiles, represented by Rome, which ruled the world at the time. As Jesus predicted in Matthew 20, he was delivered *"to the Gentiles to mock and to scourge and to crucify."*[75] The entire world was present in the crucifixion through the Romans. Thus, the entire world was also given an opportunity to participate in Jesus' resurrection, which now gave hope to the whole world.

Another teaching that backed the accusation of the murder of God was the *Supersession Myth,* which says that Israel had lost its place in God's plans, and that Christians were now God's new Israel. Simply put, according to this notion, the Jews had been a bad chosen people, and God needed a better one to replace them. Hence, we now call this myth *Replacement Theology*. The more the Jews suffered, the more it was thought that the Supersession Myth held truth. The church fathers thought the Jews deserved to be punished. Either their complete destruction or continuous migration and suffering were considered appropriate punishments for them. If we consider the situation from the point of view of one Jewish person, we understand that a Jew was never really counted as an individual. He represented his people, which in turn represented "otherness," which is frightening. Therefore, he was seen as a demon, greedy and immoral, not as a neighbor nor a member of the same human community. An individual Jew could not have his own special characteristics or accomplishments in the society of that time.

The anti-Semitic reading of the Gospels was found in all denominations and their leadership. It spread to the Catholic, Orthodox and Protestant churches. The church fathers during and after the Nicaean Council systematically denied the covenant between the Jews and God. They included *John Chrysostom* (307-407), who was important to the Greek Catholic Church; *Saint Augustine*, the bishop of the city of Hippo (354-430), who is often called the father of the Catholic Church; *Eusebius* (263-339), who wrote the history of the church from Jesus until 325; *Jerome,* who translated the

Greek New Testament; *Cyril of Alexandria* (376-444); and *Ambrose* (330-397). What united these scholars? They all believed God had canceled His covenant with the Jews. The first known expression of this doctrine was presented very early by *Justin Martyr* (100-165). According to him, the Jews had lost their right to the Scriptures and the prophets, which now belonged to the church.[76] According to this theological view, the Jews could not have any independent position or existence before God, and they did not have a relationship with God. The church fathers perhaps did not understand the far-reaching consequences of their views. Possibly, they misread the Bible, spiritualizing the promises meant to be taken concretely. They did not understand the Hebrew background of the Bible authors, which differs completely from the Greek mentality. They allegorized and interpreted, but such an examination has hardly ever been the purpose of the Word of God, which is meant to be understood by any person from whatever cultural or educational background. It is unambiguous and in no need of allegorical interpretations, which only theologians know how to make.

Unfortunately, this refined theology soon had practical consequences, since it became the law in the Medieval society. Through the Middle Ages, the Church grew in power, not only as a religious institute but especially as a political influence, putting under its power both the European part of the former Roman Empire and a part of Russia. Medieval people understood that they had a kind of dual identity: they were the property of and subject of the king on the one hand, and of the church on the other. This development partially explains why anti-Semitism in church art and liturgy could be transferred into social structures, and subsequently into social laws of different confederations and neighborhoods. The Jews could not appeal to the law or its representatives, so they had to live in insecure, secluded communities. Therefore, they were an easy target for violence, a condition that continued throughout the Middle Ages. One allegation targeted at them was the *Blood Libel* or *Ritual Murder* accusation, which has its roots in 1147 in Norwich, England, and appears in various forms even until this day. According to the Blood Libel, Jews murdered Christian children in order to use their blood in their Passover rituals.[77] The accusation led to many violent pogroms against the Jews. *Pope Innocent IV* released a statement about the issue in a papal bull of September 1255, saying the following: *"Jews are not to be accused of using blood in their rituals..."* This sentence is repeated in Jewish museums around the world because it aptly describes the situation in which the supreme leadership of the church knew very well that the allegations were a lie.

As Christianity expanded, the Church gathered a huge amount of property, and new church buildings were erected around Europe. A popular theme in Christian art was a comparison between two religions: "*Ecclesia*" and "*Synagogue.*" Strasbourg Cathedral, located in that beautiful city, dating from 1230, is a classic example of this comparison, in which Judaism, in the likeness of a woman, flees the scene ashamed, whereas Christianity is represented as a flowing, triumphant heroine. The famous wood carvings in *Efrut Cathedral* in Thuring, Germany, and the baptismal place in *St. Mary's Church,* in Prestbury, England, are other well-known examples of this kind of anti-Semitic art. Examining European art will open your eyes to see history in a different light, centuries later. The Church Law, which sought to isolate Jews from the rest of society, is a model example of how far anti-Semitism went. Its effects on later times are apparent. The Fourth Council of the Lateran in 1215, the bishops' synod, ordained a Europe-wide decree, the implementation of which varied by country and degree, that Jews were to be marked with a yellow piece of cloth – in 1941, they were marked with a yellow star. In 1267, Jews were forced into ghettos – in 1939, *Reinhardt Heydrich* gave the exact same order. Heydrich, however, was not a church leader but a Nazi SS leader who was responsible for the planning and implementation of the Final Solution while acting as the Head of the Security Police. He was born in Halle an der Saale, Germany, in 1900. He is one of the most famous Nazi leaders, partly because the Czechoslovakian Resistance Movement assassinated him in 1942. However, the question here is: why is it so difficult to see the difference between Heydrich and those who ordained the church law? The very thought is abominable.

One of the fiercest anti-Semitic theologians was *John Chrysostom*, the Archbishop of Constantinople and a church father, whom the Eastern Orthodox and Catholic Church revere as a saint.[78] As a matter of fact, he was called *Golden Throat* for his wonderful oratory eloquence. Chrysostom says the following about God's grace: *"God is called a God of consolation, a God of mercy. Because he is constantly working to encourage and console those who are distressed and afflicted even if they have sinned ten thousand times."*[79] However, this same meek man accused the Jews of giving a home to the Devil in their synagogues and of worshipping idols, which, of course, is one of the most terrifying sins in Judaism. Chrysostom said: *"Jews are dogs, stiff-necked, gluttonous, drunkards. They are beasts unfit for work… The Jews had fallen into a condition lower than the vilest animals… The synagogue is worse than a brothel and a drinking shop; it is a den of scoundrels, a temple of demons, the cavern of devils, a criminal assembly of the assassins of Christ…. I hate the Jews, because they violate the Law… It is the duty of all Christians to hate the Jews."*[80] He also said: *"Do you see that demons dwell in their souls and that these demons are more dangerous than the ones of old? And this is very reasonable. In the old days the Jews acted impiously toward the prophets; now they outrage the Master of the prophets... Must you share a greeting with them and exchange a bare word? Must you not turn away from them since they are the common disgrace and infection of the whole world? Have they not come to every form of wickedness?"*[81] It would be possible to quote more of his thoughts, but we can already get an idea of how he saw the Jews.

Saint Augustine, whose thoughts later became the church precepts concerning the Jews living under its authority, regarded the matter in this way: the Jews were not to be physically murdered, but it was to be ensured that they lived their lives in agony. His thoughts were mainly based on the Bible, in reference to Cain: *"The Bible does not say: 'Cursed is the earth,' but rather: 'You (Cain) are cursed from the earth, which has opened its mouth to receive your brother's blood at your hand.' So the unbelieving people of the Jews is cursed from the earth, that is, from the Church, which in the confession of sins has opened its mouth to receive the blood shed for the remission of sins by the hand of the people that has chosen not to be under grace [i.e., salvation through Jesus Christ], but rather to exist under the law [i.e., embracing Jewish law]."* He continues: *"And this murderer is cursed by the Church: that is, the Church admits and avows the curse pronounced by the apostle: 'Whoever are the works of the law are under the curse of the law...'"*[82] Yet Paul explicitly states: *"For I do not desire, brethren, that you should be ignorant of this mystery, lest you should be wise in your opinion, that blindness in part has happened to Israel until the fullness of the Gentiles has come in. And so all Israel will be saved... For the gifts and the calling of God are irrevocable."*[83]

The Protestant Reformation of the 16th century was a backlash against the worst overkills of the Catholic Church, dividing Western Christianity in two. It ushered on stage such persons as *Jan (John) Hus* (ca. 1369-1415), *Martin Luther* (1483-1546) and *Jean (John) Calvin* (1509-1564). Grace was put at the center of Christianity, and the Bible began to be translated so that each person could read the Word of God for themselves. Even though the Reformation largely rejected the Catholic tradition, it retained its anti-Semitism in many respects. After many centuries, the violent and terrifying speech of the church fathers was continued by the great 16th century German Reformers, who brought about Protestantism. Luther began his work against the sale of indulgences by nailing his 95 Theses to the Wittenberg Church door on October 31, 1517. Soon, his thesis and other writings were widely disseminated. The Catholic Church saw him as a big enough threat to excommunicate him from the Catholic Church in 1521. By this time, Luther was already receiving wide support from the German peasants; later, the princes ruling various parts of Germany joined the Reformation and the ensuing battles. The end result of all this was that many other Reformers modeled his teachings, so that Luther led the whole of Europe to Reformation and the birth of Protestant Christianity.

Luther apparently did not start his journey as an anti-Semite, nor did he primarily oppose the Jews. Quite on the contrary, in his book *Jesus Christ was Born a Jew*, published in 1523, he specifically emphasizes the Jewish roots and background of Christianity. Luther believed that Catholicism and its doctrines repulsed the Jews. He also believed that Jews would instead turn to Protestant Christianity, which he himself now offered. In other words, Jews would comprehend en masse that his thoughts were right, and would then convert to Christianity. But as years passed and the Reformer got older, the

Jews still did not convert to his Protestant Christian faith. So, Luther became an enemy to the Jews, bitter and disappointed. He wrote strong polemics against the Jews, culminating in *The Jews and Their Lies*, published in 1543. Besides his disappointment in the presumed blindness of the Jews, we naturally cannot forget his background. Luther was a Reformer, but he came from the old Catholic tradition. As a child of his time, who had received a Catholic education, he knew the anti-Semitic thinking very well.

Luther's anti-Semitic statements and writings were often used as a foundation for subsequent anti-Semitism. Even many centuries later, they were repeated in fully secularized anti-Semitic contexts.[84] He presented the Jews as greedy blasphemers and murderers. As the foundation for his contempt, he used the word *Verjudung*, referring to some kind of basic Judaism, which, according to him, also stained those Jews who had converted to Christianity.

Asking the rhetorical question, *"What should be done to this rejected and condemned Jewish race?"* he answered: *"First to set fire to their synagogues or schools and to bury and cover with dirt whatever will not burn, so that no man will ever again see a stone or cinder of them... Second, I advise that their houses also be razed and destroyed... Third, I advise that all their prayer books and Talmudic writings, in which such idolatry, lies, cursing and blasphemy are taught, be taken from them... we should eject them forever from this country."*[85] Just like many of his predecessors, Luther saw, in the sufferings of the Jews, a confirmation that God had rejected the Jews.

The more we study these facts, the more we understand how the Church fathers inspired anti-Semitic thinking centuries later – including the Nazi ideology. For example, Nazi leaders cited the thoughts of Chrysostom and Luther in their own speeches, and despite Hitler's Catholic background,

Luther was his special favorite. The works of Luther (and the Church fathers) were republished in Nazi Germany. In the post-war trials, *Julius Streicher* (1885-1946), who was the editor of the anti-Semitic Nazi tabloid *Der Sturmer*, gave interesting insight into something important. He was originally a teacher, but ascended high in the Nazi party. The main *"news"* of his paper consisted of stories of ritual murders committed by the Jews, the financial problems of the Jews and other such propaganda. In the war trial, Streicher said that if he was accused, then Luther should be dragged to court alongside him as well.[86]

One concrete show of anti-Semitism that has continued for centuries is the *Passion Plays*, originally from the Middle Ages. When the Bible had not yet been translated into common languages, the church wanted the people to understand its teachings. These plays, especially when performed during Easter, provoked the people to engage in violent attacks on Jewish neighborhoods. The role of Jews as murderers of Jesus was underlined by various visual means, whereas Jesus and His disciples were considered to represent the Christians. Perhaps the most famous passion play is the *Oberammergau Passion Play* from Germany. In 1942, though the Nazi government was pressed by the immense war efforts, Hitler himself took time to travel to see the play. He expressed his sentiments on the play as follows: *"This presentation portrays the menace of Jewry... for this reason it is vital that the Passion Plays be continued."*[87] This is probably enough to explain what the play was all about.

Who, then, is this Jesus, whose Jewishness was denied? Jesus, perfectly human and simultaneously God's Son, was born into this world as a Jewish man. He said that *"salvation is of the Jews."*[88] The face of Jesus is a Jewish face. Jesus could walk the streets of Jerusalem today among His brothers and not stand out from the crowd. Jesus is the suffering servant and the conquering king, but He is also a Jew. Christianity cannot exist without Judaism, but Judaism stands alone without Christianity. What, then, is anti-Semitism? It is not hatred toward the Jews, but hatred toward Judaism. It is rebellion against God's election, thus rebellion against God. It is astonishment and outrage at the fact that the Messiah came into the world through David's lineage, as a Jewish man. It is denying the truth, for if Christianity wants to remain faithful to God, it cannot deny its Jewish roots. If there were no Jewishness in Jesus, nothing would connect Judaism and Christianity. Anti-Semitism can work only if Jesus' Jewishness can be denied.

But what did Jesus himself say? Matthew 5:17-19 describes the attitude Jesus had for the Bible and the laws God had set: *"Do not think that I came to destroy the Law or the Prophets. I did not come to destroy but to fulfill. For assuredly, I say to you, till heaven and earth pass away, one jot or one tittle will by no means pass from the law till all is fulfilled. Whoever therefore breaks one of the least of these commandments, and teaches men so, shall be called least in the kingdom of heaven; but whoever does and teaches them, he shall be called great in the kingdom of heaven."* Jesus dressed in a Jewish man's outfit, and He celebrated Jewish feasts: *"But when His brothers had gone up, then He also went up to the feast, not openly, but as it were in secret... Now about the middle of the feast Jesus went up into the temple and taught."*[89] This was the Feast of Tabernacles: *"On the last day, that great day of the feast, Jesus stood and cried out, saying, 'If anyone thirsts, let him come to Me and drink. He who believes in Me, as the Scripture has said, out of his heart will flow rivers of living water.'"*[90]

In order to understand what Jesus meant by this, we need to understand what this great feast was. One custom associated with celebrating the Feast of

Tabernacles concerned water. The priests in a procession used to draw water into a pot from the pool of Siloam and bring the water into the temple as a great throng of people followed them, singing the worship psalms (Psalms 113-118). On the seventh day of the feast, seven processions made the same journey, which climaxed with the priest pouring the water on the altar in the temple. Water, naturally, is related to the much-awaited rain in the Fall, but its meaning here was purely spiritual as they waited for the words of Isaiah to come to pass: *"Therefore with joy you will draw water from the wells of salvation."*[91] The name of Jesus comes from Joshua's Hebrew name, *Yehoshua*, which means *God is salvation*. His name *Yeshua* means salvation, so Jesus offered himself as the salvation and living water of whom Isaiah prophesied.

John also tells of another feast: *"Now it was the Feast of Dedication in Jerusalem, and it was winter. And Jesus walked in the temple, in Solomon's porch."*[92] How amazing it is that this feast is mentioned in the New Testament! It is not a feast set by God to be celebrated in Judaism, but a day celebrating a historical event outside the Bible. Why did Jesus celebrate Hanukkah? Jesus, who Himself was the light of the world, celebrated Hanukkah, the feast of light, because he was part of the Jewish people. But Hanukkah, which remembers the redemption of the Jews and the purification of the Temple, is clearly also a Messianic feast. Therefore, it is highly remarkable that it was precisely during the feast of Hanukkah that Jesus revealed himself as the Messiah.[93] The word *Mashiach*, "Messiah," means "anointed one." Anointing is done with oil, and the theme of this feast has to do with oil.

What is most astonishing is that the death of Jesus occurred at the time of the Jewish Passover. It is celebrated to commemorate the liberation from Egypt, and the word *Pesach* literally means *passing by* or *over*, referring to the angel of death passing over the Jewish houses. One of the key elements of Passover is eating of the unleavened *matzah* bread. As the Jewish people were getting ready to leave Egypt, they had no time to prepare bread, so no leaven was used. This is commemorated in the Feast of the Unleavened Bread. Passover is a feast that commemorates and honors the Prophet Elijah, who is expected to return before the coming of the Messiah. At Passover, Jews have prayed for thousands of years for their return to Jerusalem. The banquet feast of Passover is called the *Seder*, meaning "order." So, Jesus prepared either the Seder or the practice meal preceding it, which we know now as Communion.[94] It must also be noted that there is a strong tradition in Judaism that during Passover, the drinking of wine and the breaking of the bread brings the Messiah to us. Rabbi *Menachem Brod* of the *Chabad* Movement, an Orthodox branch of Judaism, started a huge discussion in the Jewish world in April 2012, when he proposed that in Judaism, bread and wine specifically symbolize the body and blood of the Messiah – as it really is.[95] The *seudat Mashiach* or Messianic Feast, on the seventh day of Passover, requires the breaking of bread and drinking of wine, but how many Christians actually know about this tradition?

Despite the original Jewish nature of the New Testament, Christianity soon began distancing itself from its roots. There is something frightening about how the Church fathers created Christianity, but at the same time hated its Jewish roots. In other words, they were unable to fulfill the thought found in the letter of *James*: *"Out of the same mouth proceed blessing and cursing. My brethren, these things ought not to be so."*[96] But even more frightening is the thought that God would have rejected His people. The reasoning that the Church was the new Israel, and that Jews no longer had a connection to God, is fearsome, because it indicates a disregard for God's own words and covenants. This reasoning is also fearsome because it was implemented with violence and acts that opposed God's Laws. The thought is all the more terrifying because it has survived to this day. Derek Prince summarized it by saying that he had found the word "Israel" or "Israeli" 79 times in the New Testament, and after researching them all, he found that the apostles never used the word "Israel" as a synonym for the church. The expression "New Israel" does not appear anywhere in the New Testament. If preachers use this expression, they need to define it carefully. They also need to explain that it is not an expression the Bible uses.[97]

What did God Himself say?

"Thus says the Lord: If heaven above can be measured, and the foundations of the earth searched out beneath, I will also cast off all the seed of Israel for all that they have done, says the Lord."[98]

"Moreover the word of the Lord came to Jeremiah, saying, 'Have you not considered what these people have spoken, saying. "The two families which the Lord has chosen, He has also cast them off"? Thus they have despised My people, as if they should no more be a nation before them. Thus says the Lord: "If My covenant is not with day and night, and if I have not appointed the ordinances of heaven and earth, then I will cast away the descendants of Jacob and David My servant."'"[99]

Is it unnatural, then, to present views that are completely different from the truth of the Bible – the truth so simply and clearly put that anyone can understand it? How is it that these views are presented in churches, despite the dire warnings of Jesus found in the fifth chapter of the book of Matthew? If it were so that the promises God had given to Israel had been transferred to the church, then, according to logic, this also would have happened with the curses following disobedience. But as Eusebius himself said, even though the promises had been transferred to the Christians, the curses remained with the Jews. I believe that the same spiritual laws apply to us as Christians and to the people of Israel. The promises have not been taken away from them, but the same spiritual laws apply to us. This principle is crystal clear on the pages of the New Testament. Just as Paul wrote: *"Do not be haughty, but fear. For if God did not spare the natural branches, He may not spare you either."*[100] This makes our situation very serious, for our churches have been all but obedient to the Word of the Lord, and the situation today is worse than ever. Appreciation for the Word of God in churches has deteriorated to such a point that the consequences will be unpredictable. Instead of the Word, entertainment has become a significant part of church gatherings. The truth is, however, that everything originates from the Word, and God created the world by His Word.[101]

History clearly proves to us what happened to the church in the centuries after Jesus' death. The Medieval Church drifted further and further away from the Bible. It became a political institution that ruthlessly gave immense economic power to rulers and royalty. The distancing of the church from the Word of God had serious repercussions: violence, murders and all kinds of corruption spread and became commonplace among the clergy, and even in the hearts of the people. The more the church fathers claimed that God had cursed the Jews, the more the church received real and concrete curses upon it. Church history proves the legitimacy of this observation, despite the fact that the church was too blind to see the actual state of the matter.

The same applies to our own time. But the Jews also paid a price for the Christians' contempt of the Word of God, since the wrath of the church was targeted at them. Next, I want to consider examples of the real consequences of anti-Semitism. What happens when thoughts become words and words become actions?

4 Persecution of the Jews in the Middle Ages – From Crusades to Black Death

"The way of peace they have not known,
And there is no justice in their ways;
They have made themselves crooked paths;
Whoever takes that way shall not know peace."[102]

Some years ago, the Israel Museum in Jerusalem held an exhibition on the Crusades. It was protested by both Jews and Muslims, but the exhibition was held anyway. I did not go to it, because it was too disturbing to me that these cruel self-seekers might somehow be considered as part of my faith – as if I, as a Christian, would think that there could be anything good about the Crusades. Were the knights really motivated by religion? Were they seeking financial interests? Did they just love fighting? We can never go back and know people's thoughts, so we do not know the answers to these disturbing questions. Can we judge the people in the past on the basis of what we know today? We know that the Crusaders were known for one distinguishing factor: cruelty.

What exactly does it mean to carry the name of Christian? Does it have the same meaning for me as it does for my Jewish friends? I know that the fathers of my faith are -in reality- the prophets and fishermen of the Bible, but am I connected also with the Crusaders?

Is there something similar in me, even though I live centuries later?

As I said earlier, Jews in the Middle Ages were required to live in certain neighborhoods and often wear a yellow mark on their clothing, so they could easily be recognized as Jews. Different kinds of yellow marks are on display at the Yad Vashem Museum, and visitors are often surprised when they realize that the Nazis did not invent the yellow star. On the contrary, Jews were already secluded by the Church in the Middle Ages. They were deemed responsible for natural disasters, as well as for all kinds of cruelty prevalent during medieval times. These days are called the Dark Ages for a reason. In such religious and cultural atmospheres, where discrimination against the Jews was not only accepted but also wished for, it is no wonder violence against them was also considered desirable. Generally speaking, no matter the age or society, all kinds of persecution and violence erupt and are emphasized in times of social change and uncertainty. Therefore, the Middle Ages offered many opportunities for both unorganized or spontaneous expressions of mass hatred and more organized campaigns. At the same time when immense hatred spread in the churches, important texts and interpretations of the Bible were created in Judaism. Many of the prominent rabbis lived in that age. It is interesting how the Dark Middle Ages and the Golden Age of Judaism overlap this way. Why? Did the Jewish community turn inward and become more creative, and introspective, the more it was persecuted?

The Crusades are a phenomenon closely linked to persecution of the Jews. They were a series of violent expeditions (or in modern terms military campaigns) from 1095-1291 against those who were seen as the enemies to Christendom. *Pope Urban II* is the one who launched the crusades that have remained a disgrace to church history to this day. European Christian armies participated in the crusades with a special purpose to liberate the Holy Land, then under Muslim rule. Eight large war expeditions/campaigns were organized to achieve this particular goal. At the same time, many smaller crusades were organized against the Spanish Muslims, Turkish Ottomans, Pagan Slavs of the Baltic Sea and various other so-called heretics at the heart of Europe.[103] The knight culture typical to Medieval Europe was part of the crusades. Knights participating in the crusades may have felt that their participation held some religious significance, but they also satisfied their need for hostility and adventure. These belligerent men had an opportunity to rob, kill and destroy, yet to receive forgiveness for their sins from the Pope – or perhaps they even considered these sins as virtues.[104]

Even before the knights had left Europe, they destroyed Jewish communities on their way. Hatred toward the Jews, along with their hatred toward Muslims, was a motivation the leaders of the crusades openly expressed. It was said, for instance, that the purpose was to take revenge on Jews for the death of Jesus and to eradicate the Jews completely from the face of the earth. For example, the Jewish communities along the Rhine and Danube Rivers were completely destroyed, and these were communities with thousands of members. In Jerusalem, the Jews living there were herded together like cattle and forced inside a synagogue, which was then set on fire. There are many such stories. At the same time this atrocity took place, hymns to the Jewish Messiah were sung outside the synagogue. These are incomprehensible events, but then again, they can be understood in the light of what we know from our own age. This passing along of bloodlust from one era to another is horrendous. History repeats itself – only the means vary.

There were three main crusades to the Holy Land, in addition to many more crusades of other kinds. The first crusade to the Holy Land was more of a modest bunch of peasants with their wives and children. Muslims destroyed this group easily, in Anatoly. But a larger group of knights followed this peasant procession, and in 1099, they captured Jerusalem. Four Crusader States were established in the Holy Land at that time. Fortresses were built in them, and they were ruled under the same feudal system that operated in Europe. The second crusade took place in 1147-1149 as a protest against Muslim conquests on the European front. Several decades later, *Saladin*, the new Muslim ruler and warrior, entered the picture and captured Jerusalem in 1187. This was followed by the third crusade, led by European kings: the Holy Roman Emperor *Frederick I Barbarossa* (who drowned on the way), *Richard I The Lionheart* of England and *Philip II Augustus* of France. They did not succeed in taking over Jerusalem. These first crusades were followed by later crusades, with the express purpose of attacking Egypt because it was the center of Muslim rule. Various Crusader States were established here and there, but even the last of them collapsed in 1291.

Then there was the Black Death. The Black Death (1348-1351) originated in central Asia, but as trade expanded, it spread all around the world along the sea routes. As a matter of fact, it spread to humans from flea bites, and fleas, in turn, traveled from village to village with black rats. The disease first appeared in Europe in Messina, Sicily, but spread quickly to Italy, France, Spain and southern England. The Black Death was lethal: it is estimated that in the worst-infected areas 50% of the population died. Of the entire population of Europe, about one third died of the illness, and during the next 350 years, it broke out again and again across Europe. Financial chaos was one of many consequences of the depopulation caused by this sickness.[105]

The Black Death is closely connected with Jewish history, since Jews were soon blamed for the deaths and sufferings caused by the sickness. Apparently, more Jewish communities survived the plague, percentagewise, than their contemporaries. The Jews were very often secluded from others, living in their own communities, which in itself protected them from plagues. Secondly, it is believed that the precise regulations of Jewish hygiene, as well as their way of processing and handling food, protected them. It seems that what was meant as punishment turned out to protect them. The problem was that their contemporaries knew nothing about hygiene or the spreading of plagues due to poor hygiene. They saw only what was apparent: for some reason, the Jewish communities seemed to be protected from the Black Death. Because of this, the accusation arose that the Jews had poisoned wells or used other means of magic to make the main population sick.

The Black Death became one more reason for hatred towards the Jews, which led to Jewish massacres around Europe, as the plague raged in dirty conditions. People died of this disease, yet interestingly, the accusation of poisoning wells has survived in various forms to this day. Poisoning, along with the accusation of ritual murder, is a recurring theme in anti-Semitic propaganda.

The Spanish Inquisition

"If that is the case, our God whom we serve is able to deliver us from the burning fiery furnace, and He will deliver us from your hand, O king. But if not, let it be known to you, O king, that we do not serve your gods, nor will we worship the gold image which you have set up."[106]

I travel to Spain in 1992 to participate as a worker in the Seville World Fair. What a special year that is! The Seville World Expo takes place in 1992 because one Christopher Columbus sailed to America in 1492. The theme for the expo is "new world." I am startled as I see how the theme is displayed everywhere. That particular year meant something quite different to me, because 1492 was also the year when the Jewish suffering, in the grip of the Spanish Inquisition, climaxed. In 1492, Jews were expelled from Spain. The year 1492 is one of the culminating points of a dark time in history. This underlying darkness, however, does not show through in Seville in 1992.

On my days off, I walk the streets of Seville. I look at the doors to which the expelled Jews still have keys. The name of Barrio de Santa Cruz, Holy Cross District, reminds us of one Jew, but at the time, it was a neighborhood populated by Jews. How peculiar that even though they do not want to remember the Jewish expulsion, that area named for one Jewish man is part of a former Jewish neighborhood. I notice that many synagogues have been turned into churches. The truth has been masked. Seville is a city of sunlight, yet it is also a burial place of cruelty, torture and hidden truth.

The finding of the New World may have come about because of the expulsion of the Jews. Why do we remember only Columbus? Why do we not remember the expulsion of the Jews? And who was Columbus? Some researchers suggest that Columbus might have been a Jew who, in order to save even a part of his people, sailed the ocean in search of distant lands. The evidence is plentiful. It is said that he marked his letters with the Jewish way of referring to the name of God. It is apparent that he delayed his departure so that he would not have to leave on the day of Tisha B'Av. This is a day that has always signified some catastrophic event for the Jewish people. It is a day of fasting. It was the day when Columbus was supposed to sail, and it was the very day the Spanish Jews were expelled. Columbus sailed away the very next day. It is said that the explorer dedicated the last years of his life to studying prophecies. Not a sign of this is seen in Seville. But stolen synagogues, torture poles and burned converts are a part of the city's soul.

It is as if the whole of Europe turned into one huge graveyard. I feel chills on that hot summer day.

It is believed that Jews have lived in Spain since the First Temple was destroyed. Old Spanish Jewish families claim they can narrate the story of those families all the way back to the Bible. Anti-Semitic parish registers identify their coming to Spain during a time of Great Migration, around the fourth and fifth centuries. The story of the Jews of Seville is only one of many Spanish Jewish stories, but I think that in some way, all stories follow the same pattern. When Seville flourished, the Jews also flourished: in medicine, in trade and as landowners. But one significant factor affecting not only the history of its Jewish population but Spain itself was the birth of Islam. *Mohammed* (ca. 570-632) founded Islam on the Arabic peninsula, but once its position stabilized, it began to spread to other expanding regions. During the years 632-661, Islam spread quickly. Arabs and Berber tribes conquered Spain in 711. When the *Berbers*, a Muslim people living in northern Africa, began conquering more areas in 1013, the city of Seville offered asylum to Jews fleeing persecution. But the new religion spread, and soon Muslims arrived in Seville, too. Even though Jews flourished under the *Almoravid* dynasty, *Almohads*, in turn, destroyed them. Both were Muslim dynasties, which in turn conquered parts of Spain.[107]

After destruction and uncertainty, Jews welcomed the Christian *Reconquista*, "Re-conquest," believing better times had arrived. In their mistaken trust, they even presented the key of Seville to King Ferdinand III of Castile (1199-1252). All was well in the beginning, and Jews were allowed to practice many kinds of trade and even own land. But dark clouds were already gathering in the sky. The Church had begun an orthodoxy campaign, and the situation began to worsen. *Archdeacon Martinez* began to incite the people against the Jews; he was a well-known inquisitor, whom even future generations would know by name. Starting in 1391, almost the entire Jewish community and their synagogues were destroyed. The vibrant community never recovered from the terrors it experienced, and in 1483, the Jews of Seville were sent into exile. At the same time, all other Jews were expelled from the Andalusian region.[108]

The Spanish Inquisition was established in 1478. *Inquisitio Haereticae Pravitatis* was an existing branch of the Catholic Church whose task was to examine heretics. Its original purpose was to study the orthodoxy of Catholic converts. The Inquisition introduced torture in the 12th century as a tool against heretics; the Church was the only institution to determine what was pure, Orthodox doctrine and what was heresy. The Spanish Inquisition had the unique feature of being started by secularized rulers, *King Ferdinand II* and *Queen Isabella*, with the consent of *Pope Sixtus IV.*

This ruling couple had created a major world power in which two old dynasties united: the families of *Castille* and *Aragon*. So great was the political power of this couple that in 1492, they were able to conquer Granada, the last fortress held by the Muslims. That same year, Isabella sent the Columbus (1451-1506) to the New World in search of a new area for the Spanish royalty. It is amazing to think that he discovered a continent, which later became an asylum for the persecuted, and which has been such a remarkable supporter of the Jewish State. The sending of Columbus is a very significant factor in our story, as it seems to support the idea that the rulers were originally only interested in increasing their assets, including Jewish property. When the Inquisition united with the already existing anti-Semitism, all the ingredients for bloodshed were ready. The main inquisitor *Tomas de*

Torquemada (1420-1498) was a Spanish Dominican monk and a leader of the fight against heresy. He was a personal priest to Isabella, receiving her confession. He was also extremely fierce in relation to the so-called *crypto* or hidden Jews and Muslims. When the expulsion of the Jews was decided in 1492 with the *Alhambra Decree*, Torquemada was the chief advocate for the act.

A special feature of the Spanish Inquisition was that for the first time, an element called "*purity of blood*" was emphasized, which has a certain direct connection to later racial doctrines. Purity of blood meant that Jews were unable to have or acquire the pure Catholic blood of the Spaniards, and therefore, their conversion to Christianity was an inadequate act. Many Jews were converted, becoming *conversos, new Christians.* Any *old Christian*, meaning a Catholic Spaniard, was able to expose them to the Inquisition. They were called *marranos*, "pigs," which referred to converts who continued to practice Jewish rituals in secret.

Being exposed to the Inquisition was an extremely serious matter, leading to the torture and death of those exposed. For the informant, it meant wealth and good status. New Christians rose to important positions and the favor of the royal court, yet they were always subjected to terrible prejudice. One reason for exposing them was financial gain; another was simple envy, since new Christians could possibly become serious competitors for positions in court and trade. These denunciations could be completely devoid of truth, but torture brought up information, which in turn caused children, parents and entire neighborhoods to endure torture. The Inquisition's rule book gave advice on various forms of torture, including how to force the victim to confess to a crime.[109]

One special reason for exposures was often the observation of the Sabbath. The Sabbath became a hidden ritual to be held behind closed doors, in cellars, far away from curious eyes. The Sabbath day of rest was an essential part of the order God established for mankind, taken from His own example. The attack on the Sabbath is directly linked with how seriously or lightly the Word of God is received. *"And on the seventh day God ended His work which He had done, and He rested on the seventh day from all His work which He had done."*[110] Observing the Sabbath is one of the most essential parts of Judaism. It is about revering God, because it refers to the fact that, according to the ordained order, humans need rest. It also refers to the belief that God is ultimately the One in whom life is founded. The Sabbath in Judaism is an example of the Messianic era. In addition, many Christian researchers have proposed that the Sabbath, in the way Paul expresses it, also refers to the future.[111] However, observing the Sabbath, the day God Himself decreed, was now a crime. Other similar offenses were owning a Hebrew Bible, circumcision, and observing other Jewish holidays and feasts.

Out of all Catholic courts of law, the Spanish Inquisition was the deadliest. Orthodox doctrine was studied and observed elsewhere too, but the brutality of the Spanish Inquisition and the good status and simultaneous paradoxical insecurity of the converts has shaped our understanding of Spanish history. The final climax of everything was expulsion. The bloody and cruel inquisition began in November 1478 and lasted until 1492. Even though we do not have an exact list of its victims, we know they numbered in the thousands.

Many Jews converted to Christianity, believing they would avoid the worst in this way, but because the Inquisition believed many converts were still practicing the Jewish religion, they were burned at stakes and subjected to other atrocities. The only thing that could really protect them from torture and flames was the Spanish Royal Court, whose favor some were able to receive as a result of the growing foreign trade.

But suspicion and fear cast a shadow on life inside and outside of the court. There was no safety from the bloodlust and anger of the hooded priests. The Golden Age of Spain, the flourishing of its art and culture, and its might in trade went toward an inevitable decline as the condition of the Jews became even more hopeless.

A Spanish Jewish poet, *Anton De Montoro*, born about 1404, and a convert himself, became a poet of all converts as he described their sorrow in his poem:

"O sad, bitter clothes-peddler, who does not feel your sorrow!
Here you are, seventy years of age, and have always said to the Virgin: 'you remained immaculate,' and have never sworn by the Creator.

I recite the credo, I worship pots full of greasy pork,
I eat bacon half-cooked, listen to Mass, cross myself while touching holy waters – and never could I kill these traces of the confeso.

With my knees bent and in great devotion in days set for holiness I pray,
rosary in hand, reciting the beads of the Passion,
adoring the God-and-Man as my highest Lord,
Yet for all the Christian things I do, I'm still called that old faggot Jew."[112]

Persecution of the Jews by the Spanish Inquisition culminated in 1492 with the expulsion of Jews. The fortunate ones fled to Turkey, where *Sultan Bayezid II* welcomed them, understanding immediately the significance of this new people group who was educated and often engaged in international trade. The hapless ones, however, fled to nearby Portugal, which also soon expelled them. Spanish Jews, known as *Sfaradim* (or *Sephardim*) after the Hebrew word for Spain, *Sfarad*, spread throughout the world. Jews considered their expulsion from Spain as a great betrayal. The land where they had lived so happily betrayed them, and even though expulsions happened in about a dozen nations, it was Spain's expulsion that stuck in their minds as the most horrifying.

In every sense, Spain faced the fatal results of Jewish expulsion: since that time, Spain has never reached a leading position in the world. Some of the Sephardim later went to the South American colonies, but they experienced inquisition there as well. Many of the Jews who went there hid their Jewish identity completely and assimilated into the Spanish people and other migrants. In Argentina and other Latin American countries, during the military junta administrations of the 20th century, anti-Semitism was part of the persecution.[113]

It is remarkable, however, that in recent years, a movement has started in South America in which many are searching in their backgrounds for the Jewish roots of their families.

Well-known poet *Yehuda ha-Levi* lived in Toledo, Spain, around 1080-1141. He wrote prose in Arabic and poems in Hebrew, expressing the situation in Spain at the time as a meeting place for three religions and cultures, years before the horrors of the Inquisition.

Ha-Levi's poems tell of the faith and longing of a Jewish soul, far away from their homeland. He was blessed, for he actually made it to the land of his longing and died on Israeli soil. But his longing still remained, for his people were not as fortunate. Their story in Spain came to a cruel end. Ha-Levi could not see into the future, as he wrote, and did not know that tears would be shed not only for the destruction of Jerusalem, but also for the end of Spain's Golden Age.

This poem has been translated into English under the title *In Remembrance of Jerusalem*:

"Beautiful land,
Delight of the world,
City of Kings,
My heart longs for you from the far-off west.
I am very sad when I remember how you were.
Now your glory is gone, your homes destroyed.
If I could fly to you on the wings of eagles,
I would soak your soil with my tears."[114]

The Crusades, the Black Death and the Spanish Inquisition are not the only anti-Semitic acts from which we can learn history. As we think of Jewish history in Europe, we need to take into account similarities in different countries, perhaps at slightly different times. The expulsions of Jews took place in England in 1290, France in 1306, Hungary in 1349, Spain in 1492, Portugal in 1497 and Warsaw in 1942. In other words, the existence of Jews in Europe is like a black symphony in which the composer has written only a few high notes. Suffering, violence and expulsions make the composition a *Requiem*, or a Death Mass dedicated to ghettos and death. We could think of the lighter notes, those times when the Pope or a king, in some country, protected his doctor, banker or artist. He and his family were allowed to live.

But I doubt in my heart if we can really call such protection a high note. It is true, after all, that the inability to choose the direction of one's own life is a challenge to our sense of justice.

The later Nazi hatred of Jews is not a separate era in history. It is not an exceptional state of affairs, nor is there anything astonishing in it, on reflection. For centuries, the majestic church had taught anti-Semitism and allowed violence, and it had even been the instigator of acts of violence. People had stood on the city squares watching hangings, burnings and implementation of all kinds of brutality. Centuries later, anti-Semitism oozed into each European child through the breastmilk. The hatred of Jews had become a special part of European ideological heritage, not to be disputed. This is a part of church history in particular, since only the time of secularization, during the Enlightenment era, brought civil rights to the Western European Jews. However, the freedom brought by the Enlightenment was short-lived. It was only a sort of pause in between the movements of a symphony.

The grand finale was yet to come.

5 From Enlightenment to World War – Impact of the Enlightenment Era on the Jewish History of Europe

"To everything there is a season, a time for every purpose under heaven: a time to be born, and a time to die ... a time of war, and a time of peace."[115]

Westminster Abbey is one of the world's finest and most famous churches. It is known everywhere in the world as a stage for celebrations of the British royalty. It is splendid on the outside and full of history on the inside. I do not know how many come to Westminster Abbey for church services, but it is full of tourists every day. I come to this magnificent church on my work trip to meet a high-ranking clergyman. We have a discussion over a cup of coffee. I sit with a man whom the entire world saw in Prince William and Kate's wedding. Suddenly he announces, in the middle of his busy schedule, that he wants to take me on a guided tour of the immense church. I protest as a matter of form, but the truth is that I can hardly contain myself. What could be more amazing than a private guided tour in such a historical place?

After walking around for a while, I start to grow tired of the enormous crypts, statues and pictures of royalty. I begin to feel more and more that these people received all possible earthly honor and grandeur as a result of their mere birth, but in reality, their lives were miserable. Since so many of us, including myself, waste so much time, I immediately think of a question: how many of them used their time and position properly? In my weariness, I ask questions and answer my host politely, but quite honestly, I am grateful for the fact that the tour must come to an end at some point.

Then something happens! We come to a memorial plaque of a certain man. His name was William Wilberforce. I know him from the history books. I also know his story from the movie Amazing Grace. Wilberforce was ahead of his time and very much alone in his fight against slavery. He was opposed in the British Parliament by his own party members, because slavery was a huge moneymaker to many. He had to endure and stand firm behind his cause, even when it only produced loss. Who stood by him? A pastor, the former captain of a slave ship. This captain, after repenting, wrote a song called "Amazing Grace." We all know this great song.

My guide smiles when he sees my sudden enthusiasm. We continue our tour now that all fatigue is gone. People whose time was not wasted are indeed remembered in this church.

One of the main achievements of the Enlightenment philosophers was the *Encyclopedia*. (For those too young to know, it is a large book printed with different entries for different topics.) This one was printed in France between 1751 and 1766, in which different intellectuals presented their knowledge on various fields. Their goal was to collect existing information from various fields of science and other categories into one piece of work and, at the same time, to fight existing medieval superstition through common sense. The *Encyclopedia* was revolutionary, for it emphasized tolerance and rationalism, and also presented religion as one way of thinking among others, not as the ultimate source of all information. The French government banned the Encyclopedia for many years, but it was read in secret all the more.[116]

Enlightenment philosophers had a revolutionary effect on Western European society and government. The freedoms we take for granted are all the result of previous eras and people who had a vision for a better-functioning society. For instance, the French intellectuals would have a wide and lasting impact on the French and American Revolutions. It can be said that the Enlightenment era brought us freedoms and democracy. Issues we take for granted – such as freedom of assembly and religion, the right to an impartial trial, the end of torture, abolition of censorship and the battle against slavery – were all radical changes at that time, all promoted by the French philosopher *Voltaire*. Voltaire, whose actual name was *François-Marie Arouet* (1694-1778), is perhaps the most famous of the Enlightenment philosophers.[117]

Not only was Voltaire an extremely prolific writer, he also fought steadfastly for these freedoms, while ignoring opposition. His compatriot *Baron de Montesquieu* (1689-1755) was an influential lawyer and writer who enforced separation of powers so that political and societal policy-making would never be in the hands of only one decision-making body. *Denis Diderot* (1713-1784), *Jean-Jacques Rousseau* (1712-1788) and the English *John Locke* (1632-1704) and *Thomas Hobbes* (1588-1679) were other philosophers of that time who pursued similar changes. However, the era was marked by one terrible injustice. The slave trade was a deep, dark evil, which these philosophers confronted in their work. The African slave trade had increased exponentially during the 17th century, when the British, French and Dutch colonies sought labor forces for their coffee, cotton and tobacco plantations. It is estimated that during the time of slavery, Europeans transported about twelve million slaves from Africa to the Americas. About two million perished on the way.

The Enlightenment intellectuals had an immense impact on the American Revolution in the years 1763-1783. Civil rights became a part of the "ethos" of the United States – how the role of society was understood and written into the law of the new nation. The Enlightenment philosophers created a state whose principles of justice and the self-determination of each person's rights were written into its law. The French Revolution was also a direct consequence of the thinking of the Enlightenment philosophers, who had enforced the end of absolute monarchy and governance based on the principle of representation. Jews received civil rights in Western Europe primarily as a result of the French Revolution. A little later, *Napoleon Bonaparte*, the famous military leader who ruled France after the revolution with an autocratic hold, also emphasized the revolution's ideas. Wherever the armies of Napoleon arrived, he asserted the power of law by enhancing equality and human rights. Even though we cannot be sure of how much he wanted to preserve the Jewish religion or to what extent he only wanted to assimilate the Jews, the significance of Napoleon as a liberator of Jews, especially in Italy, can hardly be overestimated. As a matter of fact, Napoleon was possibly the first to think of establishing a Jewish nation, and it was he who also opened the gates of the ghettos for the Jews.

The Enlightenment era is a critical point in history. Most obviously, this is because of the human rights it gave, but for the purpose of this book, there is another reason for its importance. The Age of Enlightenment revealed the true face of anti-Semitism, often called *the oldest hatred*. Now that we have been through history from the Roman times until the time of inquisition, we believe we understand the nature of anti-Semitism. Throughout the entire time of the Diaspora (the dispersion), Jews had suffered specifically from Christian anti-Semitism. But now, when Jews received civil rights in Western Europe, which took little interest in the beliefs of the Church and was instead enthralled with scientific enthusiasm, something strange happened: anti-Semitism did not disappear, but only changed its shape.

To Christian anti-Semitism, which many still nurtured in their hearts, was added a new form of anti-Semitism, which was birthed as an opposition to the Jewish *emancipation*, i.e., liberation. It was socioeconomic anti-Semitism, which said that Jews had too much power in the society; that Jews could not be loyal citizens, since their primary loyalty was towards the *Torah* and their own people; and that Jews controlled trade, banks, media and politicians. People who disliked the modernization of society blamed Jews for the entire process, forgetting that at the beginning of the process, Jews had no influence on politics whatsoever. We can safely say that even though Western European governments had now given the Jews their civil rights, there have been so many regrettable anti-Jewish incidents recorded, it clearly proves that anti-Semitism was an ideology strongly rooted in the minds of many people.

In this context, it is necessary to address the so-called *Dreyfus Affair*, the story of a Jewish officer in the French army, which is one of the turning points of history reflecting the spiritual climate of the time. The story began in 1894, when a French army officer, Alfred Dreyfus, was suspected of disclosing secret information to the German army. The army urgently had to find the culprit and call him to account, and as can happen in such a situation, anyone who seemed to fit the description would be accused, so that the situation could seemingly be taken care of. So, most obviously because of his Jewish background, it was decided that Dreyfus was to be blamed for the act. Since Dreyfus's defense was denied the right to examine the documents on which the spying charges were made, it is clear that the outcome of the trial had already been decided before it began. Dreyfus lost his military rank and was shamefully imprisoned outside of France. A famous French writer, *Emile Zola* (1840-1902), published in a newspaper an open letter called *J'accuse* ("I accuse"), in which he expressed his disapproval of the dishonest trial and his trust in the innocence of Dreyfus. The letter was published in *L'Aurore* on

January 13, 1898. Zola, despite his reputation, now faced a sentence himself and fled into exile. Soon a new investigation was begun, and it is largely due to Zola's moral integrity that in 1899, the name of Dreyfus was cleared of all false accusations.[118]

It is possible that the Dreyfus incident would have simply been forgotten if something greater had not been attached to it. As often happens in history, the situation concerning Dreyfus led to other, even greater developments in that period. At the same time Dreyfus was falsely accused in Paris, an Austrian Jewish journalist named *Theodor Herzl* (1860-1904) happened to be living there. Herzl wrote to a Viennese newspaper called *Neue Freie Presse*. He had already encountered anti-Semitism earlier, as a student in Vienna, but the series of events connected with Dreyfus were the ultimate watershed for him. Not only the dishonest sentence given to Dreyfus, but also the horrendously open anti-Semitism evident in the French society during and after the trial, convinced Herzl that anti-Semitism was almost like an unchanging part of society. It could not be removed as long as the Jews lived among other nations and not in a national home of their own. Herzl decided that it was time to establish a Jewish State, so he wrote his famous pamphlet *Der Judenstaat* ("The Jewish State") in 1896. As a result of his action, the first Zionist Congress met in Basel, Switzerland, in 1897.[119]

Herzl was not the first to write or think that Jews should return to their own land. It does seem that he was tireless once he began searching for political and financial support for the establishment of the new state. Among the most important supporters of Herzl were Christian Zionists who, after searching the Bible, had come to the conclusion that the Jews would, at some point in history, return to their own land. In Great Britain and in the United States, there were Christian Zionists who gave their support to the *Balfour*

Declaration in 1917. In this declaration, the British government promised to help the Jews in establishing their own homeland with the Palestinian Mandate. As early as the 1860s, significant Christian leaders, especially in Great Britain, introduced the thought that Jews should return to build their own land. Many of the major British politicians of that time were Christian Zionists. The chaplain of the British Embassy in Vienna, for example, was someone who helped Herzl with great personal enthusiasm.

It seems appropriate to point out here that the first *Aliyah*, Jewish *immigration*, to the then Ottoman-held area had already begun in 1882 and continued without interruption until 1903. The second Aliyah occurred in 1904-1914 and the third in 1919-1923. Naturally, immigration occurred between and after these years as well. These migrants were true pioneers who cleared malaria swamps and built settlements. In other words, the migration of Jews to the future Israeli State had already begun before Herzl's vision, but he actively sought support for the establishment of the new state. The Hebrew word "Aliyah" literally means *ascent*, for you always ascend to Jerusalem. Jewish migrants, no matter where in the world they come from, make Aliyah – ascend to Israel.

In the 1870s, a new development took place when religious and socioeconomic anti-Semitism aligned itself with racial doctrine. Right about this time, *Charles Darwin's* Theory of Evolution began to gain a strong foothold. Darwin (1809-1882) was a British natural scientist whose theory stated that all species come from the same origin. Reportedly, Darwin himself did not apply his theory to humans, but it was during his time that racial doctrine became a field of science. According to Darwin, species that adapt the best to a certain environment will most likely survive. According to racial doctrine, Jews were placed at the bottom in the battle between races. This view was taken even further with the racial hygiene doctrine, which gained a footing in universities around the Western world in the 20th Century. According to racial hygiene, the number of births should be controlled in order to bring congenital defects under control. According to these theories, the Jewish problem was racial and genetic, so it could not be changed by any measure. The Jewish race, therefore, was the reason for world problems and calamities. It was in the 1870s in Germany that the term *anti-Semitism* itself was coined. The purpose was to put a scientific cloak over the old hatred of the Jews. Because Hebrew is a Semitic language, the word *Semitic* refers to Jews. Even though Jews are not the only ones speaking a Semitic language, it is clearly understood that anti-Semitism is an expression of anger towards Jews.[120]

When Jews received their civil rights, their status soon began to improve. At the same time, anti-Semitism seemed to act like a virus. Just as viruses always evolve whenever an anti-viral drug is developed, anti-Semitism evolved gracefully and elegantly, according to the times. When the significance of Christianity decreased, socioeconomic and political anti-Semitism was birthed. When natural sciences became an important part of European society, anti-Semitism evolved into a racial discipline. In the end, it made little difference to anti-Semites what their beliefs were called: all the various forms of anti-Semitism lived in harmony with each other. The virus of anti-Semitism has survived even until this present day.

As new ways of thinking were developing in Western Europe, the situation was quite different in Eastern Europe. We can truthfully say that in Russia, for example, hatred toward the Jews was part of its official national policy. (At the time, my native Finland was part of Russia, too). The czars focused much of their attention on the Jews, who served as scapegoats for the problems of the nation. The Orthodox Church performed forced conversions and also incited crowds to violence and anti-Jewish attacks. Beginning in 1791, the majority of Eastern European Jews were forced to live in a special area known as the *Pale of Settlement.* It was established by *Catherine the Great,* who forced the Jews either to convert or to move away from her lands. When the Jews lived in one secluded area, they were an easy target for continuous violent assaults known as *pogroms.* During the time of the czars, Russian Jews suffered not only from the smaller, local pogroms, but also from wider attacks that took place in waves, in 1881-1884, 1903 and 1906, and after the revolution in 1917-1921. One of the most important developments in the history of anti-Semitism occurred in Russia between 1895 and 1899, when the Russian Secret Police produced a counterfeit writing called *Protocols of the Learned Elders of Zion*. This book describing the Jewish conspiracy started to spread in 1905, when Jews were blamed for the unpopular reforms in the Russian economy. *The London Times* proved the writing to be a fraud in 1921, but it still became one of the main arguments the Nazi Party used against the Jews. Sadly, new copies are still being circulated.[121]

At the same time that the hatred of the Jews developed in its various forms, Jews also had an influence on the culture and development of Europe in many ways. It can be said that despite continuous opposition and persecution, Jewish communities were a positive economic and cultural power in each country where they lived. Even in Eastern Europe, where the Jews lived in seclusion, spoke Yiddish and in all ways led a conservative life, the Age of Enlightenment managed to push aside some of the boundaries separating them from other citizens. In Western Europe, Jews took quick steps to advance the financial, political and cultural life. In 1866, a new synagogue was inaugurated in Berlin, and even the Chancellor, *Otto Von Bismarck*, participated in the opening. This gesture was seen widely as a sign of how the Jews had broken social barriers and become part of modern society.

"But, what is the truth?" the *German Conservative Party* queried in their political program in 1892: *"We desire the preservation and strengthening of the Christian life-view in the nation and the state... State and Church are institutions ordained by God... We fight against the often obtrusive and corrosive Jewish influence on our national life."*[122] Influential journalist *Theodor Fritsch* (1852-1933) campaigned to unite all existing anti-Jewish parties, accusing Jews of many kinds of conspiracies. He could not stand the rapid urbanization and new industry, and the Jews were his scapegoat. Fritsch's mission was, in practice, impossible, as anti-Semitism was so popular as an ideology that there were over 190 anti-Semitic parties in Germany by 1890.[123]

The line between anti-Semitism and murder is like a line drawn in water: it can be crossed easily, and the line is not actually seen on the surface. We understand today that anti-Semitism is prejudice against the Jews, on the basis of either their national or religious identity. The best minds of academia have researched anti-Semitism, its birth and also the ways it could be eradicated. Anti-Semitism is defined as a hostile view of the Jews, including their possessions and their religious institutions. However, no one has been able to develop a counter-solution for it, because if we discard the spiritual aspects of anti-Semitism, we cannot fully understand it.

In pre-Holocaust Europe, anti-Semitism was an ideology deeply set in the minds of the people, the roots of which were Christian and the manifestations multifaceted. Just before World War I, there was a short intermission on the stage of world history. Before World War I broke out, the

European nations seemed to sense its coming, as they prepared for war and organized their armies. The war began on July 28, 1914, and quickly escalated into a global war, because European powers had made complicated alliances, resulting in a global conflict. When nations needed all their economic resources for the war, civilians also became a part of the conflict. At the beginning of World War I, Jews fought in the armies of their own countries. Many German Jews received medals for bravery, many were wounded and many died. About 40,000 Jewish veterans were members of the First World War Veterans Association.[124]

The war was lethal, as it is estimated to have taken over ten million lives and wounded about twenty million people. The war ended on November 11, 1918, when Germany signed the peace treaty that the Allied Forces had drawn up.

The seeds of World War II were partially sown in that peace treaty. A new era had begun.

The Weimar Republic

"But you, brethren, are not in darkness, so that this Day should overtake you as a thief. You are all sons of light and sons of the day. We are not of the night nor of darkness. Therefore let us not sleep, as others do, but let us watch and be sober."[125]

The city of Weimar is a beautiful German city. The houses of famous people – musicians, writers and artists – are adorned by metal plaques.

The cultural city of Weimar is only about six miles from another historic place. You can take a bus there, and the journey will not take long. The name of the stop is simply: Buchenwald. The rest of the way to Buchenwald is driven on a road called the Blood Road. Concentration camp slaves built the road with no tools, uncovered, unsafe, and in all weather conditions. The road truly is a Blood Road, for the slaves did not last long. Sometimes they were given their freedom by Death. I am terrified as I notice how close Buchenwald is to the homes of people.

I am horrified to see that people are living, even now, right next to the former concentration camp. The atmosphere there is horrendous. Evil hovers in the air, like gray clouds covering the aspiring sun. I watch the people walking around me, laughing.

But I am distressed. I feel like opening my mouth and yelling: "Dear people, do you not know where we are?"

World War I ended in November 1918, and in June 1919, the *Versailles Peace Treaty* placed the blame on Germany for the war. Germany was partially demilitarized and lost some of its territory, including colonies, and was made to pay war reparations to the Allied Forces. This resulted in deep shame and rage as feelings smoldered under the surface in between the two wars. Only in 1925 was there an attempt to remedy the situation, as the Allied forces left Rhineland and Germany was accepted as a member of the League of Nations, which had been established in 1919.

In this time of national defeat, the Weimar Republic was birthed and ousted the former imperial administration. The fall of imperial rule meant a new beginning for the Jewish community. Even though there were many opponents of the Weimar Republic, for Jews, it meant an opportunity to rise and move on as a community and as individuals.[126] The constitution of the republic guaranteed every citizen's right to participate in public life, as well as to be elected to public office. Because the Jews went into political life and rose to high places in the new administration, their enemies soon began connecting them with the policies of the Weimar Republic. Two parallel phenomena occurred simultaneously: Jews quickly integrated into the republic and the wider society, but elsewhere, anti-Semitism grew into a strong power in different political and armed movements. Even though these movements were relatively small, immediately after World War I, everyday anti-Semitism was common. For instance, university student unions and many spas declared themselves proudly to be *judenrein*, "free of Jews."[127] One significant phenomenon of the Weimar Republic was its special cultural, a kind of restless, and creative force. Jews were a very big part of this creative and cultural stage.[128]

In the following years, Jews were included in several governmental positions, mainly they were in the Socialist and Democratic Parties. One of them was a man called *Walther Rathenau*. Rathenau was an industrial leader who first served as Minister of Economy and later became Foreign Minister. His role was especially significant in terms of then current war reparations and the post-war economy. In June 1922, right-wing radicals murdered the Foreign Minister. This murder was a dramatic way to draw attention to a campaign launched at the end of the war, claiming the Jews were principally or even solely responsible for Germany's defeat. The myth that Germany lost the war because it was *stabbed in the back* was a myth that was uppermost in anti-Jewish propaganda.[129] The myth also blamed the Jews for the terrible post-war social and economic difficulties, which grew into an outright crisis, especially in 1922 and 1923. Inflation in those years was totally out of control. At the same time, the extremely poor Eastern European Jews, *Ostjuden*, who stood out because of their strange religious clothing, poured into Germany in the hope of better conditions. They later became the primary cause of and attraction for anti-Semitic propaganda and provocation.

A phenomenon of this time, which would play a significant role in the future, was the *Bolsheviks'* Communist revolution in Russia. World War I was a very difficult challenge to the administration of *Czar Nikolai II*. Food and many basic supplies had run out, and the Czar was openly blamed for these deficiencies. In March 1917, a revolt broke out, which the Czar tried to suppress, but it ended with a full-scale revolution. The Bolsheviks came to power. Fear of Communism took over Western Europe, and this fear increased support for far-right parties. Extremist national ideologies, which united under the banner of Fascism, became popular in many European countries.

Among the fascist and nationalist movements, some of which were very anti-Jewish, the National Socialist Party (NSDAP), founded in 1919, was easily the most radical, despite its then small size. It did not hide its goals, as its entire party program was more or less founded on anti-Semitism. Its goals included removing civil rights from the Jews and using various means in order to eliminate Jews from public life. The party leadership – especially Adolf Hitler, leader of the party – used extremely radical expressions in their speeches and printed materials as the party declared its goal to be nothing less than the complete elimination and extermination (*Ausrottung*) of the Jews. Hitler wrote in 1919: *"Purely emotional antisemitism finds its final expression in the form of pogroms. Rational antisemitism, by contrast, must lead to a systematic and legal struggle against, and eradication of, the privileges the Jews enjoy over the other foreigners living among us (Alien Laws). Its final objective, however, must be the total removal of all Jews from our midst."*[130] It could be assumed, on this basis, that the number of Jews in

Germany was very high, but the reality was quite different. In the 1925 Census, there were about 564,379 Jews in all of Germany, which is 0.9% of the population. On top of that, they were fully assimilated, mainly among the middle class, and many were married to non-Jews.

Although Hitler's party was national socialist, highlighting a heavily nationalist country and the role of a nation state, its anti-Semitism crossed all national borders. The party did not offer a solution to the so-called Jewish question only in Germany but wanted to liberate all of humanity from this curse. Therefore, the party did not stop at Germany's national borders, but insisted on a radical new solution for the benefit of all mankind.

The entire ideology of the Nazi Party was based on racism, racial doctrines and inequality between races. The party advocated a battle between species, where the Jews were the lowest one. Jews represented a source of biological evil that would defile the whole world. In addition to this, Hitler marketed two main lines of thinking: the upcoming victory of the Aryan race over the Slavic race and the need for living space (*Lebensraum*) for Germans, especially in Eastern Europe.

The Nazis had four main themes:

1) **Racial doctrines**, which believed history was about the battle between races, with the Aryans as the dominant race that the others would serve;

2) **Racial anti-Semitism**, which says Jews are not only the lowest level on the racial hierarchy, but a sort of *Untermensch*, lower than human, thus below all other races;

3) **The fight against Communism**, alleging a link between

Jewishness and Communism, in which the fight against the spread of Communism is a fight against the Jews;

4) *Lebensraum*, **fight for living space**, arguing that it is natural for the Aryan race to spread eastward and take space for itself.[131]

The last years of the Weimar Republic, when the economic crisis deepened all the more, were the years of political rise for the Nazi Party. The streets were often full of violence, and the crisis birthed many side effects. In the 1928 elections, the Nazis received only about 3% of the vote. In 1929, the situation changed drastically: the economic crisis was no longer only local, but global, and the Nazi party received about 18% of the vote in the September 1930 elections. The year 1933 was pivotal, with the Nazis receiving over 37% of all votes. They were now the largest party. During these last years, anti-Semitism became part of society, for its effect was not limited to the Jews, but also to the surrounding society. After all, anti-Semitism was a key element of the Nazi Party. It would be too easy and simple to study the anti-Semitism of those years only through the violent events. Violence affected the Jews, of course, but it was not the only effect of anti-Semitism. What made this process so historically significant? What I know of, for the first time in history, a party, fighting against a democratically elected government, succeeded in making anti-Semitism, the so-called Jewish question, a central and main election theme. Germany's assimilated Jewish community started examining itself, for there was a dangerous change in the air. We know from testimonies that at this stage, many Jews began pondering their own identity as Germans (citizens) on the one hand, and as Jews on the other.

It is imperative to look at Hitler's rise to power in light of everything above. The first edition of his book, *Mein Kampf*, was published by chance –

or perhaps as an expression of history's irony – in 1925, the same year when *Paul von Hindenburg* was elected President of the Weimar Republic. Hindenburg had been the Field Marshal of the German Army during World War I, but unfortunately, great economic hardships occurred during his two presidential terms, which reduced his support. After it was published, Hitler's book like his speeches, was not taken seriously. His writings were laughed at when they should have been feared. From the beginning, Hitler talked about all he intended to do, but the truth is that the society around him behaved like it was blind and deaf. Had the society been alert to the indications, Hitler's rise to power could have been prevented. In the unstable atmosphere of Weimar, such a man as Hitler could possibly be dangerous, but at least in part, the people wanted to close their eyes to the dangers. Jews were assaulted and synagogues vandalized. The support for the National Socialist Party grew.[132]

So, how did Hitler become the chancellor? The answer is very simple: the old chancellor, Paul von Hindenburg, appointed him. There was a misconception at that time, as is very fashionable even today, that evil could be put down by making compromises. If we did not see the same phenomenon so clearly in our own time, we might think it shocking and unbelievable that smart people could not see Hitler for what he truly was. Also, the Jewish journalists lived in complete, partly self-created ignorance. Nothing had changed, according to all of society, when in reality, an era had come to an end.

A new time of fear and terror had already begun. On February 27, 1933, the *Reichstag* building was burned down – to this day, it is believed the Nazis were themselves behind the arson – and the very next day, Hitler's administration declared the *Enabling Act, Decree on the Protection of [Volk] and State,* which canceled citizens' basic rights for the time being,[133] and which gave a suitable excuse for retracting the freedom of assembly. Similarly, it was now possible to conduct home searches without permission and to confiscate property. All of this happened quite lawfully, since Hindenburg, when giving these rights to Hitler, had acted according to the Weimar Republic Constitution, which gave the president such rights in certain situations.[134] History proves this same sly process birthed by evil, occurring time after time, in different countries and cultures. (This is a process that for instance happened years later in many Latin American nations.) After partly receiving and partly usurping power, Hitler was now, at the beginning of the year 1933, one of the most influential men in Europe, and there was no limit to his lust for power.

Hitler Governing Before the Outbreak of World War II

"His power shall be mighty, but not by his own power; he shall destroy fearfully, and shall prosper and thrive; he shall destroy the mighty, and also the holy people. Through his cunning he shall cause deceit to prosper under his rule; and he shall exalt himself in his heart. He shall destroy many in their prosperity. He shall even rise against the Prince of princes."[135]

After the arson of the Parliament building, Hitler had more power than the democratic government, which had been his original aspiration. When we examine the 1930s, we notice the German society changing rapidly, mainly through new legislation and administration. Although the changes were swift, what makes them especially interesting is the fact that in each phase, people were offered, as if on a platter, an opportunity to say: *"That is enough. This policy does not represent the people."* However, this did not happen. It is seemingly useless for us to examine history and lament the behavior of those who preceded us. But, if we are honest with ourselves, we know that in a similar situation, we would be just as surprised and frightened. The real purpose in specifically detailing history is that we might learn from the past, in order to recognize the events when they appear in our own time. We can ask God for mercy that we, unlike most of Hitler's contemporaries, would be ready to pay the high price that might be demanded of us. Let us now examine how the events evolved.

Hitler became Chancellor of Germany at the end of January 1933, and by March, the first violent anti-Jewish riots had started in different parts of Germany. The riots were arranged. As we already know, anti-Semitism was already widespread in German society before the Nazis came to power. But we also understand that with the Nazis, many quiet anti-Semites were encouraged to add action to their words. At the same time, the first concentration camp, *Dachau,* near Munich, was built. The purpose was to subdue possible opposing voices, and also to intimidate the German citizens. The first people taken to the camps were members of the political opposition, mainly the Socialists, the Communists and the Liberals. So, Dachau was already built in 1933, while Buchenwald, for example, was built in 1937.[136]

In April 1933, the Nazis tested the German people using the first boycott of Jewish businesses. The boycott lasted only for a day, so its goals could not have been primarily economic. It was more of an experiment by the government to test the people's reactions to harassment of the Jews. Reactions by the people would anticipate the course the government would take from then on. Very significant elements were present at the April boycott: this was the first time the German Jewish population as a whole would be the target of an openly anti-Semitic action, and secondly, the boycott could not and did not even attempt to be camouflaged as a spontaneous national action. It was an operation organized and pushed through by the government. Reactions from the public were not on the Jewish side, at least not to such an extent that would have worried the government. As armed SA paramilitaries stood guard outside the shops, very few had the courage to do business in them. I have heard many times that one of these brave ones was the grandmother of *Dietrich Bonhoeffer*.

At the time of the boycott, new laws were announced, including the first so-called "racial laws," which prohibited Jews from civil service and public medicine positions. As I suggested with the April boycott, I believe the purpose of these laws was not primarily economic, even though they naturally had an economic effect on the dismissed Jewish officials. The primary purpose was to create a social boundary between German Jews and "Aryan" Germans.

When the Jews were openly isolated from the rest of society, it was difficult for people to continue their attitude toward them, even when that attitude was the acceptable one. When the government's opinions were expressed all the more clearly, and the atmosphere became suspicious, few had the courage to think and act in an independent way. Along with social goals, one aim that was realistic at that time was to make the life of the German Jews so difficult that they would decide to go abroad on their own initiative, leaving their property behind for the government to seize. As late as January 1939, *Hermann Göring* wrote: *"Jewish emigration from Germany should be encouraged in all possible ways."*[137] As a matter of fact, about 275,000 Jews fled the country before emigration from Germany was declared illegal in 1941.

In May 1933, new things happened. Now, books that met the criteria of having been written by Jews or of being democratic in nature were publicly burned in the streets. Such books included the anti-war masterpiece *All Quiet on the Western Front* by *Erich Maria Remarque* (1898-1970). At the same time, pieces of art, including paintings by *Pablo Picasso* (1881-1973) and *Marc Chagall* (1887-1985), were banned from museums. Burning books might seem harmless, maybe even a jovial use of time, but the truth is quite different, for in most dictatorships (even after the Nazis), burning books and the destruction of printing machines are precursors to violence against people. Even though all dictatorships – both before and after the Nazis – and mass murders have their own characteristics, it is similarly true that the development toward mass murder often occurs in a certain order. So it is not surprising that by a month after the May 1933 book burnings, about 27,000 opponents of Hitler had been taken to concentration camps or prisons.

In September 1935, yet another major step was taken when the actual Racial Laws, the *Nuremberg Racial Laws*, were published. At this stage, Germany became what historians call a *Racial State*. Jews were isolated from their German neighbors, since according to the new laws, they were second-class citizens, which were to be completely segregated from the economic and social life of the society. By 1935, about 25% of the Jews had already lost their businesses, either because they had been ordered to close their store or because their businesses had been given to Aryan owners. Because the laws emphasized the purity of blood, Jews had no possible way of circumventing them. The ban on marriages between Germans and those of "lower blood" prevented Jews and Aryans from marrying each other – although Gypsies were counted in the same lot.

As the law was directed toward the Jews, a massive propaganda campaign was targeted at the Germans. The role of propaganda cannot be overestimated, since in all dictatorships, influencing attitudes is a procedure occurring simultaneously with legislation. All the media of the time, including radio, press and public events, was now under Nazi rule. Posters around the country portrayed pictures of beautiful Aryans on the one hand, and on the other, sly and creepy-looking Jews. From these tools of propaganda, a slight, yet noticeable change in the attitudes of officials and other public servants was soon evident. They behaved, almost instinctively, in different ways toward Jews and Aryans. Since the change occurred so quickly, between 1933 and 1935, it heaped even more cruelty upon the victims.

There has been much debate on just how the Nazi regime and its security forces were able to coerce the people to isolate the Jews. In some incidents, people acted even more abhorrently than what was expected of them. Public dishonoring of German-Jewish married couples was common, even though it had not been ordered.[138] Up until 1938, Jewish children had attended German schools, but as the society turned more anti-Semitic, the atmosphere in schools also changed. Isolation, discrimination and all kinds of disturbances became a normal part of everyday life.

All of this was, of course, only the beginning. Much worse things were about to take place. Professor *Israel Gutman,* a Holocaust survivor, was one of the oldest researchers at Yad Vashem and a world authority in Holocaust research. He said: *"Jews were certain that things could not get any worse. But the truth is that each step was worse and more horrendous. This developmental dynamic is the very essence of horror."*[139] One horrendous step taken was the Nazi *euthanasia program,* which began in 1933 with the forced sterilization of people suffering from "genetic weaknesses.". In August 1939, a new order was given, requiring the doctors to report the children born between 1936 and 1939 who suffered from various congenital disabilities or illnesses. Children were taken from the institutions, and thousands were murdered in facilities built specifically for this purpose. The entire German psychiatric medical profession participated in these murders. Doctors usually did not even see their patients; with just a glance at their papers, children were sent to six different murder facilities, escorted by SS-personnel dressed in white doctors' clothes. Disabled children were murdered first by starving them to death, then by poisonous injections or by overdosing them with sleep medication, and finally with the most popular method, gas.

At the same time, about 15-20 children were murdered by doctors. The bodies were burned.[140] It was stated at the Nuremberg War Trials that about 275,000 Germans were murdered through this program.[141] Although the Catholic Church protested, since many children lived in church-maintained institutions, the program continued until the end of World War II. It had to go underground, but still it continued.

Perhaps the most important question concerns the lawyers, doctors and others who worked on this program without remorse or moral and judicial doubts. Why were they not expelled from churches, or excommunicated, as it is done in the Catholic Church? It was, after all, a murder program. In fact, it was the first stage of Jewish mass murder. The events proceeded fiercely. When the people increasingly turned their eyes away from the reality of this horrendous scene, they became brutal and inhumane, just like the government. The key to further events lies in the reality that they refused to see. If Germans were not ready to rise up in revolt when their own children were murdered, it is clear that they would not do so for the German Jews either. The more the government terrorized the people, the closer they advanced to the mass murder of Jews.

The process that led to genocide was simultaneously, as Professor

Michael J. Bazyler said, "*legal and criminal.*" That is exactly where the most terrifying aspect of the entire process lies.[142] Law reflects the society. It reflects not only the will of legislators, but also that of the citizens who have elected those legislators. Law is never neutral; it embodies the values of the society. It is true that existing laws were both used and changed according to need, so that everything was covered with an obscuring fog or curtain of the law. The soil of society was prepared to view some people groups as subhuman, who only then were to be murdered. At the Nuremburg War Trials, the Nazi criminals claimed to have acted completely lawfully, and that, therefore, they were not criminals. Fortunately, the Military Tribunal was able to argue that the entire Nazi State had turned into a lawless nation, so following its laws did not indicate true law.[143] In other words, law and justice are not synonyms, and it is possible that in some situations, man has to act against law in order to act for justice.

It is possible that when historical processes advance at an accelerating pace, they eventually reach a point where they can no longer turn in the other direction. It is as if the events have reached such a speed that the brakes no longer function and driving into a chasm is unavoidable. Reviewing Nazi Germany, historians call the year 1938 the Fateful Year. 1938 was truly exceptional in the sense that we can see clear changes in the German society taking place. In domestic politics, by 1938, Germany had been subdued under the absolute control of one party, meaning that its governance was totalitarian, and the governing party did not stop until its power covered all areas of the citizens' lives. With regard to the Jews, Germany had advanced a long way in the process it had started, which was seen as an ever-growing part of the overall goals of the state. Over 150,000 German Jews had already left Germany, but the *Anschluss,* the annexation of Austria, subjected 185,000 additional Jews under the Nazi rule.[144] At this stage, Jewish passports had already been confiscated. The few who managed to get a passport were required to have it stamped with the letter J to reveal their Jewish background.

In foreign policy, Germany had changed from the disarmed state of the Versailles Peace Treaty into a nation on its way to war. In 1938, Germany had successfully displayed its military power before the Western nations. The German army marched to Vienna in the Anschluss Operation and was welcomed by the Austrians. After the Anschluss in March 1938, the persecution of the Austrian Jews began immediately – not by the Germans, but by the Austrians, of their own initiative. By August 1938, 2,732 Austrians had been arrested, of whom 2,033 were Jews, most imprisoned at the Dachau Concentration Camp.[145] The small country of Czechoslovakia had been sacrificed to Hitler in order to avoid war – another example of a compromise made with evil out of the belief that this would protect the world from further assaults. Czechoslovakia had to give up the zone between itself and Germany, called the *Sudetenland*, where many Germans lived. Germany, recognizing the weakness of the surrounding world, was ready for war and not afraid of governments, which offered it peace at any cost.

This all was understood by *Winston Churchill* (1874-1965), who at that time was not yet the Prime Minister of Great Britain. When Prime Minister *Neville Chamberlain* (1869-1940) returned from Munich, where the treaty was made to sacrifice Czechoslovakia, Churchill warned Chamberlain that the decision would be *"the choice between war and dishonor,"* and that as the Western nations chose dishonor, they would get the war as well. Unfortunately, the gravity of Churchill's words was not appreciated at all in 1938.

More was to come! On October 27, 1938, a group of Polish Jews were brutally and violently forced to move into No Man's Land, an area between Poland and Germany, where there were no livelihood opportunities, and where they suffered indescribable agonies and hunger, with no chance of escape. One man among them, *Sendel Grynszpan*, managed to send a letter to his son *Herschel*, living in Paris, describing the horrible living conditions of this Jewish group. On November 7, 1938, German diplomat *Ernst vom Rath* was murdered in Paris, the murderer being the Herschel Grynszpan.

Kristallnacht, "the Night of the Broken Glass," occurred two days later, and for a long time, many believed that it was a reaction to the murder of the diplomat. However, Kristallnacht was a very well-organized night of vandalism, violence and arson, which began in some cities on November 8. Nazi leaders had gathered in Munich to celebrate the anniversary of Hitler's previous, though unsuccessful, *putsch* or coup. In addition to the 1923 coup, World War I had ended in defeat on November 11, 1918. So, most likely, the night of anti-Jewish vandalism had been planned far in advance, although the diplomatic murder offered the most convenient explanation.[146] During that night, Jewish shops were destroyed, and private homes intruded upon, and most importantly, synagogues were burned. Over 30,000 Jewish men were taken to concentration camps.

A priest in Berlin said that *"even the synagogues are houses of God."* About 400 years had passed since the order given by Luther to set synagogues on fire, and now the horrible act had come to fruition. This was the beginning of an end for German Jews. Perhaps the situation of the German Jews was an alarming sight even to their contemporaries in 1938, but it had not yet been perceived that, in fact, all of Europe was on the verge of destruction.

The Night of the Broken Glass was the beginning of the end. Evil never begins at the point to which it ultimately comes. Many historians have estimated that in the 1930s, it would have been possible to engage in an effective resistance against Hitler, because his power was uncertain, and the war had not yet begun. But at that time, resistance was limited to a few courageous individuals. Anti-Semitism was so deeply rooted in society that anti-Jewish actions had no meaning in creating resistance. Where there was resistance, it was when the people felt that Hitler was a threat to Germany's own national interests. The night, which had such a striking name, received international press. The endangered position of the Jews in Germany was a well-known fact, but at the time of the Night of the Broken Glass, the world had begun to close its gates to the Jews, who were desperately knocking on them, seeking safety. For example, Great Britain received Jewish children who arrived through special *Kindertransport*, "children's transport." These children said goodbye to their families, since they had to come alone. They left without realizing that they would never see their parents again. Thousands of children were saved in this way.

In July 1938, an international conference was organized to discuss the alarming situation of the German Jews. The conference was President Roosevelt's initiative and is known as the *Evian Conference*. Most nations, including Roosevelt's administration, sent lower-level representatives who had no mandate to make decisions. Thus, governments were able to create the impression that they were following the development of the situation in Germany but in reality no attempt was made to find a solution. A member of the Australian delegation said: *"since we do not have a racial problem, we are not desirous of importing one."*[147]

Chaim Weizmann, who later became the first President of the State of Israel, said to the *Manchester Guardian: "The world seemed to be divided into two parts – those places where the Jews could not live and those where they could not enter.*"[148] The significance of the failed Evian Conference as a step that led toward genocide cannot be overstated. It is also noteworthy that anti-Semitism was widespread in many nations. The idea of a Jew as the enemy did not relate to the present only but to the kind of future nations wanted for themselves.

The world's indifference showed in various ways. In May 1939, a ship called *St. Louis* left Germany for Havana, in order to bring a group of about 900 German-Jewish refugees to *Cuba*. However, the government in Cuba changed and their permit was canceled. The captain of the ship counted on the United States or Canada to come to their rescue, but in the end, the ship had to return to Germany. European nations such as *Belgium, Holland, Britain* and *France* received a few of these refugees, but most of them perished in the Nazi "Final Solution."

Thus, we have arrived at the very threshold of World War II. As the war broke out, Hitler's first target was Poland, the country where the largest Jewish population of Europe lived. Over three million Jews were now left at Hitler's mercies. The Final Solution, which had for so long been a theoretical goal of the SS, had now become an easily attainable reality. Millions of Jews were at the mercy of the Nazi regime. We know only a fraction of their stories.

As a survivor, author Primo Levi said in his famous statement, which is featured in the Anne Frank Museum in Amsterdam: "*One single Anne Frank moves us more than the countless others who suffered just as she did, but whose faces have remained in the shadows. Perhaps it is better that way; if we were capable of taking in all the suffering of all those people, we would not be able to live.*"

As many elderly Holocaust survivors have said to me, unless you have actually been "there," you cannot fully understand.

But there is one thing we can do: we can remember that each victim was an individual, a family member and a human being. Nazis tried to destroy the humanity of these humans by turning them into numbers. This is where a great secret is hidden, for the God of the Bible deemed the names of men so important that He changed the destinies of some by giving them a new name. So, we remember the six million, but we also remember one individual.

An Israeli poet, *Zelda Schneerson Mishkovsky* (1914-1984), wrote a poem called *Everyone Has a Name*:

"Everyone has a name given to him by God
and given to him by his parents.

Everyone has a name given to him by his stature,
and the way he smiles
and given to him by his clothing.

Everyone has a name given to him by the mountains
and given to him by the walls.

Everyone has a name given to him by the stars
and given to him by his neighbors.

Everyone has a name given to him by his sins
and given to him by his longing.

Everyone has a name given to him by his enemies
and given to him by his love.

*Everyone has a name given to him by his holidays
and given to him by his work.*

*Everyone has a name given to him by the seasons
and given to him by his blindness.*

*Everyone has a name given to him by the sea
and given to him by his death."*

6 The Nazi Final Solution – Steps on the Path of Genocide

"And I, Daniel, alone saw the vision, for the men who were with me did not see the vision; but a great terror fell upon them, so that they fled to hide themselves. Therefore I was left alone when I saw this great vision, and no strength remained in me; for my vigor was turned to frailty in me, and I retained no strength. Yet I heard the sound of his words; and while I heard the sound of his words I was in a deep sleep on my face, with my face to the ground... Now I have come to make you understand what will happen to your people in the latter days, for the vision refers to many days yet to come."[149]

We drive toward the Wannsee Villa to the most beautiful neighborhood of Berlin. We pass by very well-kept gardens. We see glimpses of great sailing boats. As we get out of the car when we arrive, we see a beautiful path leading to a white villa. We are surrounded by old green trees. The atmosphere is sophisticated and calm. The area is elegant.

The white villa is now a museum. We see elegant rooms. This is where the representatives of the different branches of the Nazi administration gathered in January 1942. They met together to make a decision about the mode of cooperation through which a genocide could be executed painlessly and within a reasonable timetable. One must not forget the German railroads, for they had an especially important part to play in this plan. The meeting did not need to take long, since the participants had a shared understanding about the importance of the goal. The estimated number of Jews in Europe was too high, but even that was not a problem. This regime could take on any challenge.

The Wannsee Villa, if anything, represents the everyday nature of evil. The representatives of the Nazi regime were average men to whom this sudden historical situation gave power. They discussed the genocide as if it were transportation of munitions to the front lines or any other delivery. They did not understand that their days were numbered. Even though there was still time left, the clock was inevitably ticking. Naturally, they did not understand whose possession they had touched.

The Wannsee Villa does not impress me. I would not move anywhere near this area, even if I were paid to live there. I leave quickly, as for some reason I feel nauseated. Perhaps the thought of the Nazi leaders having breakfast connects in my mind with an image of an open mass grave.

What do we actually mean when we use such terms as *genocide* or *mass murder*? When the acts of the World War II culprits were defined in the Nuremberg War Trials, the judges said: *"They (the defendants) conducted deliberate and systematic genocide – viz., the extermination of racial and national groups – against the civilian populations of certain occupied territories in order to destroy particular races and classes of people, and national, racial or religious groups, particularly Jews, Poles, Gypsies and others."*[150] The United Nations defines genocide as follows: *"Genocide is a denial of the right of existence of entire human groups, as homicide is the denial of the right to live of individual human beings; such denial of the right of existence shocks the conscience of mankind... and is contrary to moral law and to the spirit and aims of the United Nations."*[151] Genocide is not only against the spirit and aspirations of the UN, it is a crime against humanity itself. Genocide is an unnatural state to which certain factors lead. It is not war, even though it might take place during a war. History offers us plenty of examples of genocide, with both common and unique features.

The word *Holocaust*, which is used in most languages to describe the persecution of the Jews in Germany, comes from the Greek, where it has a profoundly religious meaning: *burnt offering.* In Hebrew, Germany's persecution of the Jews is described with the word *Shoah.* It is a Biblical word meaning *destruction* or *catastrophe.* These religious words were brought into use because there were simply no suitable words in our colloquial language to describe what happened, since it was so shocking and enormous in proportion.

In the German persecution of the Jews, the world was taken to a point from which it has never fully recovered. After all, the persecution of the Jews raises serious questions. What is the responsibility of an individual in a society? How should we respond to the persecution of innocent people around the world? What is our personal responsibility in society, and how far should we obey the state apparatus? How is individual responsibility connected to the fact that before a society tolerates the existence of concentration camps, the essence of that society has to change?

The Holocaust, genocide of the Jews, was an extreme genocide, as its open and proclaimed purpose was to murder the entire Jewish population. It took place just recently, and it is the most documented of all genocides in world history. In other words, we have an enormous amount of associated evidence from the perpetrators of the Holocaust as well as the victims and survivors. Along with individual stories, part of this material relates to entire communities that were murdered. The Holocaust encompasses every element of genocide, from its initial plan to its final implementation. These elements include the following:

- **discrimination** against a particular group;
- **financial steps** such as confiscation of property;
- **negative thoughts and descriptions** of a particular group in the form of propaganda
- specific **racial doctrine;**
- **government bureaucracy** and administrative practices in the service of genocide;
- **the reactions of the intended victims** in an intensifying atmosphere of danger.[152]

Many Holocaust researchers have struggled with the definition for this special genocide, the Jewish Holocaust. Should it be seen as one event that has a unique nature, with no predecessors or parallels? Or should it be seen as an event that has coherence with other similar events, so that it would be easier to learn from and draw conclusions from it?[153] What about the Armenians or Rwandans; what did they face? The entire genocide concept opens up frightening horizons to which even the researchers do not know how to react nor to give exhaustive explanations.

We are used to thinking about the Holocaust from the viewpoint of genocide; therefore, we connect it, in a narrow manner, to the years of 1941-1945, when the genocide mostly took place. This was between the attack by Nazi Germany on the Soviet Union in June 1941 and the end of the war in May 1945. The events of the war brought more and more Jewish communities under German rule. Since we cannot review all of Europe here, we can consider Poland, and especially the city of Warsaw, as an example of this series of events.

Before the war broke out, the world's second-largest Jewish population was in Warsaw, with about 375,000 Jews, about 30% of the city's population. As Hitler's army accomplished an easy victory over Poland's ill-equipped, though brave army, a process started concerning the Jews. Immediately after Poland's surrender, the Jewish community of Warsaw became the target of brutal attacks, forced labor, vandalism and robbery; thousands of Jews died during the first weeks of German reign.

Officially, Reinhardt Heydrich gave orders regarding the Jews in September 1939. According to the orders, Jews living in small cities or towns were to be taken to ghettoes, which were to be established in large cities. Well-known Jewish personalities were to be sought for and ordered to be contacts between the Germans and the Jews, in the so-called *Judenrats* or *Jewish councils*. These were orders that concerned the so-called transition stage: Jews were to wear a badge of identification, they were to do forced labor, their possessions could be confiscated, and they could be transported to labor camps. The Jews were registered during this stage, so that their exact number and address were known. Often, they had to give up their radios etc.

The Warsaw Ghetto was established in November 1940, and during World War II, it was the largest Jewish ghetto in Europe. Because about 500,000 Jews lived in a cramped area, many died of epidemics, starvation and the coldness of winter. Since the ghetto was surrounded by a wall, it was impossible for its inhabitants to do any kind of business with the Polish legally, and illegal business was very dangerous. But even though the Jews were isolated from the rest of the world, they had the strength to organize schools and cultural activities, all of which formed a kind of resistance to the Germans – often called spiritual resistance.

In July 1942, Germans started deportations from the ghetto. In practice, this occurred in a very simple manner. The Jews whose names were on the list were forced to come to a place called *Umschlagplatz*, "transfer/loading place", which can still be visited in today's Warsaw. They were forced into freight wagons and then to trains heading for concentration and extermination camps.

By September 1942, about 300,000 Jews had been deported, of which about 254,000 had been taken to *Treblinka* Extermination Camp, where they were murdered upon arrival. Were the Jews able to influence their own fate? The president of the ghetto's Jewish council, *Adam Czerniakov*, committed suicide when the deportations began, realizing that there was absolutely nothing he could do for anyone.[154]

Henryka Lazawart was a Polish-Jewish poet who also acted in the underground organizations of the Warsaw Ghetto. She wrote her poem *Little Smuggler* just before her death in the extermination camp of Treblinka in 1942. During the Holocaust, children had to take on adult roles, but the poem describes this from the child's perspective. I do not think that there is any way we can imagine what the life of a child during the Holocaust was really like.

We cannot comprehend it fully, but we can respect it by listening:

"Through walls, through holes, through sentry points,
Through wires, through rubble, through fences...I flee, dart like a
cat...A hundred times I risk my life, I risk my childish neck.
And if the hand of sudden fate
Seizes me at some point in this game.
It's only the common snare of life...
The dust of the street will bury

The lost youngster's fate.
And only one grim thought,
A grimace on your lips:
Who, my dear Mama, who
Will bring you bread tomorrow?"[155]

Who cared about the children? We know the Jewish teachers and children's workers, dedicated to the well-being of the children, did all they could do to ensure that the children might continue a normal life for as long as possible. Sometimes dedication to children required sacrifices I dare say few of us would be ready to make. One of the most well-known persons to make such a sacrifice was *Janusz Korczak* (1879-1942), the pen name of the pediatrician, teacher and children's author *Henryk Goldszmit* from Warsaw. He left his reputation and honor as a well-known, respected author in order to dedicate himself to orphans, and when he was expelled to the Warsaw Ghetto like many other Jews, he was ready to set up a children's home for hundreds of ghetto orphans. As a well-known author, Korczak could have received help left and right to leave the ghetto, but he refused to abandon the orphaned children. When the Nazi occupiers ordered the orphans to be sent to their immediate death in Treblinka, Korczak was offered an opportunity to save his own life. However, he refused, selflessly deciding to go with these children on their last journey.[156] What makes this case so special is that Korczak knew the hopelessness of the situation. He knew the journey would end in certain death. But only his presence would calm the children, and he saw that this was important enough to sacrifice his own life.

"Greater love has no one than this, than to lay down one's life for his friends."[157]

As the events proceeded, because of the Germans' brutality, there were young people in the Warsaw Ghetto who decided to form a band of organized resistance. In pictures, these young people look very young and very beautiful, in the way we associate with the portraits of that time. It is impossible to understand or imitate their bravery. It is one thing to act courageously in a situation where it is possible to be saved, but their courage was different; it was the kind of moral bravery that acted even when facing an almost certain death. *Mordechai Anielewicz*, the young commander of the *Jewish Fighting Organization* (ZOB in Polish), looks especially sad to me, but at the same time determined. Under his command, the group of young people immediately began to search for weapons that could be used against the Germans at the appropriate moment. In January 1943, they wrote an appeal to the Jews of the ghetto, explaining to them that all the German talk about working and being saved through work was only a lie. When deportations began again in January 1943, the group understood the time was close. In fact, they thought it was time for the last deportations before the entire ghetto would be destroyed. So, therefore, this was when they attacked the Germans. Deportations did, in fact, end for a while. However, we know that the fighters realized they were outnumbered. Anielewicz is quoted on the wall of the Yad Vashem Museum: *"Jewish armed resistance... is [a] fact. I have been a witness to the magnificent, heroic fighting of Jewish men in battle."*

Indeed, it was only a respite. The last ghetto battle and the ultimate destruction of the ghetto began on the eve of Passover, April 19, 1943.

Conducting attacks, the so-called *Aktion*, during Jewish holidays was a commonly used method favored by the Germans. The heroic, yet desperate fight of the Warsaw Ghetto Revolt against the Germans began at that time of celebrating freedom in 1943. The Jewish fighting spirit surprised everyone, including the Germans, but in the final battle, exhausted and fighting with inadequate weapons, they were no opposition for the German troops led by General *Jürgen Stroop,* who had been sent from Berlin for this very purpose. The German troops were well armed. At this stage, they knew they would face resistance, and Jewish resistance was not looked well upon by Berlin. On May 16, 1943, the battle was over, and according to reports sent by Stroop to Berlin, 56,065 Jews were killed. The young commander and most of the fighters died in battle. Some of them managed to escape into sewage canals, and some walked to the other side from under the ghetto wall. A few made it safely, but some were killed by the poisonous gas the Germans purposefully put in the sewage to prevent them from escaping.

We know that in many ghettos, the Jews were singing *Ani Ma'amin* (I believe) right before their death. It is part of the Jewish "morning prayer," and according to *Rabbi Maimonides,* one of the thirteen basic pillars of Judaism. The lyrics go like this:

"Ani Ma'amin
BeEmuna Shlema
Betviat HaMashiach
Ve afalpi sheyitmameha
Im kol ze ani ma'amin
Im kol ze yechake lo
Be kol yom she yavo'

"I believe

With complete faith

In the coming of the Messiah.

Though he may delay

Nonetheless, I will believe

Nonetheless, I will wait

Still every day

I believe"

The young Warsaw Ghetto fighters remind me of another heroic story, even though the heroes of these stories never met each other in reality. Perhaps it is fitting at this point to remember a heroic young woman called *Hannah Senesh* (1921-1944). Senesh, a well-known figure in the history of the Holocaust, was originally from Hungary and had moved to the Jewish community in the Palestinian Mandate before the years of World War II. This young woman volunteered in the British Army to be dropped into Europe. Her purpose was to help the Jews in Budapest so that they would not be sent to concentration camps, just as the war was coming to a close in 1944. For this purpose, the British dropped her from a parachute in Yugoslavia, but she was captured and executed after being tortured. Before her execution, Senesh wrote the words that are found today in Holocaust museums and memorial events around the world. They are strong words, for they challenge each of us to think about our own lives. Is anything more important than our life?

The words fit not only Senesh herself, but also the young Warsaw fighters:

"Blessed is the match consumed in kindling flame.

Blessed is the flame that burns in the secret fastness of the heart.
Blessed is the heart with strength to stop its beating for honor's sake.
Blessed is the match consumed in kindling flame."

But are there any more matches? Are we just out for ourselves, or are we a part of something greater? Would we answer the challenge as young Hannah did?

As we review the Warsaw events as single incidents, we understand the bigger picture taking place in different parts of Europe. First, Jews were forced to leave their homes and move to cramped conditions in a designated isolated area. When all this had been accomplished, they were often used in forced labor, in factories or on the streets. The direction was already clear at this stage. They were not wanted, and neither was there any intention to keep them alive longer than necessary for administrative or practical reasons. Later, when Nazi Germany occupied one country after another, they implemented the same process everywhere with slight local variations. Let us consider Germany itself for a moment. In many cases, not only at the outbreak of World War II but also in the 1940s, Jews had effectively been isolated from the rest of society. Their possessions were confiscated, making them poor; they received only very little portions with their ration cards, and they were not able to use public transportation. They had been isolated from the rest of the world even by the confiscation of their radios. In September 1941, their isolation was completed when they were forced to wear a yellow star. Their transportation to the East (a term used as a code name for concentration and extermination camps) began just one month later. The German people had received many hints as to what was actually happening. Hitler's so-called prophecy from 1939, in which he threatened to destroy all Jews during the war, was publicly placed all around Germany in 1941. That same year, his propaganda minister *Josef Goebbels* wrote in the weekly *Das Reich* that Hitler's prophecy was being carried out.[158] Who would not have noticed the sudden disappearance of neighbors and acquaintances? Trains traveled east filled with people instead of goods, and returned empty...

At the same time, Churchill was preparing Britain for a difficult war that would possibly take a long time. He said, for instance: *"You ask, what is our policy? I can say: It is to wage war, by sea, land and air, with all our might and with all the strength that God can give us..."*[159] The triumphal march of the German army was inevitable. The Allies would indeed require all the strength that was bestowed upon them. As the German army proceeded deeper within the Soviet Union and Yugoslavia, certain factors were present that contributed to the implementation of genocide:

- It was clear from the beginning that **the Eastern Front did not comply with any moral rules** or **rules dictated by international law**;
- **Human rights violations** against the Slavic population were accepted or even encouraged;
- **Prisoners of war** were treated cruelly or murdered;
- **Local administration** was destroyed;
- The existence of the local population was allowed only to ensure **economic exploitation;**
- All under German rule lived under constant, **intentional threat and terror.**[160]

It was in Poland, in the Soviet Union and in the former Yugoslavia where the civilian population saw the most death, so it can be rightly stated that the war was waged especially against civilians. The aim was to subordinate the local population to the status of slaves and murder all Jews living in the area.

The German army was the first to reach the occupied areas. Although the myth of the respectability of the German army, the *Wehrmacht*, has been raised up on many forums in the past, the truth is that the Wehrmacht accepted Hitler's policy in the areas it had occupied. Here is an example of the army orders, signed by *Erich von Manstein*, the Commander-in-Chief of the 11th Army: *"Jewry constitutes the middleman between the enemy in the rear and the still fighting remainder of the Red Armed Forces and the Red leadership. More strongly than in Europe, it [Jewry] holds all the key positions in the political leadership and administration, controls trades and guilds and further forms the nucleus for all unrest and possible uprisings... The soldier must appreciate the necessity for harsh punishment of Jewry, the spiritual bearer of the Bolshevist terror. This is also necessary in order to nip in the bud all uprisings which are mostly attributable to Jews."*[161] It is estimated in current research that Wehrmacht units murdered about 10 million civilians; not in fighting but in mass murder and burnings of entire towns and wider areas.[162] Logically, it is also clear that different parts of the army and other military units would have exchanged information.

Right behind the army came *Einsatzgruppen*, or Mobile killing units, whose task was to follow the army deep into the land captured from the enemy. Their aim was to destroy influential individuals, such as the Commissars, Communists and especially the Jews. So, when the army arrived at a village, the Jews were taken outside the village and shot. Because over

90% of the victims were Jewish civilians, it is appropriate to use the word "Jewish" to describe them. Usually, before the shootings took place, the victims themselves were forced to dig a deep mass grave into which they tumbled on top of each other as they were shot to death. If the number of victims was very large, locals were used as labor force. We know from local witnesses that there was often movement in the graves from those who were still alive after the shootings. Sometimes a surviving victim escaped at nightfall, but this was rare. In mass shootings, it was not always possible nor desirable to ensure the death of the victims. In one instance, a German soldier arrived at the murder scene and managed to film the process. His film can be seen in the Yad Vashem Museum, and it is absolutely horrendous. The Einsatzgruppen, who carried out the shootings, were often loyal to the party idealists and SS members, so these operations did not astound them. The *SS* (*Schutzstaffel*) was Hitler's elite group and security guard, whose training was aimed at unrestrained use of violence. But so-called ordinary men and ordinary police officers were also present at the shootings, and many studies have been conducted in order to understand their role and motivation. Is it possible that just anybody can become a mass murderer?

What did the shooters see in the event? How did they feel about the situation and their task? A fair amount of witness accounts has been preserved. One former soldier recalled: *"Today I still remember the horror of the Jews who saw the corpses in the pit. Many Jews were shocked and screamed."*[163] Even though most of the men participated in the shootings, there was always someone who refused: *"Sometimes some of the men refused to take part in the shootings. I refused a few times. None of our overseers did anything to us, nor to any other who refused to shoot. We were given other tasks. We were not threatened with any punishment, especially not during the executions.*"[164]

Implementing large-scale mass murder by shooting was extremely problematic, as it required a great number of men. It could not but have an effect on the men's mood, and in addition, mass graves were difficult to keep secret. A new way of murdering had to be developed quickly, and it was essential that the murderers did not need to be so physically close to those being murdered. Distance would make killing easier. Watching people die close-up might cause feelings of pity to arise, even reluctantly, causing guilt. Mass murder had to be made easier for the murderers. There were experts in this field in Germany, since the euthanasia program had already been started years earlier, which operated in a similar manner. The experts of German euthanasia institutes were invited to establish new units in the East. Doctors who had taken part in murdering disabled children were now promoted.[165]

In 1941, the Chief of Security Services and Police, Reinhardt Heydrich, decided to summon a special meeting so that different administrative sectors could agree upon actions directed at solving the Jewish question. In the invitation, he said: *"In order to reach a common agreement on all aspects connected with this final solution among the central agencies concerned, I suggest that we make these problems a matter of joint discussion."*[166] The German governor in Poland, *Hans Frank*, wrote in his diary before the meeting: *"One way or another – I will tell you that quite openly – we must finish off the Jews... the Jews will disappear. They must go... In January there will be a major conference on this question in Berlin...We cannot shoot these 3.5 million Jews, we cannot poison them, but we will be able to take measures that will lead somehow to successful destruction; and this in connection with the large-scale procedures which are to be discussed in the Reich."*[167]

Extermination of the Jews, as a goal and official policy of all government bodies in the state, was discussed at a breakfast meeting in Berlin's luxurious Wannsee neighborhood on January 20, 1942. The discussion was chaired by Reinhardt Heydrich; there were high-ranking representatives of the SS, the police and different government departments present. The decision to be made was in reality not about whether to exterminate the Jews, but about planning the cooperation between different government bodies and agencies in order to fulfill the goal of genocide in the easiest and quickest way possible. Fifteen representatives of the National Socialist Administration elite participated in the meeting. Many of them had academic education – eight even had a doctorate degree – and most had built successful careers. Many came from middle class homes. Many were of a Christian religious background; one was the son of a pastor. Their average age was 43. They represented, it could be argued, the elite of Nazi Germany at its best.

Most likely, Heydrich wanted to be sure that he, as the leader of the organization, would be responsible for the fate of the Jews, not the Ministry of the Interior, which was his competitor. Heydrich explained in the meeting that deportations of the Jews to the East had already begun, on the basis of Hitler's earlier decision, and therefore only Heydrich himself was an authority on the Jewish Question, no matter which European nation was discussed. No actual written order with precise instructions on the implementation of genocide has ever been found, but it is assumed Hitler gave such sensitive orders verbally. From the surviving memos, we know that the decision about Jewish deportations had been made earlier. If, up until January 1942, Jews suffered exhaustion due to forced labor and were subjected to cold, hunger and heavy physical punishment, now, the goal was clearly murder. After this, exhaustion through work was no longer an actual part of state policy. The operation that was discussed at the Wannsee Conference was called *Operation Reinhardt.*

As a result of the Wannsee Conference, large-scale deportations and the systematic murder of the Jews began. The following provides only a partial overview of the timeline of events (taken from different sources and by no means an exhaustive list):

- **February-March 1942**: Permission for deporting Jews from France and Slovakia was issued;
- **March-October 1942**: 58,000 Jews from Slovakia were brought to Auschwitz;
- **March 1942**: Deportations from occupied France began, followed by deportations from occupied France in August of the same year;
- **July 1942**: Deportations of Norwegian Jews began;
- **March 1943**: Deportations from Greece and Macedonia began;
- **September 1943**: Deportations from occupied Italy began;
- **October 1943**: Deportation of the Jews still living in Denmark;
- **May-July 1944**: 430,000 Hungarian Jews were deported to Auschwitz, often directly to the gas chambers.

Almost all branches of the Nazi German government took part in the deportations; therefore, all took part in the genocide.[168]

Instead of slow and difficult shootings, new and more efficient ways were developed that would put less strain on the troops and enable the murder of larger masses of people in a shorter time. Death camps were built in occupied areas of Poland: *Belzec, Sobibor, Majdanek, Chelmno, Treblinka* and *Auschwitz*. Belzec was the first camp of Operation Reinhardt, situated conveniently along the Lublin-Lemberg railroad. Jews of many different nationalities were transported there, and half a million were murdered. Sobibor, which had become famous for the October 1943 prisoners' rebellion, was located closer to Warsaw; 250,000 Jews were murdered there. Treblinka was along the Warsaw-Bialystok railroad. It operated for 14 months, during which 900,000 people were murdered. Majdanek was located in the Lublin area, and it operated as both a concentration and extermination camp. About 74,000 Jews were brought there, about 60,000 of whom died there. Chelmno, in turn, operated from December 1941 to March 1943, and again from June 1944 to January 1945. About 152,000 people were murdered here.[169]

It has been estimated that about 15,000-20,000 people could be murdered every day in just one camp. In order to understand the magnitude of the matter, think of this: between March 1942 and November 1943, two million Jews and 50,000 Roma (Gypsies) were murdered.[170] Common to all camps was their isolated location, especially in Poland, and their connection to railroads. Their location was kept a secret from the Germans who had no direct connection to them, and from the locals. Only Majdanek and Auschwitz were also concentration camps; all the others were extermination camps, meaning that human transports were brought there only to be murdered. Usually, the Jews transported to the camps had been in cattle cars for several days without water, food or any kind of hygiene; sometimes the journey could take over twenty days. Of course, many of the people died on the way. After descending from the train, the remaining ones lived for a few hours at most, unless they were chosen for slave labor – and even this possibility included the ever-present death.

In a sense, the trains carried all of humanity, as each of us can find ourselves there. Any one of us could have been there. The following poem is written by an Israeli poet, a Holocaust survivor, *Dan Pagis*. The poet waited for twenty-five years before he was able to describe the railway carriage, the cattle car, where he placed not himself, his parents and relatives, but the first created ones, the world's first family. The theme of Cain and Abel is commonly used in connection with the Holocaust. It reflects envy, hatred and murder, sentiments which are not distant motives in connection to genocide. It is as if an explanation for the Holocaust is sought from the first murder:

Written in Pencil in the Sealed Railway-Car
here in this carload
i am eve
with abel my son
if you see my other son
cain son of man,
tell him that i[171]

The poet has intentionally left out the last sentence. We do not know what mankind would have said. What would the mother have wanted to tell her other son, who was a representative of the entire human race? And why exactly is it Eve who is speaking? Naturally, there are no right or wrong answers to these questions.

"How shall I console you? To what shall I liken you, o daughter of Jerusalem? What shall I compare with you, that I may comfort you, o virgin

daughter of Zion? For your ruin is spread wide as the sea; who can heal you?"[172]

The crimes continued, even at the last stage of the war, just before freedom. In fact, the deportations of Hungarian Jews to Auschwitz in the spring and summer of 1944 showed that Germany was waging war on two fronts: war in a military sense and war against the Jews as a people. During the deportations of the Hungarian Jews, Germany had practically lost the military conflict, and in this state of national distress in Germany, all available trains and resources were needed to transport military supplies. But when a choice needed to be made, valuable trains were used to transport Jews to Auschwitz, where they often lived for a few hours as they awaited the gas chambers, since the chambers could not handle such large numbers of people at one time. Even at the very end of the war – only days before the Allied Forces came to the camps – the so-called death marches were organized. Prisoners had to march in the bitter cold of winter without shoes or outdoor clothing, pushed forward by the armed guards towards the inner parts of Germany, away from the liberators. The purpose was to hide all evidence of the crime in this way. Thousands of prisoners died on these marches, without food, drink or shelter, as blood stained the snow red around Eastern Europe in the winter of 1945.

In 1945, the architects of the murder were aware of the turn the war had taken. What, then, happened to the participants in the Wannsee Conference afterwards? Did they live happily ever after? The answer might depend on the viewer's perspective. Heydrich himself died that same year in Czechoslovakia, in the resistance movement's attack. *Adolf Eichmann* fled, but we will return to his story later. *Heinrich Müller* was never found, though it has been claimed that he was able to escape through the Vatican to somewhere in Latin America. Two participants had already committed suicide in 1945. All in all, we know that about a third of the Wannsee Conference participants died during or immediately after the war, and another third died quite soon after the war. The rest were able to return to their (apparently) comfortable middle- class lives, avoiding all punishment.[173]

The Holocaust victim *Joseph Wolf,* an Auschwitz survivor who lived in post-war Germany, said in 1974 – the same year he committed suicide: *"I have published eighteen books on the Third Reich, but to no effect. You can print books in Germany till you are blue in the face. There can truly be a democratically elected government in Bonn, but the mass murderers are allowed to walk free, live in their own houses and raise flowers."*[174]

Clearly, the Holocaust was a process. It proceeded through the first wavering steps toward the final goal. That goal would never have been reached without the beginning. Those living through that time were able to see only a collection of confusing, independent events, whereas the events all around Europe were aimed at one and the same goal. Evil comes to a climax because of the first compromise. The time of the first compromises is a time when citizens, communities and societies could still take action. Holocaust researchers use the so-called "triangle of hatred" to describe this setting. I have seen it used for instance in schools in different variations. On the solid foundation of the triangle are the people's attitudes, in this case the anti-Semitic attitudes. Above the foundation are the first actions, such as anti-Semitic newspaper writings or the supposedly harmless funny jokes told among friends, In the middle is discrimination, which is a more serious situation of which the local authorities or government must be aware. Moving upward to the narrower part, anti-Semitic acts of violence begin to occur. But at this stage, the anti-Semitic acts are targeted at property, such as tombstones or synagogues; only at the top of the triangle do we see violence aimed at people and possibly mass murder. We understand two foundational facts from this: first, the triangle cannot stand if turned upside down, so without the firm foundation of anti-Semitic attitudes, mass murder would never have taken place; second, resistance is easiest to do when is the hatred has only developed to the level of speech.

One of the Holocaust witnesses, *Corrie ten Boom* – a Christian Dutch woman who saved Jews – describes this time through the experiences of one person. The ten Boom family had a clock store in Haarlem, where a young German man called Otto came to work just before the German occupation. Right from the beginning, Corrie was perplexed by Otto's rudeness toward an old man, Christoffel, who worked in the store. This rudeness did not show in what he did, but in what he did not do. He did not hold the door open for the old man, nor did he help him with his coat or pick up a dropped tool. Corrie's brother Willem had lived in Germany, and he explained to Corrie that Otto's actions were deliberate. According to Willem, Otto acted in this way because Christoffel was old. The Germans were systematically taught to despise old age and to believe that the elderly were of no use to society.[175]

If we want to understand the years of the Holocaust and the time preceding it through a simple and clear chain of events, this is what it could look like:

- **1933-1938:** Establishment of Nazi government; Anti-Jewish propaganda; boycotts targeted at Jewish stores; legislation to isolate the Jews from the rest of society;

- **1938-1939:** Destruction of Jewish synagogues and communities; vandalism and arrests;
- **1939-1941:** Jews no longer have any rights; deportations to the East;
- **1941-1945:** Murder of the Jews (and others) in extermination camps.

Auschwitz-Birkenau: The Soul of Genocide

"In the day that you stood on the other side – in the day that strangers carried captive his forces, when foreigners entered his gates and cast lots for Jerusalem – even you were as one of them. But you should not have gazed on the day of your brother in the day of his captivity; nor should you have rejoiced over the children of Judah in the day of their destruction; nor should you have spoken proudly in the day of distress... For the day of the Lord upon all the nations is near; as you have done, it shall be done to you; your reprisal shall return upon your own head."[176]

The city of Krakow is located relatively close to the Auschwitz-Birkenau concentration camp. Most visitors interested in Jewish history begin their journey there. The city has survived well, as it was not bombed from the air during World War II. On a summer eve, the atmosphere in Krakow is just like any other European city, but we, the visitors, are awkwardly aware of where we are. The more the days pass by, the more awkward this awareness becomes. We are aware, as a group, of anti-Semitism in the past and in the present. In addition to the Christian group, I have Clila and Hadassah with me. If you have seen "Schindler's List", you have seen their parents. Joseph and Rebecca Bau were secretly married in the concentration camp – just like the movie portrayed. Clila and Hadassah were born of this marriage only because one man, Oskar Schindler, saved their parents from certain death. Their names were on the list!

On guided tours, we see the houses that belonged to Jews in the area of Kazimierz. They look dirty, and I assume this is because of the time of Communism. Our Polish guide tells us that because the owners do not want to pay compensation to the Jews for these houses, they are kept in the worst possible condition. Thus, the new owners believe they can avoid the claims of the old owners. And truly, I remember reading that thousands of private homes were taken from Polish Jews, and immediately after the war, the Communist government took possession of them. Their collective value now would be so very much.[177] Ordinary people live also in the ghetto apartments. There is a flower shop on the square. I ask the guide if the people think about the past and who lived in the apartments. She says that she is not a religious woman, "but evil spirits must live in this area." We are close to Schindler's factory, a refuge in a world filled with terrors.

We travel to Auschwitz. Again, evil hovers in the air. We see a torture chamber, prisoners' gallows, watchtowers, barbed-wire fences, mountains of hair and children's little clothes. We see the execution wall against which the tortured prisoners were shot. Our guide tells us that a gas chamber could hold up to 2,000 people, screaming in terror. But here, the commander of the camp also had a pool. He invited friends to spend a holiday with his family. I remember a letter in the Yad Vashem Archives in which a family thanks the commander of Auschwitz for "the best vacation we have ever had." A vacation in Auschwitz, this place of horrors.

It is impossible to forget for even a moment where we are. We are at the heart of the Holocaust.

Auschwitz was situated at a very suitable place for its intended purpose, as it was a remote location. There were useful rail connections there, and it was surrounded by a river, which restrained any attempt to escape. As a matter of fact, we know the SS leader *Heinrich Himmler* favored the place because it was both isolated and easily accessible. In 2011, Yad Vashem received the original blueprints of the Auschwitz-Birkenau concentration camp as a gift. The blueprints had been found in Berlin in 2008 and had come into the possession of the German *Bild* magazine, which decided to submit them to Yad Vashem.[178] In the subsequent event where I was present, it was emphasized again that someone actually drew Auschwitz; it was a designed institution. In photos of the time, men who look like architects sit at drawing tables and design buildings that are going to become a concentration camp. This is how easily the planning of the world's largest industrial-like murder institution was done. Ultimately, Auschwitz-Birkenau, or simply Auschwitz, as it is commonly known, is the symbol of all evil to people around the world. The murder machinery in Auschwitz never stopped, even as they began to restrain murder in other camps in 1943, assuming the labor force was possibly needed for some purpose at this critical stage of the war. In Auschwitz, human life had no value.

Yechiel Dinur, who wrote under the pseudonym *Ka Zetnik*, was a writer of Yiddish poetry and an Auschwitz survivor. His pseudonym actually means "'concentration camp prisoner." I became acquainted with his story for the first time at the Eichmann exhibition organized by Yad Vashem. The general public learned about his story at the Eichmann trial in 1961, where he testified and suffered an attack, shocked by the case. Dinur died in Israel in 2001. According to Dinur, Auschwitz was another planet! There is, according to him, no answer or explanation for Auschwitz – hell on earth.[179]

This account is largely based on my several guided visits of Auschwitz-Birkenau. In the early days, Auschwitz-Birkenau, the largest of the extermination camps, functioned simply as a prison and the place where people sentenced to death by German courts were brought to be executed. Of the approximately 150,000 Poles who were sent to the camp, about 75,000 died. From 1941, approximately 15,000 Russian prisoners of war were brought there; almost all perished. From 1943, about 23,000 Roma (Gypsies) were brought to the camp, and about 20,000 of them were murdered. Other prisoners of war, members of resistance movements and abducted persons were also there. These are the numbers, but they were human beings, just like us.

Auschwitz-Birkenau was not just one camp, but an immense complex with several subcamps. The camp grew roughly like this: Auschwitz I was the main camp whose commander was of a higher rank than the other commanders. It was established by Himmler's order in April 1941. In August 1944, there were about 16,000 prisoners in this part of the complex. Auschwitz II is the camp we know as Birkenau, and it was established in March 1942. It was the largest of all divisions, a center for mass murder with gas chambers, and later also a place where possessions stolen from the prisoners were collected. Prisoners from Birkenau were chosen to perform exhaustive forced labor, but those too weak to work were murdered, their bodies burned in Birkenau. In August 1944, there were about 88,000 prisoners in this part of the complex. Auschwitz III was a camp made up of satellite camps, where the prisoners were used as slave labor for different companies and industries. In the summer of 1944, there were about 31,000 prisoners in this part.[180]

Between 1940-1942, Auschwitz was a concentration camp, where the prisoners died as a result of hunger, intense work and executions. At that point, the Poles were still the single largest prisoner group, followed by the Jews. This state of affairs is understandable if we consider the purpose of the concentration camps in more detail. Of course, they were institutions of forced labor and murder, but in a psychological sense, the mere awareness of their existence frightened the population into silence. The first to be gathered there were the intellectuals and ideological leaders. To my understanding, the large number of Poles among the prisoners is connected precisely with this ultimate purpose.

In the fall of 1941, gas was tested on the basement of barrack 11 in Auschwitz, after which, in the spring of 1942, two former farm houses in Birkenau were altered to suit the purpose, and they began functioning as extermination sites. Additional buildings were soon ordered from a German company producing them. Thus, in 1942, the nature of the camp changed, and it was turned into an extermination camp as well as a concentration camp. Even then, out of all the incoming transports, only the Jews were targets of immediate extermination. In 1944, the nature of the camp changed again, and it became only an extermination camp.

Jewish concentration camp prisoners were the slave labor force, whose labor input was not supposed to save them but to exhaust them to death. Anyone visiting Auschwitz-Birkenau can understand this very simple truth by just realizing the vast distance the exhausted, hungry, sick and weak prisoners had to walk daily, back and forth, in order to come to the work camps. The purpose of work was to murder the prisoners. It is apparent that using slaves was also a question of economic gain, as the SS was paid a compensation from German firms for using slave labor. But we must understand that not even economic gain was able to save the prisoners in a situation where there was an unlimited number of them available. They were too easily replaceable. Over a million Jews were murdered in the camp, with estimates ranging from 1 million to 1.35 million.

In addition to the survivors' testimonies, we know Auschwitz-Birkenau from the visual evidence in the *Auschwitz Album*. The photographs were taken in May or June of 1944. When the invasion of Normandy occurred on June 6 of that year, Nazi Germany had practically lost the war. However, the hurried transports of surviving Hungarian Jews to Auschwitz, and from there directly to the gas chambers, continued. It is thought that photos of the transports were taken by one of the SS photographers, *Ernst Hoffmann* or *Bernhard Walter*, whose task was to take photos of the prisoners.

From the photos, we see the arrival of the Hungarian Jews to the camp and the process following their arrival. In fact, an extension was built especially for these trains, and many of the photographs were taken immediately after the Jews had descended from the train. After their arrival, they went through a selection process, after which some might live for a while through work, and others went straight to the gas chambers. The album shows the entire process and is the only visual material we have. What is the most terrible is to look at mothers and children who sit or stand, waiting to be taken to "showers and barracks." Perhaps some of them anticipated that they had only a few hours left to live – only until the gas chambers would again have room. The Auschwitz Album is kept at the archives at Yad Vashem.

The numbers make one dizzy. They are too vast to be understood. As it is with the entire Holocaust, we should keep in mind when studying this large camp that we are thinking about millions of people, but also about individuals. There are words that were left behind, words we see in Yad Vashem Museum, perhaps without thinking about the context in which they were said. Just like the words of *Benjamin Fondane*, a Romanian Jewish philosopher murdered in Auschwitz in 1944:

"Remember only that I was innocent and that, like all of you, mortals of this day, I had, I too had a face marked by rage, by pity and joy, an ordinary human face!"[181]

When we contemplate the vast number of the victims, the poem of a young Jewish boy (who later died in Auschwitz) about his own dream is a necessary reminder of the significance of an individual. The work of *Abramek Koplowicz*, who was born in *Lodz* in February of 1930 and died in Auschwitz in 1944, is presented at Yad Vashem.

This is part of Abramek's poem *Legends of My Own "Dream"*:

"When I will be 20 years old,
In a motorized bird I'll sit,
And to the reaches of space I'll rise.
I will fly,
I will float to the beautiful faraway world
And skywards I will soar.

The cloud my sister will be
The wind is brother to me.

I will fly, I will float over rivers and seas.
I will marvel at the Euphrates and Nile.

I will gaze at the Sphinx and Pyramids
In the goddess Isis' ancient land.
I will glide over the mighty Niagara Falls,
And soak up the warmth of the Sahara's sun.
Over the cloud-covered Tibetan peaks will I ascend
Above the mysterious magic land of the Hindus.

And when extricated from the sun's heat,
I will take wing to the Arctic north,
And I will whir above the giant Kangaroo Isle,
And then over the ruins of Pompeii.
From there I'll set my sights to the Holy Land,
Where our Covenant was given.
I will even reach the illustrious Homer's country,
And will be so amazed by the beauty of this world.

To the heavens I will take off.
The cloud my sister will be
The wind is brother to me. "[182]

Auschwitz is not just one place in Europe's cruel history, nor is it just one memorial of the Holocaust. To most people worldwide, Auschwitz *is* the Holocaust, both the symbol and venue of it. Therefore, the following historical moment took place there, too. On September 4, 2003, the Israeli Air Force made a historic flight on F-15 aircrafts over Auschwitz. With them, they had a group of Holocaust survivors and a person I later personally met in Jerusalem: an American Jewish fighter pilot, *Al Weber*. I understand that this event was one of a kind. Although I was not there myself, there a movie was made of the event, showing the expressions, faces and emotions of these people. This event reminds us that Israel, as a state, has risen from the ashes and is a miracle.

Visibly moved, the Commander of the Israeli Air Force gave a speech right before the aircrafts took off: *"We came here to learn about the mass murder, the past, the vibrant Jewish life, the culture and the rabbis learned in the Torah. We came to close our eyes and to picture a Jewish city once alive. We came to walk in the ghetto, on the gravesites of genocide and on the forest paths before the gate leading to death. We came to see a place which was an indescribable tragedy to a people and individuals. We came to speak to the victims. To those who were killed instantly, to those on whose ashes we stand, to those who died of hunger and cold, to those who ended up in the battle for existence. We came to say to the victims that despite all, we are here. Jewish resistance has become a powerful modern army whose fighting spirit is alive."* Between the commander's speech and the singing of Israel's national anthem, *Hatikva*, the fighter pilot, spoke directly from the cockpit: *"We, the Israeli Air Force pilots, who are flying above the death camp, Auschwitz, are here as our people rose from the ashes. We came to pay our respects to the courage of the victims, and we carry your silent cries of pain on our shoulders. We promise to be a shield protecting the Jewish people and its state, Israel."*[183]

Who would have believed during the dark years of World War II that in September 2003, the Air Force of the independent State of Israel would be here? Who would have believed that there would be survivors of this place of terror present there? In the darkness of the 1940s, it seemed as if no one would be able to survive and that the powers of hatred could not be overcome. Who would have believed, then, that the Israeli pilots would sing, together with the survivors, a very special song? The value of this moment to the survivors cannot be described in words. The song sung as a sing-along at the event was written by, once again, our young heroine Hannah Senesh. As we know, she wrote it without full information about what was happening in Europe at that time, and the lyrics are prophetic. The entire world, as it was known until World War II, came to a kind of end point during that war. Jewish communities were eliminated, and millions of people vanished. Entire villages no longer existed in 1945.

Unaware of all this, Hannah Senesh presented her prayer:

"Eli Eli
She LoYigamer leOlam
HaChol ve HaYam
Rishrush shel HaMayim
Barak beShamayim
Tfilat HaAdam"

"My God, My God
May these things never end:
The sand and the sea
The rustle of the water
The lightning in the sky
The prayer of Man"

7 Contemporaries of Genocide – How Did People React?

"Then He will answer them, saying, 'Assuredly, I say to you, inasmuch as you did not do it to one of the least of these, you did not do it to Me.'"[184]

In August 2009, my friend Carrie flies from Chicago to Amsterdam, while I fly there from Israel. We have decided to travel to Holland to deepen our knowledge of the Holocaust by seeing some of its original developmental stages in Europe. We chose Holland as our destination because there are many suitable sights there. After arriving in Amsterdam, we immediately begin our program. Without planning it in advance, we find that each place we visit includes a different aspect of the Holocaust.

Our visit to Anne Frank's House begins in a special way. I had written to them in advance, thinking that perhaps they would free us from queuing for hours outside (the lines to visit the home are always very long). They confirmed that we could come for a visit on August 2. Suddenly, I receive a new message from them, asking us to move our visit to August 4. This suits us fine. It is only when we arrive at the house that we realize the significance of this day. August 4, 1944 was the very day when the Frank family, and their friends who were hiding with them, were arrested as a result of betrayal. The **informants** constitute a group among the Holocaust contemporaries. Somehow it feels special – as a sad privilege – to be in Anne Frank's house on that date. We know that each year on August 4, Miep Gies, who helped the Franks, spends the day behind closed doors, mourning. She was a **rescuer**. In some small way, we feel like we become one with her grief.

We visit the Resistance Museum. **Resistance** was another part of the contemporaries' reaction. We visit a Jewish theater, where the Jews were *gathered before being sent to camps. The Nazi **perpetrators** made up a large part of the contemporaries. We visit the Jewish Museum and many other sights. It feels very strange that, at the same time as the persecution of the Jews is remembered, we are in the middle of a terrifying human rights violation. Amsterdam is a center for human trafficking, and you cannot miss seeing this phenomenon of modern slavery as you move around the city. However, the local people to whom we mention the matter seem to find our disapproval strange. A similar paradox is that the Dutch do not know much about the story of the ten Boom family. We visit Haarlem, where the ten Boom home functions as a museum and the clock store still stands. It is upsetting to think that the heroes of World War II are mostly forgotten.*

According to the guide, only foreigners come to visit the ten Boom home.

I have to say that the trip is good, but it does not mean relaxation and seeing only good things. Rather, we return from Holland to our homes upset and deep in thought.

Has anything changed in people's behavior?

A Jewish man and carpenter named *Mordechai Gebirtig* (1877-1942) lived in Krakow, Poland, where in 1938, he wrote the very well-known Holocaust poem title *S'brennt* (*It burns*). Gebirtig could not have possibly known in 1938 that the following year, in September 1939, German troops would flood Poland, and the life of its Jews, the largest Jewish community in Europe, would be destroyed forever. In the poem, Gebirtig makes a petition to his non-Jewish neighbors, the only ones who can put out the fire of violence:

"Our town is burning, brothers, burning,
Our poor little town is burning.
Angry winds are fanning higher,
The leaping tongues of flame and fire,
The evil winds are roaring! Our whole town burns!
And you stand looking on with folded arms,
And shake your heads.
You stand looking on, with folded arms,
While the fire spreads!"[185]

The poem was also a prophecy, because its writer Gebirtig, our poet, died in the winds of evil as the Germans occupied Poland. He was like the prophets of the Bible, as he saw into the future and tried to give a warning – but even more like the prophets in that his warnings fell on deaf ears. His neighbors stood on the side watching, some perhaps rejoicing, others suffering, and some foolish, completely indifferent to what was happening. Gebirtig's brothers died in the flames of fire. Perhaps he understood what we need to understand today: existing anti-Semitism enabled the persecution of Jews. Anti-Semitism is not a detached thought. The Holocaust is a story about people, like a play, directed, written and produced by people, whom we divide in three groups:

1. Perpetrators;
2. Silent bystanders;
3. Rescuers.

We can clearly see that majority of the surrounding society watched as their neighbors became victims of violence, looting and death. Some collaborated with the criminals, while others only benefited from the possessions they took over. Although some clearly rejoiced over the destruction of their neighbors, many were simply indifferent. Indifference is often caused by fear and a lack of understanding. Sometimes it is moral blindness or outright hatred, both of which readily contributed to the fate of the Jews. Churches, which should have led the moral fight, very often remained silent. How could it have been otherwise, when the way had already been prepared by their false teachings? We see a contrast between the majority and the minority – only an extremely small group of people had the courage to stand for the truth in a situation that might have led to death. The gray area of neutrality is tenuous, hard to maintain, as it does not exist in reality. The invisibility of evil does not mean the presence of goodness.

"I call heaven and earth as witnesses today against you, that I have set before you life and death, blessing and cursing; therefore choose life, that both you and your descendants may live."[186]

Every student of the Holocaust knows the three categories, which are now used to explain a variety of situations, such as bullying. The categories are an excellent and wonderfully accurate way of understanding human nature. Human nature does not change, and for that very reason, studying the contemporaries is one of the most interesting queries about the Holocaust.

The Perpetrators

We know the most about the perpetrators of the Holocaust, the Nazi criminals, as their faces are familiar to us. We have watched their faces for one important reason: the Nazi criminals represent ultimate evil to us. Their well-ironed clothes and even their polished boots represent order. How often have I seen a person changing in front of my eyes, as they start wearing a uniform? They become an authority, one who gives orders, reliable and commanding at the same time. The Nazi criminals represent this change brought on by a uniform. It is even more pronounced, as we see them as the opposites of the victims; they were a glossy image in the vicinity of the hungry, beaten and dirty prisoners. Removing a uniform produces a mindless moment in which a person is changed into something entirely ordinary. This kind of incident is documented at the Eichmann Exhibition produced by Yad Vashem. Here is what happened in the case of Adolf Eichmann.[187]

Often called the Architect of the Holocaust, Adolf Eichmann was held as a prisoner of war by the United States, but he managed to escape early in 1946. For a time, he lived under false names in different parts of Germany. At the beginning of 1950, he traveled to Italy and lived by hiding in monasteries. A famous escape route, the *ratline*, operated in the Vatican. The name refers to the routes the Nazis took to escape through Italy, and more precisely the Vatican, to South America. Another famous helper may have been the ODESSA Organization, established to help former SS officers. In Eichmann's case, he was helped by Bishop *Alois Hudal* (1885-1963), originally from Austria. Bishop Hudal, with the help of his vast contact network, arranged visas, hideouts and everything else necessary to aid well-known Nazis. Eichmann's family followed him to Argentina some years later, and until 1960, he was in hiding, working different jobs in the vicinity of Buenos Aires.

As early as 1954, *Simon Wiesenthal* (1908-2005), a Holocaust survivor known as the "conscience of the world," had received information in Vienna that Eichmann was residing in Argentina. Wiesenthal may have been one of the most well-known survivors, having been liberated from the Mauthausen camp. After working first for the American liberators, he began searching for the war criminals, and with his help, over a thousand Nazi criminals were brought to justice. In addition to Wiesenthal, the Chief Prosecutor of West Germany, *Fritz Bauer,* received similar information concerning Eichmann in 1957 from German Jewish sources living in Argentina. The story is long and complex, and very exciting, but I will share it only briefly. After learning of this, the Bauer hinted at Eichmann's whereabouts to the Israeli security service. Israeli agents kept an eye on Eichmann, who now used the pseudonym *Ricardo Klement.* The agents of *Mossad*, the Israeli Secret Service, hijacked Eichmann on May 11, 1960, and he was brought to trial in Israel.

The Eichmann trial was immensely significant for many reasons. First, it opened the reality of the Holocaust to the general public. The survivors, silent for years, the living witnesses of a crime, were finally able to have their voices heard. The Eichmann hearings gave researchers and historians much more information on the Nazi regime's actions and hierarchy. The world press was freely able to follow the trial, which ended with Eichmann's conviction, despite his defense that he had only *followed the rules.* Eichmann was executed by hanging in 1962, and his ashes were scattered over the Mediterranean Sea, outside Israeli waters. The most interesting thing for us is the change that took place in Eichmann between the Holocaust and 1960. There are not many photographs of Eichmann during the Holocaust, and the ones I have seen portray him at the height of his power, in uniform, with the SS skull hat and boots. But when we look at the photos of Eichmann taken by the Israeli Secret Service agents as they were watching him in Argentina, we see a worker in civilian clothes. He took the bus to work, which most likely was quite a shock to a man used to chauffeurs. He was, in fact, quite pitiful, poor and working whatever jobs were available. The change we see illustrates what philosopher *Hannah Arendt* aptly describes as the *Banality of Evil*. What was banal about this man was that in Jerusalem, they were awaiting the epitome of evil, which Eichmann was during World War II, but during the trial, many made comments that he was *"so common."* He was average in height and weight, and he also wore glasses. *Leonard Cohen* wrote a poem about Eichmann's commonness, and this commonness was shocking to all observers.

It is true that in the human mind, extreme evil is easily connected to people who are "not like us". Who else but an exceptionally cruel or evil person could commit horrific human rights violations? However, research from various parts of the world, does not support this view at all. Among the Nazi criminals, some may very well have had sanity issues, but for the most part, they were ordinary people. As far as existing research, no specifically cruel type has been identified among them. Considering other human rights violations, such as the military junta in Argentina in the 1970's or the genocide in Rwanda in 1994, we can clearly see that the perpetrators of cruelty in many (if not all) cases returned to normal life afterwards. No particular difficulty was seen, at least on the outside. It seems that persons committing human rights violations received their power during a time of war or persecution, which gave them an incentive to perpetrate crimes. For us, the challenge lies in that the criminals belong to the same human race as you and I. They often had families, and they were conscientious parents.

Theodor Adorno (1903-1969) conducted pioneering research on a human type capable of serious human rights violations. Adorno studied in

Frankfurt but later went into exile. His science was presumably colored by his experience in a totalitarian government, although his most famous sociological research, on this very issue, was completed in the United States. In 1949, he returned to Frankfurt. Adorno coined the term *authoritarian personality*; according to him, this personality type has certain psychological features that make someone easily unsympathetic but an even more conscientious criminal. Adorno did not focus on the environment or society in his research, but on a person's characteristics. This authoritarian personality does not see blind obedience as cowardice, but as a virtue. Therefore, the dictator coming to power or a totalitarian government can use people with this personality type. Of course, many researchers do not agree with Adorno.[188]

Researchers have also analyzed the thinking of the previously mentioned "ordinary" men during and after the mass shootings. How were they able to execute their part in this shocking genocide? The explanations given by various researchers[189] include at least the following perspectives:

1) **Killing during the war was legitimate**, as the Germans only defended themselves from their enemies;

2) **Wartime brutalizes and gives too much power** to people, making them unable to see things the same way as in normal times;

3) It was important to **obey orders**; murdering was part of their duty and had no connection to individual persons;

4) **Environmental pressure** made these men not want to stand out from the masses.

To these explanations, we can add mechanisms that helped the perpetrator not to see the victim's humanity or his own responsibility. First of all, the victims looked different; they were hungry; they were not able to wash themselves. Secondly, the perpetrators were trained and educated to obey, meaning that orders were to be obeyed without question. Thirdly, it is possible for man to "create several worlds" for himself that do not coincide with each other, as with a separation between home and work. Therefore, it was possible for the Nazi criminals to act in the utmost brutal manner in the concentration camp but to return home as loving husbands and fathers.[190]

Frankfurt Auschwitz Trials (*der Zweite Auschwitz Prozess*) took place between December 20, 1963 and August 19, 1965 in Germany. Former SS and other perpetrators (who had been active in Auschwitz) were tried; this process was made into a TV documentary *Auschwitz Trial The End of Silence* by *13 Productions, France Television*. The main defense argument was that there had been no choice because everyone had been following their orders. Fritz Bauer, the prosecutor thought that this had nothing to do with historical reality. According to him, Hitler would never have been in power without men like these.[191] In a trial held in Düsseldorf, Germany, in 1964, several testimonies related to this very topic were given. What did the people see, and how were they able to stay in their roles despite the suffering of others? When discussing the perpetrators, we usually think of only the well-known Nazi leaders, the brutal camp guards, the SS men and professional murder units. The reality is quite different, because an immense number of professions, from state bureaucrats to doctors, lawyers, industrial leaders and many others, participated in the murder. European railroads will always be connected to the Holocaust because they played a central role in this genocide. What, then, did the railroad workers say at the trial?

"I dealt with these matters only from my desk. My sole activity was

technically taking care of train timetables."[192]

"I made appropriate reports on the corpses found at the tracks in my jurisdiction. The reports then were submitted to the management. By this I had fulfilled my duty."[193]

"I heard the shootings along the train, but never saw them. I never turned my head and looked back. I always looked forward."[194]

Needless to say, not everyone in this larger group was personally ready to execute brutal human rights violations. Not everyone was forced to stay at a workplace that required them to act against their conscience. But, at the same time, most of the people chose silence, which enabled the human rights violations. The largest group of Holocaust contemporaries were not the perpetrators of the crime but the silent bystanders.

Who or what enabled the crimes, then?

The Silent Bystanders

We call them "bystanders" because they really did not do anything but stand by and watch the daily victory of evil. Just as survivor *Kurt Messerschmidt* says: *"Some of the people disapproved, but their disapproval was only silence."*[195] Silence never helps the victim, but instead protects the perpetrator. Existing research on various mass murders proves the undisputed truth of this claim.

Researchers have stated that human rights violators always strive to keep the bystanders unaware. When this is no longer possible, they will scare them into silence, whether before, during or even after the crime. On whose side are the silent bystanders, then? When they continue their normal lives in conditions terrorized by daily atrocities, they become useful to the executors of crime. That makes them an accomplice to the criminals. Depending on the incident, silent bystanders might be individuals, societies, churches, organizations or international players. For example, was the UN a classic silent bystander during the genocide in Rwanda? If you are interested in comparing different events, I highly recommend watching the movie *Hotel Rwanda*; then you can decide for yourself.

Elie Wiesel describes one classic bystander:

"Since the war, it has been the main thing I have wanted to understand. Nothing else. How could someone be indifferent. The criminals, I was able to understand them. Also the victims, albeit less easily. But the others, all the others who were not for or against...." Wiesel continues: *"He does not say no, nor yes, nor maybe. He does not say a word. He is there but acts as if he was not. Even worse, he acts as if we were not there either."*[196]

We need to bear in mind that persecutions did not take place in a vacuum. They were part of a certain historical era and its set of values. Essentially, it can be said that man does not have a right to determine the outcome of the life of another human being – in contrast, man has a direct responsibility to preserve life. Elie Wiesel said, after experiencing Auschwitz: *"We, who were forgotten by Creation and perhaps abandoned by its Creator, must demonstrate our faith in both... We, who inside the barracks and the darkness saw all those paths leading to death... [we, who] were dominated by death, still proclaim our belief in the Jewish tradition with every fiber of our being: Everything about life is in life, however frail and vulnerable it may be."*[197]

In a society where man has the right to decide between life and death, it is a short journey to contempt for life. This tendency, which is seen very clearly in Western society today, was taken to the extreme in Nazi Germany, where the value of human life was measured with very tangible standards. Moral values and human dignity were not a consideration. *Zvi Gill*, who chaired the Organization of Holocaust Survivors in Israel for a long time, said: *"We who staggered through the valley of death... struggled to extract a message of meaning and renewed purpose for our people and for all people, namely: a message of humanity, of human decency and of human dignity."*[198]

If we think of the bystanders as a community, we cannot bypass the Christian churches, which had much more power and much more of a say in Europe during the Holocaust than they have today. Priests and pastors and church hierarchy were all silent bystanders. Even as late as 1945, the churches were declared innocent concerning the Holocaust, but we have come a long way since those days. From the days of total denial, we have come to a time when we can admit the possibility of evil. The church was not only guilty because of its actions, but even more so because of its silence. This era was marked by the sin of silence, and this was true of both the Catholic and the Protestant churches.

The poet *Nathan Alterman* was born in Warsaw in 1910 but moved to the British Mandate in Palestine in 1925. Although he became known in Israeli politics, his true legacy was in poetry. In 1942, he wrote a well-known Holocaust poem, *From All Peoples,* which relates to Pope Pius XII. Thousands of Catholic priests, monks, nuns and ordinary parishioners all around Europe helped the Jews. At the same time, however, their spiritual leader was either silent or his rhetoric was thought to be so unclear as to consider him a classical bystander. Here is an excerpt of Alterman's poem:

"The iron devoured day and night,
And the holy Christian Father in the city of Rome,
Did not come out with the icons of Christ,
To stand one day in a pogrom.
To stand one day, one single day,
Where for years like a lamb, A small
Unknown
Jewish kid
Stands alone."[199]

An interesting change took place in Nazi Germany in 1933. The Catholic Church in Germany opposed the Nazi Party even before its ascent to power and warned parishioners not to join the Party. Several Catholic priests and theologians predicted that the Nazi Party would become an enemy of the church. Obviously, they understood well that Hitler, in the end, wanted to control the entire society, to which the church also belonged. If this were to happen, the church would no longer be able to take care of her duties. Even before the beginning of Hitler's reign, there was a clear understanding within the church of how dangerous Nazi rule would be. As a matter of fact, if we look at it in more detail, it is clear that before 1933, the main opposition to Hitler came from the German Catholic Church. This changed suddenly and completely in 1933, for reasons that have to do with daily politics. In 1933, the Vatican signed a *Concordat Agreement* with the Nazi Party. The purpose of the agreement was to define the rights of the church in relation to the state. Obviously, Hitler would not have agreed to the concordat had it not been profitable for him. Even though the agreement secured the rights of the church, it also took away the most important right and responsibility: the right to address social issues. This considerably diminished the Church's actual influence in the society. It is interesting to point out that later, when Christian clergy were taken to Nazi concentration camps, there were more Catholic priests among them than Protestant pastors.[200]

Even though it is impossible to claim that the Catholic Church leadership had truly changed their mind to support Hitler, it can reasonably be said that they no longer resisted Hitler's growing power. Many priests believed the mission of the Church was above earthly power. Even Hitler's opponents, who saw the Nazi rule as a threat to the Church, did not protest against the ever-increasing threats and actions against the Jews. Similarly, in a very strange way, the Catholic Church in Germany supported the war, which began in September 1939, even though Poland, the target of the attack, was perhaps the most Catholic nation in Europe. There is something quite peculiar and inconsistent here. While some Catholic priests, nuns and monks around Europe were hiding Jews in monasteries and churches, the Church as an institution worked with their opponent. The Church as an institution was not the moral voice of the time; instead, the true face of Christianity comprised individual people, swimming against the current.

The Protestant churches did not offer any clearer moral voice. It is terrifying to think that in the summer of 1932, pastors, laymen and various leaders already gathered in Berlin to reflect on how the Nazi Party could gain more power, especially among the Protestants. This gathering was summoned by *Wilhelm Kube*, one of the leaders of the Brandenburg area and a Nazi Party group leader in the Prussian state legislature. In connection with this particular event, Hitler suggested that the pro-Nazi part of the German Evangelical

Church would be called *Deutsche Christen*, "German Christians." The name was far-reaching – it says it all. It says that Germany is as important as Christianity, and that the two go hand in hand. After a very short period of time, German Christians influenced by long national-religious tradition accepted a change called *nazification*, in which the Church adapted itself to Nazism. The anti-Jewish writings of Luther were once again relevant. The leader of the German Christians, *Ludwig Müller* (1883-1945), said, among other things, that Christianity did not rise from Judaism but in opposition to it.[201] Although it is evident that the church leadership only tolerated Hitler's administration with regard to the internal issues of the church, the treatment of Jews was never raised as a question on which Hitler would be opposed.

Even more alarming than studying Luther's writings in relation to the Jews was the *dejudaization* of the Church, a program to remove Judaism from Christianity. The spirit of that time declared that everything that was of Jewish origin was bad and evil. Therefore, the Bible, which was a Jewish book written by Jews, now represented this despised class. In the spirit of that day, measures were taken that were aimed at removing Judaism from the churches; interestingly, German newspapers have commented on this topic in recent years.[202] Christianity, which cannot interpret the words of Jesus apart from their connection with His Bible, the Torah, now had to be completely separated from the Old Testament. The New Testament had to be rewritten. The "tedious and repetitive" references to the Jewish customs, which Jesus and the apostles performed, had to be removed. Jesus was now turned into an *Aryan Jesus.* The Hymnal and Catechism were also changed, so that the entire church could get rid of her Jewish background.[203] All of this is appalling and blasphemous. It shows that the spirit of that time had completely overtaken the church, whose leaders had no spiritual insight concerning Hitler. What makes this all the more frightening is the connection it has with the present time. Even while I am writing this text, I see, from the webpages of various churches and theologians, the same attempt to separate Jesus from Judaism and remove the Old Testament from the churches.

Although Protestant pastors who expressed their opinions on National Socialism were taken to concentration camps, it also needs to be pointed out that about 85% of the German pastors swore loyalty to Hitler – and most did it voluntarily. The churches themselves decided independently that the pastors should take the oath. This was a great mistake, as it made it easier for the Gestapo to find the opposition.[204] Large Protestant churches, which had real influence in the society, were involved in the Nazi Party and all sections of the system. Before the outbreak of World War II, Protestant pastors had generally opposed the peace terms of World War I, believing in the special destiny of the German people. It was easy for them to see positive characteristics in the ideology of Hitler, who, like them, opposed Communism.

Could it be true that Hitler came dressed as an angel of light, when he so easily won the churches to his side? Was the desire for law and order so great after the chaos of the Weimar Republic that Hitler was received, even when his speeches should have scared and awakened people? Were the Christian leaders of the time completely unable to see him with spiritual eyes, or was the opportunity to ally themselves with a strong leader too tempting? And how much did the existing anti-Semitism affect them, as we know that anti-Semitic sermons were commonplace? One thing we know for sure: Hitler was certain he was able to control the pastors. When it came to the state church, it was he who could refrain from paying the pastors' wages, if he deemed it necessary.[205]

According to his own words, Hitler was ready to grant freedom to the churches, as long as they did not act against the state. As soon as Hitler had become the Reich Chancellor, Romans 13 started coming up in sermons, seemingly at the will of the pastors: *"Let every soul be subject to the governing authorities. For there is no authority except from God, and the authorities that exist are appointed by God. Therefore whoever resists the authority resists the ordinance of God, and those who resist will bring judgment on themselves... Render therefore to all their due: taxes to whom taxes are due, customs to whom customs, fear to whom fear, honor to whom honor."*[206] Paul's words were misused, as no taxes or work were insisted upon, but in this case, there was a person in power who wanted to destroy God's people. The state required actions that were against the Word of God, whereas the Word of God would have required actions against the state. The latter was not natural to the pastors, as Luther's theology of two spheres presented God as the Lord of the Church and Emperor as the lord of the Empire. This idea had deep roots in Germany.

Researchers have presented a clear connection between Protestants and Nazis that contributed to the Holocaust.[207] Many factors explain the silence of the churches at this fateful moment: anti-Semitism was clearly expressed in the sermons of the time, and there was an attempt to protect churches as institutions and buildings. This provokes questions concerning the mission of the church, which do not relate only to the time of persecution of the Jews. What is the purpose of the church during a crisis? Should an institution be protected, or should it be a voice of morality in dark times? We all know Jesus' teaching that says we are to *"Render therefore to Caesar the things that are Caesar's, and to God the things that are God's."*[208] But as we examine Nazi Germany, we see that the government no longer required only that which belonged to the emperor but also wanted that which was God's share. As Pastor *Erwin Lutzer* was pondering this problem, he came to the conclusion that the words of Jesus never required us to give to the emperor the share that belonged to God. The words explicitly say that each should be given their share. The totalitarian government, on the other hand, exceeds its share in its desire to subjugate everything under its own power. In those cases, we might be forced to carry out civilian disobedience.

Many of you might remember the story of Pastor *Martin Niemöller* (1882-1984). Dissatisfied with the Weimar Republic, he initially supported the Nazi Party, but soon realized the state was headed in the wrong direction. Niemöller was a brave pastor who spent the entire war incarcerated in a concentration camp, and who became the icon of Christian resistance in Germany. His poem about silence is a classic. It has been quoted in many different forms, as he apparently modified the poem when speaking to different audiences.

The essence of the matter is always the same, however – being silent when one should speak up:

"First they came for the socialists,
and I did not speak out –
because I was not a socialist.

Then they came for the trade unionists,
and I did not speak out –
because I was not a trade unionist.

Then they came for the Jews,

and I did not speak out –
because I was not a Jew.

Then they came for me –
and there was no one left to speak for me."

In 1933, Niemöller was already establishing a resistance movement against Hitler within the church. This group, *Pastors' Emergency League* (*Pfarrernotbund*), was the first such movement, mainly on his and Dietrich Bonhoeffer's initiative, and it later became *Bekennende Kirche,* the Confessing Church, which was the theological resistance to Hitler. However, even this opposition church was not vaccinated against the virus of anti-Semitism. The church's program declaration, the *Bethel Confession* of 1933, underlined solidarity, especially with the Jews who had converted to Christianity. The *Barmen Declaration,* drafted by the famous Swiss theologian *Karl Barth* (1886-1968), spoke specifically about protecting the Church, without demanding anything special against the persecution of the Jews. The declaration, written in May 1934, states, among other things, the following: *"the errors of the 'German Christians' of the present Reich Church government, which are devastating the Church and also, therefore, breaking up the unity of the German Evangelical Church... Therefore, they may be deemed to have waived their right to be legitimate leaders of the German Church..."*[209] The Confessing Church had all the possibilities to act as an awakener during the persecution of the Jews, but while it offered an opposing voice, the problem was that it did not go very far in its resistance on behalf of the Jews. I believe this reflects the fact that, as the two ideologies of Nazism and Christianity encountered one another, Christianity in Germany was not morally prepared to confront Nazism.

If we consider Nazism and Christianity as two ideologies or religions, we understand that an "ism" cannot be stronger than the strength of those believing in it. Supporters of Nazism were ready to take steps for their "ism" that Christians would never even consider. Hitler's position was also peculiar, as he truly was the "*Messiah*" of the Nazis, and his supporters had sworn absolute obedience to the Nazi Party. Hitler said himself that he would bring the Germans a new religion, which, unlike Christianity, would not weaken the people. He believed in reincarnation, and therefore believed he had descended from many former kings.[210] It is frightening to think that instead of fighting this ideology, Christians, including their leaders, assumed that they could lead a parallel life. They thought this despite the fact that Hitler and several other Nazi leaders hated Christianity and expressed their intentions to obliterate it as soon as the conditions would allow.[211] When Christians accepted Hitler, they accepted blatant immorality and genocide. This is tragic, as current research states: *"Most of the Jews avoided deportations in those nations occupied by or allied with Germany, where the leading church spoke publicly against deportations before or right after they started."*[212]

For centuries, anti-Semitism had been part of church doctrines. Several members of the German Evangelical Reich Church made a declaration about this issue on December 17, 1941: *"Since the crucifixion of Jesus until this day, Jews have fought, misused or falsified Christianity. Christian baptism does not change anything concerning the racial specificity, national essence or biological nature of the Jews. The German Evangelical Church must take care of the fellow German countrymen and promote their religious life. Racially Jewish Christians have no place or rights within the Church."*[213]

Martin Niemöller is one of the few persons we know of who dared oppose Hitler *in a conversation with him,* and he spent the war in a concentration camp. He behaved in a wonderfully bold manner, but this was not because of the persecution of the Jews. When the war was over, he said with remorse: *"I was an anti-Semite during the war…Christianity in Germany is more responsible before God than Nazism, SS or Gestapo. We are the ones who should have recognized our brother who was suffering… even though he was a Jew."*[214] Niemöller was willing to stand beside the Jews who converted to Christianity, but otherwise he, too, believed that there actually was a so-called Jewish question demanding a solution in Germany. He also believed the sufferings of the Jews were because of their involvement in Jesus' death – a way of thinking that had contributed to the hatred of the Jews since the early church fathers. I believe this case proves that anti-Semitism had had a crucial effect on churchmen. Even though the opposition from the church was almost the only opposition there was, we can only mourn the fact that the opposition had so little influence on the course of events. Tragically, anti-Semitism meant life or death, as it seems it often kept people from helping the Jews, even when there was no great risk involved. In addition, the ways in which countries outside Germany related to Hitler's regime seems to be clearly linked to the extent of anti-Semitism in those countries.

Some who began in the bystander role ended up making choices that raised them to resistance. Nazi propaganda toward the youth was forceful, as they wanted to recruit the youth into blind obedience, even if it meant betrayal of loved ones and spying for the Party. Therefore, each example of resistance is all the more significant. One famous and very touching case of resistance is the German youth who formed a resistance group called *Die Weiße Rose* (the White Rose). It was a non-violent group of students and one professor that operated in Munich, especially at the university, spreading anti-Nazi leaflets and making similar graffiti. Three siblings, *Inge, Sophie* and *Hans Scholl,* were part of the group, along with some of their close friends. They had begun their journey like their other contemporaries in National Socialist youth groups, but unlike their peers, they were able to see behind the slogans. They deeply disapproved of what the government was doing, including their policy concerning Jews. The student resistance movement worried the Nazi regime greatly, as they saw the youth as the key to the future of the nation. In addition, the very thought of resistance *among the Germans themselves* was scandalous and unthinkable for the government. It is no wonder, then, that they tracked the movement quickly, and Hans and Sophie Scholl were executed in 1943. If this story is unfamiliar to you, I recommend a movie called *Sophie Scholl, Die Letzten Tage* (*Sophie Scholl, The Last Days*). It is even a valuable historical document, since it is based on the Gestapo's interrogation records, so it is historically accurate and truthful.

Resistance did not always include enormous risks to life. In May 1943, churches in Holland tried to plead with the local German commissioner: *"We have no fantasies. We fully understand that your Excellency can decide not to listen to us. But what is impossible according to human laws is possible in our faith. The Almighty God can touch even your heart."*[215] This kind of polite request, which was rare, did not actually endanger anyone. But where was the Christians' courage when it was needed? Can we even talk about courage, or should we just speak of faith – faith in the power of God, the influence of religion and the sanctity of life? It is true that Christians of the 1930s and 1940s, in Germany and the occupied countries, faced a challenge to their faith. The challenge was not only about Jews, but also about what to do when facing evil. If we want to learn something from all of this, we could say, at the very least, that unless we recognize evil, we can certainly not resist it.

The Righteous Among the Nations

On my first day at work at Yad Vashem, the Holocaust Museum and Education Center, I have the honor to attend a special ceremony. A man somewhere in Eastern Europe (and I do not remember exactly where, because the whole first day is like a big cloud in my head) had saved one Jew during World War II. Putting himself in great danger, he had hidden his Jewish friend in his own home. He fed him and took care of him when he was sick. Even thinking about a doctor's visit would have been very dangerous... But both men, the rescuer and the rescued, survived miraculously until the end of the war. They separated in 1945, when the Jewish man got on board a ship taking survivors to Yishuv, the Jewish community of the Palestine Mandate at the time.

In the year 2008, the children, numerous grandchildren and some surviving relatives of this one Jewish man stand in front of a tree planted for their savior. They are one huge, loud group. A man somewhere saved one person, but here stands the whole world. Suddenly, I remember a saying from the Talmud: "whoever saves a life, it is considered as if he saved an entire world." Here, it is actually true, because the whole world is in children and grandchildren.

A non-Jewish man is now a recognized Righteous Among the Nations because he alone acted in a different way from the rest of the world around him.

It is of utmost importance that the names of the victims do not disappear. So, there is an entire area at Yad Vashem, the Garden of the Righteous, where trees have been planted in remembrance of the non-Jews who saved Jews during the war. The trees of the Righteous are the first thing a visitor sees when entering Yad Vashem. There are over 23,000 Righteous to remind us and future generations that even amidst the atrocities of the war, there was a possibility to choose. Furthermore, we perceive that as important as it is to talk about the victims, it is just as important to tell the story of the rescuers. Hungarian *Imre Bathory*, who has a tree in Yad Vashem, said: *"I know that when I stand before God on Judgement Day, I shall not be asked the question posed to Cain, where were you when your brother's blood was crying out to God?"*[216] The former Director of Yad Vashem's Righteous Among the Nations program, *Irena Steinfeldt,* said: *"In a world where Auschwitz was reality, the Jewish people and the survivors needed to hang on to some hope for mankind, something that would enable them to maintain their faith in human values and rebuild their lives after having witnessed an unprecedented moral collapse."*[217]

According to Jewish mystics, God does not destroy the evil world on account of the righteous who live in it; this belief has a Biblical origin, referring to the city of Sodom, on whose behalf Abraham pleaded before God. There may be a lot of evil in the world, but there are always those who are righteous. This was also true during the dark era of Nazi persecution, when some burned as bright candles, and some paid with their lives for their actions. They were a small minority in a much larger group. We could perhaps describe them in this way: they were ready to act, putting their lives in danger; they were ready to do what was needed, instead of only speaking about it; they did not consider their own life of more value than that of another. They understood the single most important thing: exceptional times require exceptional actions. The crime they saw taking place around them was so great that fears about personal safety paled alongside it. In other words, they were ready to share the fate of the victims in order to save someone's life.

Elie Wiesel described the Righteous Among the Nations and the general conditions this way: *"In those times there was darkness everywhere. In heaven and on earth, all the gates of compassion seemed to have been closed. The killer killed and the Jews died and the outside world adopted an attitude either of complicity or of indifference. Only a few had the courage to care. These few men and women were vulnerable, afraid, helpless – what made them different from their fellow citizens?... Why were there so few?... Let us remember: What hurts the victim most is not the cruelty of the oppressor but the silence of the bystander.... Let us not forget, after all, there is always a moment when moral choice is made..."*[218]

Historians, as well as victims of persecution, have attempted to analyze those who helped them in many different ways. It is almost impossible to find a common denominator that would explain the extraordinary courage and strength of moral values that could make a person put their life at risk for another. The rescuers came from all nations and peoples; they came from different social classes and professions; the only common denominator was their strong identification with the victims. Often the decision to help had to be made in an instant, when persecutors, such as the Gestapo, were about to arrest the victim. The *Gestapo*, *Geheime Staatspolizei*, was the State Secret Police, the state's main way of terrorizing citizens. In the darkness of night, a frightened person knocked on a door. There was no time to stop and think about the decision, as the neighbors could call the Secret Police. The decision to give asylum to the persecuted had to be made immediately. Helping did not always mean hiding; it could involve obtaining false papers, buying food or medicine, smuggling them over the border or a number of other things. But in any case, it did mean the line drawn between life and death. So, this is not a question of normal relationship with someone who asks you for help; instead, the question is more fundamental: does the person (the intended victim) have a right to continue living? In some sense, it can be assumed that a person to whom others turned must have understood their role and the fact that under the circumstances they could not run from that responsibility (morally) or place in on anyone else.[219]

The risks were enormous: most often, if caught, the helper was to share the same fate as the Jew. What did this mean in reality? In Western Europe, those who helped Jews (for instance, those who hid them) were sent to camps, like Corrie ten Boom or some of the helpers of Anne Frank. In Eastern Europe, such as in Poland, not only the helper but his entire family might be shot on the spot. The immediate risks were, therefore, highest in Eastern Europe, but we know that in practice, the concentration camp was the same as a death sentence to many rescuers. On the other hand, we need to remember that the risk did not only come from the Germans. Helpers were in danger first and foremost because of their own families and neighbors. Anyone could be an informant. There are cases in which the rescuer and the one being helped survived until the end of the war but were murdered by anti-Semitic neighbors when the war was already over. Helpers were often forced to act completely alone, and they were not able to tell anyone about what they were doing. In Austria, virtually all of them acted alone and were completely isolated.[220] If we compare these helpers to the heroes of the resistance movement, we understand the difference between them: the rescuer had to hide his activities from everyone. Most rescuers acted alone, without the support of a group, and they had no way of knowing how long the war would go on.

To get an idea of what these helpers did and what risks they faced, particularly from their neighbors, I want to mention *Romualda* and *Feliks Ciesielska*, who have been recognized by Yad Vashem as Righteous Among the Nations. They and their son were transferred to Krakow, where they were given a residence that had been taken from the Jews. They felt pity for the Jews and decided to help them in whatever way they could, so they used their store as a cover to hide Jews. They did this until the Gestapo came for them in 1942. The Gestapo apprehended them after receiving information about the Ciesielskas family from their Polish neighbors. Feliks died in Mauthausen Camp, whereas Romualda survived Auschwitz.[221] The Germans, as such, had nothing to do with this state of affairs; rather, deep-rooted anti-Semitism attracted the whistleblowers. Anti-Semitism did not disappear at the end of the war; those who helped the Jews had to move away in order to live in peace. It is believed that many who helped the Jews during the war have never told their stories, just because they were afraid of their neighbors' reactions.

In search for an explanation for selfless behavior that deviated from the norm, researcher *Eva Fogelman*[222] divided the rescuers into groups according to their motivations:

Moral Rescuers, whose sense of right and wrong obligated them to act. Danger of death did was not a factor in a situation where great injustice was taking place.

Philo-Semites, those who felt a connection to the Jews. They often had a distant Jewish background or were Bible-believing Christians.

Concerned Professionals, whose profession gave them an opportunity both to meet Jews and to help them with visas, passports and hideouts. We count, for example, diplomats, doctors and teachers in this group.

Networks of Rescuers, who were often part of the resistance movement, where helping the Jews was one action among others.

Child Rescuers, who were used as decoys when transferring people. Children avoided suspicion and were therefore able to do many kinds of tasks that the adults could not do. The need for silence and keeping secrets was a very heavy responsibility for children.

Each person recognized as Righteous Among the Nations has a story.

Jan Karski (1914-2000) was a Polish aristocrat and diplomat who acted as a Polish resistance movement's courier for the *Polish Government in Exile* in London. As an aristocrat, he was able to travel to meetings with the Western heads of state around the world. With great personal courage, he ventured into the Warsaw Ghetto and one of the camps in order to give an account to the outside world about exactly what was happening in Poland. The terrors he witnessed convinced him that he had to pass on the information. The task was extremely difficult, not so much for technical reasons, but because in reality, no one wanted to believe his words.

Karski wrote:

"The Lord assigned me a role to speak and write during the war, when – as it seemed to me - it might help. It did not. When the war came to its end, I learned that the governments, the leaders, the scholars, the writers did not know what had been happening to the Jews. The murder of six million innocents was a secret... Then I became a Jew. And just as my wife's entire family was wiped out in the ghettos of Poland, in its concentration camps and crematoria – so have all the Jews who were slaughtered become my family.

But I am a Christian Jew. I am a practicing Catholic. Though I am not a heretic, my faith tells me the second Original Sin has been committed by humanity: through commission, or omission, or self-imposed ignorance, or insensitivity, or self-interest, or hypocrisy, or heartless rationalization. This sin will haunt humanity to the end of time. It does haunt me. And I want it to be so."[223] What made Karski different from his contemporaries? Why did he see, when his contemporaries wanted not to see?

Another recognized as Righteous Among the Nations is a deeply religious Catholic man who said before the war: *"I would rather stand with God against man than with man against God."*[224] France surrendered to the Germans in June 1940, and the nation was divided into two parts: occupied and unoccupied France. Most tragic in the surrender of France was that no one in all of Europe had anticipated France's defeat, and for this very reason, refugees from all around Europe had arrived in France during the previous years of Nazi rule. When France surrendered, it was practically full of refugees, Jews and other persecuted peoples. What would the refugees do now? The march of German army boots in Paris awakened a mood of despair and defeat everywhere – the very reason these miserable thousands had fled from their countries of origin. Immediately after the German occupation of northern France, thousands of refugees tried to flee from the north to the south. Movies, literature and memoirs have all portrayed this sad scene to us. If people could not find a vehicle, they walked. Many refugees had left all their belongings behind years earlier, and now they carried with them only a few bags. Grandparents and young children all fled. It was one dreadful sight of desperation among many such situations caused by the war, but to the refugees, it meant the end of everything.

What was it that they hoped for? At this stage, Hitler had conquered practically all of Europe, since many of the unoccupied nations were his allies. For the refugees, an escape to unoccupied England had become an impossibility. Their only remaining hope was to get to the south of France, then travel through Spain to Portugal and from there, by ship, to the United States. This was the direction of the journey, but it was not a path without problems. After all, the whole of Europe was under an evil scourge at that time.

A man named Aristides de Sousa Mendes – who, years earlier, had so clearly expressed his desire to act according to the will of God – had become the Consul of Portugal to France earlier that year.[225] This is a story I have told many times when taking people to his tree at the Yad Vashem grounds. The account is also available on a film to recommend *Aristides de Sousa Mendes by Jose Mazeda, TAKE 2000*. This is what happened: in the summer of 1940, 30,000 refugees were waiting outside of the Portuguese Consulate in the city of *Bordeaux*, right outside the gates of his office. We don't know what was going on in Sousa Mendes's mind when he saw the desperate group of people. Was he perhaps thinking that God had brought him to this position for this exact moment? We only know what Sousa Mendes did. He put his position and career – virtually everything – in danger, not for one friend, but for a desperate mass of people. He decided to act against the orders of his government. With the help of his own sons and one rabbi, he set himself to writing visas or transit permits through Portugal for the refugees. After working non-stop for three days and nights, he passed out, just as he finished writing the visas. By then, the Portuguese government had been notified of him, and they sent security guards to bring him immediately back to Lisbon.

Sousa Mendes left with the security guards, knowing very well what kind of reception awaited him in Lisbon. But he obeyed anyway. He and the security guards traveled toward the Spanish border and arrived at the Portuguese Consulate in the city of Bayonne, where the same desperation prevailed on the streets. Was Sousa Mendes responsible for them as well? What is man's personal responsibility in general? Sousa Mendes is an example to follow. We have two stories of what happened next. One says that Sousa Mendes forced his way into the consulate and started writing visas. Another story, depicted in a movie recently released in Portugal, alleges that he was not allowed into the consulate, but wrote the visas in a nearby cafe. He knew the visas could raise questions and might not be respected at the borders. Therefore, he added with his own hand the following very exceptional sentence: *"The Government of Portugal most respectfully asks the Government of Spain to allow the holder of this document to pass through Spain, freely. The holder of this document is a refugee from the European conflict and is on their way to Portugal."* Sousa Mendes went with the refugees to the Spanish border himself to make sure that they were allowed to cross.

Sousa Mendes's return to Lisbon was a struggle, as he was taken before a disciplinary committee and dismissed from his post at the Ministry of Foreign Affairs of Portugal. Complete loss of position, social rejection and poverty was the story for the rest of his life. There was no way he would be able to provide for his family of thirteen children after he became known for his actions "against the State." In 1954, he died a premature death, unrecognized and unrewarded. But he never expressed remorse for what he had done, not even after paying such a high price. On the contrary, after losing everything, he reportedly said before his death: *"If thousands of Jews are suffering because of one Christian [Hitler], surely one Christian may suffer for so many Jews."*[226]

If we examine this in light of the Bible, what examples do we find of similar actions? In the beginning of this book, I mentioned Pharaoh's daughter, whom the former Israeli Chief Rabbi, Meir Israel Lau, called the first Righteous Among the Nations. The book of Exodus recounts: *"Then the daughter of Pharaoh came down to bathe at the river. And her maidens walked along the riverside; and when she saw the ark among the reeds, she sent her maid to get it. And when she opened it, she saw the child, and behold, the baby wept. So she had compassion on him, and said, 'This is one of the Hebrews' children.'"*[227] Pharaoh's daughter took the child into her own care, because she felt pity for him. Let us compare this story to something that happened in Italy in 1943. The German occupation had just begun when a woman called *Yuzzi Galambos*, a mother of three who had hid her Jewish background from everyone, became seriously ill. In January 1944, right before her death, she told her children's young Italian caretaker of her Jewishness, asking her to save her children. Germany had already occupied northern Italy, and the young nanny, *Ida Brunelli,* feared for her life and that of the children. Yet she courageously took the children to her own mother in another city, where, pretending to be Hungarian refugees, they survived until the end of the war.

In the book of Joshua, when the Israelite spies had to hide from the king of Jericho, a woman named *Rahab* hid them until the search was over: *"So the king of Jericho sent to Rahab, saying, 'Bring out the men who have come to you, who have entered your house, for they have come to search out all the country.' Then the woman took the two men and hid them. So she said, 'Yes, the men came to me, but I did not know where they were from.'"*[228] Likewise, during the German occupation of the Netherlands, especially in 1943-1944, the *ten Boom* family in *Haarlem* hid people in their home for a short time until they could be smuggled to the countryside, where it was possible to hide them more securely.

Sometimes, people had to hide someone in their own room for years, risking their own lives. 2 Chronicles tells of one such incident: *"Now when Athaliah the mother of Ahaziah saw that her son was dead, she arose and destroyed all the royal heirs of the house of Judah. But Jehoshabeath, the daughter of the king, took Joash the son of Ahaziah, and stole him away from among the king's sons who were being murdered, and put him and his nurse in a bedroom. So Jehoshabeath, the daughter of King Jehoram, the wife of Jehoiada the priest (for she was the sister of Ahaziah), hid him from Athaliah so that she did not kill him."*[229] Similarly, in September of 1943, after Germany had occupied Greece, a member of the royal family, *Princess Alice* – the mother of the current British *Prince Philip* – hid the family of the Jewish *Haim Cohen* in her own residence, and despite the Gestapo's searches, she never sent them away.

Sometimes, someone had to pretend to be one of the enemy in order to save a larger number of people, as in the case of Esther: *"Esther had not revealed her people or family, for Mordecai had charged her not to reveal it."*[230] Likewise, *Oskar Schindler* spent time with the Nazi officers, never showing his disapproval for what they did. This way, with gifts and entertainment, he was granted favor, by which he was able to save a significant number of people from certain death.[231]

Of course, there are more Biblical examples, but even from these, we can understand the principle of one person acting in order to save another person's life during times of persecution. The Bible presents these people as models and examples. They are always presented in a favorable light compared to their contemporaries. It is as if there is a law declaring that we are responsible for helping and protecting our neighbors who may be in danger. Those heroes in the Bible, as well as the rescuers during the Holocaust, are our examples of righteousness.

A Word About Resistance

Was there any Christian resistance, then? Please note that I am no longer speaking about the Righteous Among the Nations, but about resistance, which is a slightly different matter. The Righteous Among the Nations were individual persons, sometimes groups of people, who saved one or more Jews from certain death. Sometimes, these helpers were a part of a wider resistance. So, now, we are speaking only about resistance. First and foremost, we think of groups and movements that took part in various operations to overthrow the Nazi government, to prevent the actions of the German army, to save prisoners from the Gestapo and the like. Although there is purely spiritual resistance in the form of prayer and teaching of the Bible, here I mean resistance that took practical action but was also inspired by the Christian faith of those involved.

Many are familiar with the book *The Hiding Place*, which relates the actions of the ten Boom family on behalf of the Jews as part of the resistance movement during the German occupation of Holland. I sincerely recommend reading it. Some are also familiar with the rescue story of *Conspiracy of Goodness*, which took place in the Protestant village *Chambon Sur Lignon* in France during its occupation. There are other such stories from around the occupied regions of Europe.

In this context, however, I want to concentrate on another kind of story and discuss the previously mentioned German priest and theologian Dietrich

Bonhoeffer.[232] The facts here are based on several books but also the film *Bonhoeffer: The Agent of Grace, 2000*. Bonhoeffer was a Lutheran pastor and theologian, and also a member of the resistance movement, whose name has become a myth. What makes him ever so relevant is the precision with which he, unlike a large part of his contemporaries, understood the manifestations of evil around him. The decision he had to make was one the majority of mankind would not be ready to make. As a result, Bonhoeffer was executed in the last weeks of the war. His family learned about his death only when they heard about it on the BBC news.

Dietrich Bonhoeffer was born in 1906 to an aristocratic family in Breslau. His father, *Karl Bonhoeffer*, was one of the leading psychiatrists and neurologists of the time, and his mother, *Paula,* came from an old, esteemed family. In 1927, Bonhoeffer defended his doctorate at the University of Berlin, at the age of only 21. He then had an opportunity to travel, and he was most impressed by the time he spent in New York. There, he familiarized himself with the practical priestly work in the churches of the poor in Harlem, and he was drawn to the gospel music of the black population. At the same time, he also became aware of the consequences of the economic crisis in the United States.[233]

After returning to his own country in 1931, Bonhoeffer taught theology at the University of Berlin. At this stage, he was a devoted pacifist and believed that even making preparations to go to war was wrong. What makes this interesting is that Bonhoeffer's pacifism only grew as the Nazis rose to power. At this stage, he did not yet think about resisting the state with arms. The Bible gave him a reason to resist the war and to resist Hitler.[234] Bonhoeffer noticed that the Nazi Party was in conflict with the church, and he also saw the Party's problematic Jewish policy.

The power of the National Socialists quickly became established and, as we remember from the previous chapter, terrorism against citizens increased during the year of 1933. Bonhoeffer then gave a radio speech in which he appealed to the Germans, saying that Hitler was a *leader* who could also become a *seducer* – this is a kind of play on words, as the German words *Fuhrer* (leader) and *Verfuhrer* (seducer) sound the same. His speech was interrupted in the middle of the broadcast.[235] He appealed to pastors, yet it proved to be more than they could take. Many of Bonhoeffer's colleagues appealed to Romans 13: *"Let every soul be subject to the governing authorities. For there is no authority except from God, and the authorities that exist are appointed by God. Therefore whoever resists the authority resists the ordinance of God, and those who resist will bring judgment on themselves."*[236] It must be kept in mind, however, that in 1933, Bonhoeffer's attitude toward the Jews was still unclear. We know that when he was asked to perform a burial for his Jewish relative, he declined in fear, but later said that this denial was something he regretted for the rest of his life.

In August 1933, Bonhoeffer, together with other pastors resisting Hitler, said that in reality, the German church was already divided. A majority of the state church promoted Germany and Hitler. After trying without results to change the church from within, through various declarations or petitions requiring signatures, Bonhoeffer and Martin Niemöller, formed a group called the Pastors' Emergency League, a resistance movement that subsequently became the Confessing Church. In the final days of May 1934, the pastors held a meeting in Bremen, where the so-called Bremen Declaration was birthed, which became the basic document for the Confessing Church. The Confessing Church now became the opposition within the church. Bonhoeffer recognized the dangers early on, and he alluded to this conflict in his sermons, using the book of Daniel as his subject.[237]

In October 1933, after the political situation had tightened, Bonhoeffer traveled to London, believing it was time to retreat from the entire situation. Karl Barth reproached Bonhoeffer for leaving the German Church at such a moment. In April 1935, Bonhoeffer returned to Germany to lead seminaries, first in Berlin and later in Finkenwalde; in 1937, the government banned the seminary, which continued underground, with Bonhoeffer remaining as its leader. Under his leadership, the underground seminary trained pastors for the Confessing Church, who criticized the growing influence of the National Socialists in *Reichskirche*, the State Church. For example, priests of Jewish origin were no longer granted open posts.[238]

The year 1938 began in a rather peculiar (and some writers have said prophetic) way, as in January of that year, the Gestapo arrested Bonhoeffer, who was forbidden to come to Berlin.[239] The same year, Bonhoeffer made the first contacts, through his brother-in-law *Hans von Dohnanyi,* with the central figures of the conspiracy against Hitler. In September, he helped his sister Sabine and her Jewish husband to flee first to Switzerland and from there to England. In November 1938, the Night of the Broken Glass occurred. Bonhoeffer was one of the only pastors who denounced this horrible event.[240] Strangely, it was also at about this time that the possibility of a political murder began to be spoken of openly – in other words, the conspiracy against Hitler. Right before the outbreak of the war, however, Bonhoeffer traveled to the United States. On the last day before his trip, he had a discussion with Hans von Dohnanyi concerning the words of Jesus: *"all who take the sword will perish by the sword."*[241] Bonhoeffer's answer, according to a friend, was that Jesus' words had to be taken literally. Christians must understand that they will not be excused if they choose violence to solve this situation. On the other hand, Bonhoeffer saw that people were needed who were ready to take the judgment on themselves. In the light of all we now know, Dohnanyi was looking for Christian approval for the intended political murder. Bonhoeffer's answer was not unambiguous, since he understood that the weight of this heavy burden rested on his shoulders, and he could not deny that only an extreme move, such as murdering Hitler, would change the political situation.

Bonhoeffer himself would have been safe in the United States had he remained there, but as he was reading his Bible, he felt an urgency to return to Germany. Once again, another peculiarity of history: Bonhoeffer returned to Germany in the summer of 1939 with the last ship to cross the Atlantic before World War II.

After the outbreak of war, the Nazi regime closed Bonhoeffer's seminaries, and in August 1940, he received a so-called sermon ban "in the entire Reich." In March 1941, the ban was extended to publications as well. Bonhoeffer, for all practical purposes, finally joined the conspirators against Hitler at this same time. He began using his church contacts in an attempt to get in touch with the Allies for negotiations. He joined *Abwehr*, the *Army Intelligence Service*. He and Dohnanyi also used their contacts to help Jews escape to Switzerland.[242] His secrecy was noticed in the Confessing Church. He could say nothing of his activities, and a nasty rumor circulated that he was suspected of spying on the church for the Nazis.[243]

Bonhoeffer's attitude toward Hitler and his regime changed considerably during the war. Before the war, he was an advocate for pacifistic resistance. However, the continuous brutalization of the war, and the increasingly radical forms of persecution against the Jews, forced Bonhoeffer to assess the situation again. He no longer rejected an armed coup or an attack against Hitler, believing that without support from leading generals, it would be impossible to remove Hitler through mere civil resistance. As Hitler achieved military victories, the generals' confidence that he could be overthrown fell.[244] We can only try to imagine what Bonhoeffer was thinking: a murder is an extreme means, and it is not a sinless act. He was aware that after the war, he would lose his post for participating in a coup, and moreover, he was weighed down by the awareness that he would lose all his righteousness.

The conspiracy against Hitler, as we know, did not succeed. Members of the conspiracy attempted his murder in March 1943, but the attempt failed. In April 1943, Bonhoeffer was arrested because in a search of Hans von Dohnanyi's home, documents were found showing Bonhoeffer's involvement in the resistance movement. He was taken to *the Tegel Prison* in Berlin and prosecuted in the military court. At this stage, the high-ranking officials who participated in the resistance movement succeeded in suppressing the investigation, so the situation did not seem very serious. In prison, Bonhoeffer managed to be a witness of his faith to both the guards and his fellow prisoners. His letters, which were smuggled out, were later published as a book. An escape from the prison could have been arranged, but he did not want to put anyone in danger, and the escape would certainly have caused retaliation.

As portrayed in the 2008 movie *Valkyrie*, Count *Claus von Stauffenberg* (1907-1944) carried out a bomb attack on Hitler at his eastern headquarters. Stauffenberg was not just any contemporary; he had served in Hitler's war campaigns and had even been wounded on the front line. While at the eastern front, he had seen terrible violations of human rights, which he had mentioned to the army officers. Therefore, this was a well-informed and reliable person. On the morning of the attack, however, everything that could possibly go wrong did. The attack failed, and Hitler survived with very minor injuries.[245] Furthermore, a new problem emerged, as the attack revealed that the conspiracy against Hitler had spread even to the highest army leadership. Hitler had mistrusted the army from the very beginning, so this confirmed his already existing prejudices. After the Gestapo's investigations, several high-ranking officers involved in the conspiracy were arrested and sentenced in the People's Court for the attempted coup and conspiracy against Hitler. And now, we come to the very core of the story: Bonhoeffer lost his most important protectors when their involvement was exposed. So, on October 8, 1944, Bonhoeffer was taken into custody by the Gestapo and sent to their notorious headquarters on Prinz-Albrecht-Straße for questioning.

In February 1945, Bonhoeffer was transported to Buchenwald concentration camp near Weimar. From there, he was evacuated to Flossenbürg concentration camp in Bavaria. In April 1945, the diaries of *Admiral Wilhelm Canaris* (1887-1945), the Director of Abwehr, were placed in the hands of Hitler, who ordered that all members of the July 20 conspiracy were to be executed without delay. According to Hitler's order, the SS court sentenced Bonhoeffer and others to death by hanging on April 8, 1945. When the guards came to take him to be executed, Bonhoeffer wrote a message, which he left with an English prisoner of war: *"This is the end – for me, the beginning of life."*[246]

Bonhoeffer lived at a time when the majority of the people and the church leadership did not recognize evil, even though it was staring them right in the face. The Bonhoeffer who in 1933 promoted pacifism was not the same man who gave his life in 1945. He went through a transformation, but it took place on an individual level and did not extend to the entire church. The years before the National Socialists came into power did not prepare churches to face challenges, nor did the churches have a vision that this was a battle between good and evil. Therefore, individual people represented Christianity at that time, instead of the religious communities acting as a whole. Bonhoeffer himself had reputedly said that even if evil was clothed in goodness, good will and loyalty, this only would show how deep the evil was. Bonhoeffer's life offers us an example of how evil can be resisted if its essence is identified. It is also a question of taking responsibility. It is not about avoiding evil by being silent bystanders, as so often happened during the persecution of the Jews, but about taking responsibility as Christians. If, like Bonhoeffer believed, God's Kingdom is bound to what happens on earth, then God works in this world, and we should be His instruments.

Sadly, the German Reich Church, along with many priests, pastors and individuals, chose adaptation, conformity and submission to evil. It seems that no one was aware of what was happening in time to stop the evil. Manifestations of evil were visible, but they were not taken seriously. No one even thought that taking a stand against evil had anything to do with the duties of the church. Changes in society took place so quickly, and yet it happened gradually. The more that evil changed the society, the more difficult it became to react to it. This is the danger each generation has to face. Therefore, suffice it to say that Bonhoeffer's thoughts on costly and cheap grace fit our time, just as they fit Nazi Germany.

The values, pressure and depreciation of society are all elements that can drive the church to become the church of cheap grace, as Bonhoeffer described in *The Cost of Discipleship*: *"Cheap grace means grace sold on the market like cheap-jacks' wares. The sacraments, the forgiveness of sin, and the consolations of religion are thrown away at cut prices... Cheap grace therefore amounts to a denial of the living word of God... Cheap grace is grace without discipleship, grace without the cross, grace without Jesus Christ, living and incarnate"*[247] By contrast, according to Bonhoeffer, costly is the kind of grace that leads us to sacrifice our whole lives to Him who sacrificed himself for us: *"Costly grace is the treasure hidden in the field; for the sake of it a man will gladly go and sell all that he has. It is the pearl of great price to buy which the merchant will sell all his goods… It is the call of Jesus Christ at which the disciple leaves his nets and follows him… Above all, [grace] is costly because it cost God the life of his Son. Costly grace is … the living word, the Word of God, which he speaks as it pleases him."*[248]

On December 19, 1944, only a few months before his death, Bonhoeffer wrote to his fiancé and family, as a Christmas greeting. The poem called *Von guten Mächten treu und still umgeben* (Sheltered Wonderfully by Powers of Goodness) became a much beloved hymn around the world:

"Sheltered wonderfully
By powers of goodness
We are looking forward confidently to what may come
God is with us
In the evening and in the morning
And for sure on every new day…
If now the silence is spreading deep around us,
Let us hear the full sounds of the world
That is widening invisibly around us,
The high hymns of all your children.
By loving forces wonderfully sheltered,
we are awaiting fearlessly what comes.
God is with us at dusk and in the morning
and most assuredly on ev'ry day…"[249]

8 Of Faith and Knowledge After the Holocaust – Lessons

"I will give you the treasures of darkness..."[250]

I have flown over the United States, from the east coast to the west, immediately after crossing the Atlantic. I am exhausted after traveling for days, and I can hardly keep my eyes open. I have been invited to speak at a Holocaust-themed conference in a famous Department of Theology. I sit in the first row with the other speakers, the audience behind us.

Despite being tired, I listen to the speech. It does not align with my thinking, and the speaker is not a Holocaust researcher. I hear words that are ignorant or anti-Semitic. I understand that they believe that the Bible is subject to interpretation. I look around and hope that someone will stand up and object, until I understand through the fog of jet lag that it is I who must stand up. I sense a responsibility. After all, I represent Bible-believing Christianity. Silence would mean accepting the speaker's views. I am terrified. I am exhausted. My wish, my prayer of "someone else" bangs in my head. I cannot, I do not have the strength, I do not know how.

The speaker has finished, and it is time for the audience to comment. I am aware of the tedious, strange atmosphere in the hall. I am certain that I am not the only one who is bothered by the conference's arrogant academic atmosphere. Somehow, I manage to force myself to get up and take the microphone. "I just want to say that I do not agree with the previous speaker, whose comments are imprecise and on the verge of being anti-Semitic." A dead-still silence descends in the hall. Through the fog, I realize that I will never be invited here again. I do not regret for a moment speaking up for the truth.

The conference organizers treat me with icy politeness now. But a surprise that brings tears to my eyes awaits in the morning. When I enter the conference hall, the audience of ordinary Americans begins to circle me. One of the men takes his cap in his hand and says, "Well... we would like to thank you. We all would have wanted to say something to that speaker yesterday. But we just did not know how to do it."

Because the Holocaust was such an immense and almost indescribable tragedy, connected with different political events and various people groups, researching it has not been easy, and the lessons learned from it cannot be fully explained in only a few sentences. Because its consequences were so wide, not even the survivors have been able to articulate how to research or even understand it. Such gifted survivors as the author Elie Wiesel have said that the Holocaust was outside the events of world history, in its own secluded class.[251] On the other hand, one of the veteran Holocaust researchers, political scientist *Raul Hilberg*, who wrote his first book in 1961, would completely disagree. According to him, everything can be researched, measured, analyzed and presented. Others, such as *Yehuda Bauer*, an Israeli veteran researcher and leading expert on Holocaust research, have proposed that the Holocaust was a singular or highly distinct event. In these divergent views, therefore, lies the Holocaust-related mystery and its problematic research. At the same time, however, these views hold an explanation for the Holocaust, as they do not necessarily cancel each other, despite the contradictions. Questions have been asked about the uniqueness of the Holocaust: What is its relation to other mass murders or genocides? Is it unique? Some say that the

Holocaust stands alone because of the number of victims. At the same time, there is fear that due to the number of victims being so huge, it becomes unreal. What is unreal and difficult to understand is also easy to forget. Therefore, Holocaust education aims to emphasize the individuals and their experiences, within all people groups. At the same time, broader lines are taught through the lens of these individual experiences.

The Holocaust is unique because all Jews were its victims. Even Jews who did not experience the Holocaust were meant to be its victims. Not every Jew experienced the Holocaust directly, but the Holocaust was meant to be the fate of every Jew. If we think about the victims, only in the case of the Jews and perhaps the Roma (Gypsies) do we see this similar absoluteness. All the other victims were victims due to something, that is their actions or opinions. In other words, they, as an entire people, were not destined for destruction. The best researchers in the world have analyzed the historical developments and explanations leading to genocide, but I believe that all explanations are incomplete unless they take into consideration the special role of the Jewish people in God's plan.[252] The Bible explains the hatred toward the Jewish people as enmity against God and His selection. This hatred rises up time and time again. We can therefore draw a conclusion that even though the acts of violence and mass murder are not a unique event in world history, the hatred towards the Jews makes the Holocaust unique. Racial doctrine and blood purity were less important elements in the Holocaust than the attack against the God represented by the Jews.

So, God was personified in the Jews, and the war was a war expressly against the Jewish faith and spirit. Judaism had given the world thoughts of freedom, equality and justice, which the Nazis tried to destroy. These thoughts came from the Bible.[253] Therefore, the question is: did not the Nazis, like so many before them, ultimately try to destroy the Almighty, Omnipotent and Omnipresent God Himself? One of the most famous artists of the Holocaust is *Samuel Bak*, who was born in Vilnius, Lithuania, in 1933. Out of the 80,000 Jews in Vilnius, only about 250 survived World War II and the Holocaust. Bak and his mother were among the survivors, and Bak became one of the great artists of our time. Art, to him, was always a question to which he was looking for an answer. In his art, the Holocaust and Judaism are joined together in a way that is difficult to describe in words. As it is believed in Judaism that the very lettering and writings in the Bible are part of creation, then destroying the Ten Commandments or the Scriptures destroys God Himself, who has set in these Scriptures a certain order of creation. In several of his pieces of art, Bak writes the initial letter of God's name at the feet of broken tablets of the law or in the fire that kills. This symbolizes how breaking the tablets of law in the Holocaust was interfering with God Himself.[254]

Philosopher *Emil Fackenheim* (1916-2003) was one of the most gifted thinkers of our time. This German-born rabbi and philosopher was taken to the *Sachenhausen* concentration camp, but he managed to escape from the Nazis. He believed that the Holocaust of World War II resembled most closely the genocide of the Armenians during World War I. According to him, the common factors were the following:

1. **An entire nation** had been chosen to be a victim of destruction;
2. The murder took place **during a war;**
3. It was **hidden** as effectively as possible;
4. The **victims were transported** to far-away places;
5. When all this was taking place, **the rest of the world** hardly protested.[255]

There were also differences between these genocides, especially in their practical implementation:

1. In the Holocaust, the **victims were defined and selected** carefully and precisely;

2. **Legislation** was used to enable the removal of the Jews' civil rights along with their possessions, while preserving an illusion of the legality of the actions;

3. A large-scale **operation of a technical nature** was set up, including railways and the murder institutions themselves;

4. A large number of **people were recruited**, of which some acted as murderers and others as their assistants.

According to Fackenheim, all these operations were enabled by the fact that Nazi Germany was, in fact, a dual state. By this, he means that in addition to the traditional legal and academic structure, an SS structure was created, which was a state within a state.[256] The elements that had to be in place before the murder were political will, with which the SS mobilized a large part of the people; political planning, with which the murder operations were organized; and willing participants. Most likely, many participants did not understand their own role, nor its tremendous significance for the success of the whole plan. Perhaps only the contempt expressed by the world during the Nuremberg War Trials made them examine themselves in a different light. But by then, it was already too late.

As we examine the Holocaust, we come across many spiritual and emotional issues that are universal. Man is central in the story, because the story expressly brings out the choices made by man. How are choices made in extreme conditions? What makes people from the same culture arrive at such different solutions? Under no circumstances can we focus our attention exclusively on the Nazi supreme leadership or on the victims. Most of the people, living at the time, led a normal life, not unlike mine or yours. His or her story has been forgotten, but is it in that normal life and its circumstances that many answers are hidden? We must cross the gap between our daily lives and the Holocaust's contemporaries and see them as human beings. At the same time, we can learn to look at our own surroundings from a different or more critical perspective. Who or what determines our opinions? To what degree is a citizen obliged to obey the law? What is the responsibility of each citizen at a time when laws are immoral? What dangers threaten our freedoms from modern technology – for technology at the time of the Holocaust was almost rudimentary in comparison with our time, yet it still contributed to genocide? How does anti-Semitism occur today, and what feeds its occurrence? Which opinions are forbidden? Where is the prohibition of certain opinions taking us as a society? These and many other questions arise when studying the Holocaust.

I feel that the most frightening element in the whole process is the lightness and ease with which the structure of society was changed. One step in the wrong direction, one new law, one foolish person who makes a wrong decision – that is all that is needed. The truth is that life is full of choices, which we make each day. But how many of those choices are informed, conscious choices? How often do we follow the easiest path, without finding out the full scope of the situation? Nazi Germany is only one example of where wrong choices can lead. In that case, an entire process started long before the election of Hitler. After his election, things progressed at an accelerated pace, yet every new step, new law, new murder offered the bystanders an opportunity to react. Could one train driver have stopped the train in the wrong place? Could one doctor have declared the disabled healthy? Do we choose silence because we cannot bear the thought of the sacrifice we would have to make if we chose to speak the truth? The problem arises in a situation where a good society changes into one with whose values we cannot agree. What do we do in a situation like this?

Only natural catastrophes are so far outside our knowledge and control that we cannot prevent them or make plans for them. Human actions – such as destroying the Second Temple, massacres by the Crusaders, the Inquisition and the Holocaust – are planned acts, implemented and processed by humans, which require a humane answer.[257] Even though no one is saying that Christianity was a cause of the Holocaust, it is evident that it was one historical factor that contributed to the Holocaust. All the processes we have gone through, from the Middle Ages to the 1930s, contributed to anti-Semitism, which enabled the murder of the Jews. Even though we have a good reason to present Nazism as an anti-Christian ideology, we must say that anti-Semitic teaching over the centuries had conditioned Europeans to accept the thought of murdering the Jews. Even though it is possible that anti-Semitism has also occurred outside Christianity, we can unequivocally say that the hatred and hostility of Christianity toward Judaism is unprecedented in history. So, we move from this horrible thought toward understanding. If we, as Christians, have to face the past, how do we do it?

Christian Interpretations of the Holocaust

"God is Spirit, and those who worship Him must worship in spirit and truth."[258]

One way to consider faith (in this case my Christian faith) is to examine the way it relates to the people around us (me). If we accept this principle, we can implement it when we examine the situation after the Holocaust in the Christian world. It is very easy to point a finger at the past, but the problem is that we are not actually any better than our predecessors. If the Christian world *just survived* the time of World War II, what does this project for our day? Why is studying the Holocaust important in itself? Catholic priest and Holocaust expert *Michael McGarry* talked about the Holocaust being part of Christian history. He emphasized that Christians need to understand that we do not study the Holocaust just because it is Jewish history: *"Thus, we do not study what happened to them, but what happened to us."*[259]

We all know the stories of those who helped Anne Frank or the story of Corrie ten Boom's family. We remember the Christians of that time either as heroes or as horrible, non-Christian guards in the camps. But we must be willing to look deeper, so that we can see the truth. We could say that, up until the 1990s, Jews were -more or less- left alone to remember and study the Holocaust. The thought seems impossible, but the victims of the crime remembered, studied and taught the matter alone, decades after the event. Even though the perpetrators of the crime, the silent bystanders and the few rescuers were non-Jews, maintaining the memory of the crime was left entirely to the victims. Christian values did not function in that critical moment, when they should have been put into practice. We need to learn why this happened. Can our values be tested again? Sadly, yes, for values are useful only if they work at a critical time. Has there ever been a generation whose values have not been tried?

Jobst Bittner is a German pastor who has done pioneering work to break the Holocaust-related silence that has shackled German Christians. He has explained how the silence, non-encounter and evasion of the issues create a curse instead of a blessing over individual people, churches, cities and entire nations. He has done a lot of work in Germany to break the silence, for as long as silence continues, the curse rests and does not allow a new harvest to grow. Pastor Bittner has said that healing for people and communities will come only when the silence of difficult or shameful periods of history is intentionally broken. The same is true of the children of Nazi criminals, whose parents have not told the truth, and who have had to face it, in extremely painful ways, decades later. In his book, Pastor Bittner tells of a man whose father, a famous professor, had left his Nazi past unmentioned in his biography, and later developed dementia. The professor's son wrote an article in which he expressed his feeling that his father's dementia was a direct consequence of deliberate forgetting. In reality, the question was not about forgetting, but about deliberate actions. The son of the professor referred to this "forgetfulness" as an illness of an entire generation. In other words, after the war, it was simply decided that it is better to forget. Only in recent years has this situation changed in Germany.[260]

In the Christian world, certain explanations always arise when discussing the Holocaust. I will bring them up here so that we can learn from them, and perhaps gain a better understanding of why easy explanations are not enough. We cannot just tear the unfit part out of our history books. We must face the truth. How did the Holocaust take place in Christian Europe? One explanation I have often heard, when speaking at Christian (especially Evangelical) events, is that Nazism was an anti-Christian ideology. Because Christianity comes from Judaism, Christianity can never be anti-Jewish. Of course, this claim contains some truth. Nazism was anti-Christian, as we know from Hitler himself. It is tragic that the *church leaders of the time did not believe him* but instead wanted to coexist with all the compromises. The second argument, which says that true Christianity cannot be anti-Jewish, is more difficult to accept or understand. The problem is that when we examine Christianity and its history, applying this definition is hard. It is a simple statement that relates to thousands of years of violent history, and I do not believe this can be done so easily. If we go to the other extreme, we hear it said that Christianity was the root cause of the Holocaust. We have already discussed history, so we understand that this assertion is not, in itself, the whole truth. Perhaps we ought to leave individual people out of the discussion and examine only theology. Naturally, we understand that certain theological concepts had prepared the ground for the genocide of the Jews in Europe. Therefore, we must study theology if we want to be certain that the same factors are no longer present in our churches. It is evident from personal experience that in most parts of the Protestant world, there is little or no awareness of the extent to which Christian anti-Semitism contributed to Nazism.[261]

Have the churches examined their own role in relation to the Holocaust? This kind of research would mean studying the anti-Semitism of the churches and attempting to estimate how much it affected Nazism and the mechanisms of the Holocaust. Did it impact the populations that perhaps did not help the Jews, even if they could have, because they were mentally blocked by the anti-Semitism already present in their society? Here some examples of churches referring to their past:

In 1947, Jewish and Christian leaders met in *Seelberg*, Switzerland, to discuss the matter and to draw a mutual declaration. The *Second Vatican Council* in 1965 produced a declaration called *Nostra Aetate* (In Our Time). In this declaration, the Vatican distanced itself from anti-Semitism and made a strong statement that anti-Semitism is foreign to true Christianity. The document went even further in suggesting that Jews were not to be held guilty for the death of Jesus. If we think about Judaism and Catholicism as old religious communities, we understand the significance of this issue. In 1998, the Vatican gave another statement called *We Remember: A Reflection on the Shoah*.[262] Many individual Catholic churches, as well as old Protestant churches, have followed in these footsteps and issued various declarations on the topic. The *Rhineland Area Protestant Synod* drew up a declaration in 1980, the *Baden Area* in 1984 and the *German and Austrian Catholic Bishops' Conference* in 1988.[263] Many Lutheran churches took a stand on Luther's teachings in the 1970s, and the Presbyterian Church in the United States gave their declaration in 1987. The United Methodist Church, in turn, issued their statement in 1996.[264] The existing covenant of the Jews with God has truthfully been emphasized, as well as the argument that Judaism should be studied on its own terms, not just Christianity's.

In seeking to understand the Holocaust, the role of theology does not seem to be a central part of the discussion on Christian values. It may very well be that the Holocaust strengthened the perception in some circles that the Jews were cursed and no longer had a covenant with God. Therefore, the birth of the State of Israel was a shock treatment that turned everything upside down. If the prophecies about the people of Israel returning to their land were now being fulfilled, it meant that God was still operating among the Jews. Even though the declarations of the churches expressed remorse and sorrow because of the Christian anti-Semitism that contributed to the Holocaust, at the same time, a somewhat cold attitude was apparent with regard to the State of Israel. In private discussions with the leading Holocaust experts in the churches, I have also noticed this very problematic attitude.

A Catholic theologian and thinker, Father *John Pawlikowski*, with whom I have had the opportunity to discuss these matters several times, has said that moral sensitivity is an absolute prerequisite for moral thinking. According to him, God intervenes most often through humans, but we can only be part of His intervention if we are responsible. Some theologians have, in turn, expressed that, after the Holocaust, mankind can only recognize its own defectiveness, and we cannot assume that God will use us anymore. German - American activist and priest *Reinhold Niebuhr* said that when real evil is present, removing oneself from the situation is immoral. The correct response to evil is anger.[265] Truly, why did we have so little anger during the years of the Holocaust? At what stage did the bystanders cross the invisible line and turn into murderers?

Was God once again looking at the world and saying the same thing He did thousands of years earlier: *"And the Lord was sorry that He had made man on the earth, and He was grieved in His heart."*[266]

On Suffering

"But as for me, I would seek God,
And to God I would commit my cause—
Who does great things, and unsearchable,
Marvelous things without number."[267]

One thing that has been ignored in the Christian interpretation of the Holocaust is God's role during this shocking chain of events. As God is Almighty, He saw all that took place. If God was silent during the Holocaust, does this happen at other times too? One of the greatest and most difficult questions concerning the Holocaust is: where was God? One reason why Christians have ignored this extremely big question is that we rarely remember that the God of the Jews (our older brother) and our God is the same Creator of Heaven and Earth. If He was silent during the Holocaust, it would inevitably have an impact on us as well. Another reason, in my opinion, is that our perception of ourselves and how *faith should serve us* has changed dramatically in recent decades. In a way, we do not even accept the thought that God allows us to suffer, because we are the center of everything. Therefore, to many Western Christians, the thought of persecution, which Christians elsewhere are currently facing, is an absolute impossibility.

The third reason, I believe, has to do with how we understand evil and wickedness. Studying American Christian children and their views on the Holocaust, a researcher found one key factor. Based on their Christian faith, the children believed the Holocaust can be explained with supernatural elements. The Holocaust, therefore, was part of the battle between good and evil, where bad things happen when instructions are ignored.[268] What makes these children's interpretation problematic? We do believe, of course, that world events are truly part of a bigger conflict. The core idea of this entire book is the God who sees and acts in history. But the problem in the children's answer lies in the fact that they completely ignore the role and choices of the people as part of the Holocaust. The Holocaust was an inhumane event, one for which each person associated with it has a responsibility, as do governments and their leaders. Moral clarity is important, and we will lose it if we blame abstract wickedness for our own bad or wrong choices. Therefore, researchers see an immediate need to teach children about the choices they may have to make later in life.

Returning to the thought of suffering and the Almighty, linking unjust suffering and a just God is a challenge. We can study the book of Job, yet the scale of the Holocaust feels much larger. The murder of six million of whom one and a half million were children is incomprehensibly depressing.[269] How did the Holocaust contemporaries experience this very thing, then? We do not have many sources to find this out, but one very special source is called *Esh Kodesh* (Holy Fire), written *Rabbi Kalonimus Kalamish Shapiro* (1889-1943) from the Warsaw Ghetto.

Esh Kodesh is a collection of the sermons the rabbi gave during the Holocaust in the ghetto. Because the sermons were directed at his students during the Holocaust, they are a unique window to the spiritual situation in the ghetto. They were preserved because the rabbi hid them under the floor of his home before he was transported from the ghetto. As the rabbi was preaching, his own family and contemporaries were taken from around him and transported to death camps. So, the sermons are an authentic proof of how he saw God in that nest of misery during these tragic events – just before his own death. We may be quite surprised! For the rabbi does not speak at all about the daily horrors, but instead, he concentrates on speaking about the presence of God in suffering, and about the joy found in God's Presence. The rabbi sees God as being aware of the fate of the Jews. He presents the idea that this is about a supernatural conflict between the Nazis and those fighting them, as part of another, bigger conflict. But in this situation, God Himself is suffering alongside His Jewish people. The rabbi's view that suffering is part of faith, and that it turns into joy when it unites man with God, can be seen as his summary of it all.[270]

Many Jewish thinkers, such as the well-known *A. J. Heschel* (*Abraham Joshua Heschel*, 1907-1972), a Polish-born American Jewish rabbi and a leading theologian, have argued that every reason for the Holocaust lies solely with humans. According to Heschel, a process of hardening and indifference takes place in a society, which inevitably leads to something like the Holocaust. One of his central theses was seeing indifference, not wickedness, as the opposite of goodness. Heschel also argued that in Western thinking, even God has been made into someone man is looking for, whereas Heschel's view is that God is always looking for people.[271] As an answer to Heschel and his supporters, other thinkers have argued that Heschel was so traumatized no way he was able to produce any kind of theological response to the Holocaust.[272] It has also been argued that even before the Holocaust, the Jewish world had already suffered many different persecutions and catastrophes. The Jewish way was always to look for an explanation for these adversities, which was sin and the need to repent. In other words, the Jewish answer to all calamities was theological.

Personally, I would go back to the Bible and see that God "*blessed the latter days of Job more than his beginning…*"[273] But the answer for the Holocaust has been different, for it has been very practical and even secularized. One part of the answer is the State of Israel. Some Jewish thinkers, however, have responded that the State of Israel is also a theological answer to the Holocaust – in other words, the existence of the State of Israel has saved post-Holocaust Judaism.[274] If this was truly the case – if we start from the thought that the State of Israel has saved post-Holocaust Judaism – what, then, can save the post-Holocaust Christian world? If the world continues on its journey, without facing the truth of the past, it cannot avoid making the same or worse mistakes again.

Far too often, the Holocaust is interpreted as the cause for the emergence of the State of Israel. This view demonstrates ignorance of the Nazis' actual world-domination plans and what was happening in the

Palestinian Mandate at that time. Since the time of the Roman Empire and the destruction of the Second Temple, there has always been a Jewish community in the area of the modern State of Israel, irrespective of who has ruled the region. In the late 19th century, anti-Semitism in Europe, especially in its eastern parts and in Russia, pressed the Jews to move to the Ottoman-governed area, where they cleared away the malaria-infested swamps, built settlements and started cultivating the land. The largest waves of migration took place in 1882-1903, 1904-1914 and 1919-1923. Communities organized themselves, both politically and for defensive reasons. When World War I was over, Great Britain took control of the region, and Jewish migration accelerated, especially in the 1930s as the situation in Europe became increasingly unstable. The Jewish community there was called *Yishuv,* and it demanded independence, citing the Balfour Declaration, in which it was promised its own homeland. It was only a matter of time before Britain would have to give up its Palestinian mandate. This happened in 1947, when the United Nations decided to divide the region into two parts, one for Arabs and one for Jews.

It is important for us to understand that the Jewish State was already forming before World War II. Britain could not forcibly keep the Jewish State, an existing community with its own leaders, as the reluctant mandate. Sometimes it is best to express your thoughts so clearly that you will definitely be understood: Hitler did not create the State of Israel; rather, the establishment of the State of Israel is the workmanship of God. Just as it was with the enemies of Israel throughout its history, from the Pharaoh of Egypt to Haman of Persia, so it was once again: right when God's plan was about to be realized, the power of evil grew into astonishing proportions. God had decided to save the Israelites from Egypt, but right then, Pharaoh changed the conditions for the worse.

Hitler's plan during World War II, was not limited to the six million he was able to murder – it would have extended to all the Jews in the world. Hitler's attack was an attack on the establishment of the State of Israel, as the clock of world history has moved forward ever since the establishment of the nation. We must understand that the State of Israel was not birthed because of the Holocaust but in spite of it.

"Then He spoke to them a parable: 'Look at the fig tree, and all the trees. When they are already budding, you see and know for yourselves that summer is now near. So you also, when you see these things happening, know that the kingdom of God is near.'"[275]

World War II ended with the absolute surrender of Germany on May 7, 1945. Hitler had committed suicide a few days earlier, on April 30, as the Soviet troops surrounded Berlin. The Allied victory was the only reason why the Jewish genocide was forced to end. The Nazis had attempted the extermination of the Jews, coming closer to this goal than anyone else before them. The Nazis and their like-minded assistants around Europe made genocide a reality. We know the Jewish people were the target for the genocide, but let us remember that in murdering the Jews, the Nazis also murdered mankind. They also murdered us, because we can never again be humans in the same way as before the Holocaust. When I look at the pictures of young officers sending millions to death, my trust in man dies. That is the reason why I speak. I speak of something I have not experienced. I am a witness to an event that took place before my time.

Citing Elie Wiesel, I have become a witness to the Holocaust, because I have listened to the witnesses of the Holocaust.

A Witness Statement

Luna Kaufman and I meet each other for the first time in New York, in the winter of 2009. I know Luna only by her reputation as one of the Holocaust survivors who, after the Holocaust, has dedicated her life to promoting interreligious relations. We meet each other because Luna is interested in cooperating with the Christian Department opened a little earlier at Yad Vashem. She has just finished her autobiography, 'Luna's Life'.

'Luna's Life' is published in New York only three months after our first meeting, and Luna chooses me to host the events. In this role, I interview her about the book and her life. The events held at the Holocaust Museum in New York, known as the Museum of Jewish Heritage, and at Seton Hall University (a Catholic university) are a great success for both of us. Luna's book is received with interest, and I make a remarkable number of new and important contacts for my work.

By 2013, we have become close friends, and we meet every time I am in the United States on work visits. In the summer of 2013, I am Luna's guest for several days. Luna has traveled a long way from the Krakow Ghetto to Manhattan's posh Upper East Side. She tells in her book about the sad moment when her whole family had to move to the ghetto that the Germans established in Krakow in 1941. She also describes how her father and sister were taken by the Germans to forced labor camps outside the ghetto, never to return. Still, Luna recalls her life brightly. Even though the conditions were horrendous in the Plaszow camp, under the brutal power of Commander

Amon Goth, she believes in goodness. She has never lost her zest for life, nor her faith in hope. Above all, Luna believes in brotherhood and dialogue between Jews and Christians. It is an honor for me to put down in writing her thoughts on the relationship of these two brothers.

Luna was born in Poland on November 28, 1926. Her childhood in Krakow, was – in spite of existing anti-Semitism – almost free from anti-Jewish incidents. Students in her schools were mostly Christians, but Luna has good memories of that time. One of her school memories has to do with a Catholic priest who came to school to give religious instruction. For little Luna, the discussion with the priest was an especially significant weekly experience, for as she says herself, she somehow felt she was ahead of her time in that situation. The horrible times in the ghettos and camps during the Holocaust were, however, one thing that cannot just be wiped out, as a large part of her family and acquaintances perished in them. Luna left post-war Poland with her mother, as anti-Semitism was still strong even at that time. She says in her book that, even though Poland had been a home to the Jews since before the Spanish Inquisition, many Poles now resented the return of Jews in the post-Holocaust years. But for Luna, life had become much more than just surviving the Holocaust.

Luna was granted a U.S. visa in 1952, as she was already married to an American resident. She arrived in the United States via Israel, and soon realized there were many Christians in America who wanted to learn more about Jews and Judaism. When the opportunity came along, she began working as an instructor in an American organization called the *Anti-Defamation League*, which teaches tolerance in the Judeo-Christian-Muslim world. In the 1970s, Luna met *Sister Rose Thering*, a Dominican nun who was a visionary building bridges between Christians and Jews. In addition to her other public activities, Sister Rose was a professor at Seton Hall University and I warmly recommend the Oscar-nominated movie about her life, *Sister Rose's Passion* (2004). Sister Rose was a pioneer who welcomed a new alliance with Luna, and they began visiting schools together and giving joint interviews to the media. At the same time, Luna worked personally with the Governor of New Jersey to promote a Holocaust-based curriculum for schools written by Anti-Defamation League, which is used in schools across the country. In all of these tasks, Luna was motivated by her firm beliefs that religious hostility had contributed to the birth of the Holocaust, that prejudice is born of ignorance, and the key to removing prejudice is education.

Sister Rose always wore a golden Star of David intertwined with a cross, given to her by Yad Vashem, which represented her belief in unity. Following Sister Rose's death, Luna commissioned a replica and has worn it ever since as a symbol of following Rose's work.

In 1994, Luna was honored to be a participant in the Vatican's history-making concert for Holocaust survivors. The event was hosted by her University schoolmate from Poland, *Pope John Paul II.* Perhaps no one has done as much for Jewish-Catholic relations as this Pope, whose unique position made public support possible and brought change to the Catholic Church around the world. Pope John Paul II is one of the Christian leaders most recognized by the Jewish world. To this day, Luna speaks about him with great admiration.

Although Luna works among pioneers in interreligious relations, and much has changed since the end of the Holocaust, there still is a lot of work to be done. In the current generation, however, there is a new tendency among young Poles to seek and embrace their Jewish comrades. Luna is buoyed by

American Christian support for Israel and sees their tourism as a positive extension of the work she did with Sister Rose. They worked together to bring Christian groups to Israel, especially in times of crisis. No one came back from these trips the same way they left.

Luna has had to make a number of life or death choices. When things were already bad in Krakow, Luna and her family were offered a hiding place, though it would have posed a terrible risk not only to them, but also to their Christian hosts. Ultimately, the hiding place was so risky that they decided against it.

Luna remembers another case: during the last months of the war, while in forced labor in Leipzig, an SS woman gave her extra food – a small thing, but in those conditions, one that could mean the difference between life and death. Luna never understood the reason for what happened, but she felt the peculiarity of human nature in this gesture – that the same SS woman could be very cruel toward other prisoners, but for some unknown reason, chose to help Luna. The third case involved a residential building owned by Luna and her family, which was stolen by the Poles when her family was forced to go the ghetto. After the war, Luna and her mother returned to the house. A Polish tenant refused to let them in into their apartment, which was now even more valuable to Luna's family, as it was the only link to the past after the death of many family members. The woman had simply stolen a Jewish residence, as was so often the case at that time. However, another Polish neighbor living in the same building, immediately invited them in. How can such opposite reactions be explained?

The post-war situation was complicated -- the physical danger was largely eliminated, but the attitudes remained unchanged.

Luna has dedicated her life to eliminating prejudice and has set the example that Christians and Jews should extend their hands to each other. Judaism is a big brother to Christianity. Both religions hold forth the same precept, *Love your neighbor as yourself.* According to Luna, it is now time to truly expand our worldview and make each person our neighbor. [276]

Dead Bones Live – The Return

"The hand of the Lord came upon me and brought me out in the Spirit of the Lord, and set me down in the midst of the valley; and it was full of bones. Then He caused me to pass by them all around, and behold, there were very many in the open valley; and indeed they were very dry. And He said to me, 'Son of man, can these bones live?'
So I answered, 'O Lord God, You know.'

Again He said to me, 'Prophesy to these bones, and say to them, "O dry bones, hear the word of the Lord! Thus says the Lord God to these bones: 'Surely I will cause breath to enter into you, and you shall live. I will put sinews on you and bring flesh upon you, cover you with skin and put breath in you; and you shall live. Then you shall know that I am the Lord.'"'

So I prophesied as I was commanded; and as I prophesied, there was a noise, and suddenly a rattling; and the bones came together, bone to bone. Indeed, as I looked, the sinews and the flesh came upon them, and the skin covered them over; but there was no breath in them.
Also He said to me, 'Prophesy to the breath, prophesy, son of man, and say to the breath, "Thus says the Lord God: 'Come from the four winds, O breath, and breathe on these slain, that they may live.'"' So I prophesied as He commanded me, and breath came into them, and they lived, and stood upon their feet, an exceedingly great army.

Then He said to me, 'Son of man, these bones are the whole house of Israel. They indeed say, "Our bones are dry, our hope is lost, and we ourselves are cut off!" Therefore, prophesy and say to them, "Thus says the Lord God: 'Behold, O My people, I will open your graves and cause you to come up from your graves, and bring you into the land of Israel. Then you shall know that I am the Lord, when I have opened your graves, O My people, and brought you up from your graves. I will put My Spirit in you, and you shall live, and I will place you in your own land. Then you shall know that I, the Lord, have spoken it and performed it,' says the Lord."'"[277]

A Holocaust survivor tells their story to a group of Christians. I see handkerchiefs taken out. Sniffing is heard in the room. Someone is taking notes, but then all of a sudden, the hand stops. The story is told by my friend, who is already 90 years old. Leesha was a young girl in Holland during World War II. Her whole family, which included about a hundred people, was taken to Auschwitz, although she worked at the Jewish Hospital in Amsterdam and was not among the first ones taken away.

Leesha joined the resistance movement. With the code name Red Tulips, she was able to save hundreds of Jews by taking them to safe houses. There was a reward on her head, because she managed to escape from the hands of the Gestapo three times. Leesha is a true living heroine, who acted when so many hid in fear.

When the war ended, she, like so many Jews in the same situation, was the only survivor in her family. During the war, there was much action, and one had to be brave. But after the war, she was alone. What meaning was there to life, when all her loved ones had been murdered? Her entire world, as she had known it, had simply ceased to exist. And so, in fact, she wanted to die. Always, when I hear this part of the story, it upsets me greatly. No one has ever known loneliness like survivors of the Holocaust.

What could alleviate it?

We all remember seeing pictures of how, at the end of a long war, crowds of people all over the world gathered together spontaneously to celebrate, as feelings of joy and relief filled the streets. We remember women handing flowers to soldiers and members of the resistance movement coming out of hiding. But the truth is always more complex. Joy was simple and easy only to those who were able to return to their old lives. Some were now free, but others only freed. The Allied forces were anything but prepared for the greatest problem awaiting them. The post-war homeless, whom this field of study calls *Displaced Persons* or *DPs* (though, in that era, they were also called refugees) – the millions of former concentration camp prisoners, the deported, prisoners of war – all walked the roads of Europe, trying to find their way back home. When the Allied Forces first liberated the concentration camps, they had no idea of the true magnitude of the problem. Russian soldiers freed Auschwitz on January 27, 1945, the British came to Bergen Belsen on April 13, 1945, and the Americans liberated Dachau on April 29, 1945. Among all the homeless, the former concentration camp prisoners, about 90,000 of them, were only the tip of the iceberg. Enormous crowds were looking for opportunities for repatriation or a new home country.

However, the situation for the Jews was most difficult, as their repatriation was in many cases impossible. At the end of the war, the Jews, especially those in the concentration camps, hoped that their particular suffering would come to the attention of the Allies. But this wish did not materialize, probably for the simple and, perhaps it is worth adding, humane reason that it was impossible for the soldiers to perceive the very complicated problems the Jews were facing in their current situation. In fact, the military administration was quite ill-equipped for repatriating civilians. It can be said of the American occupation zone that things began to change for the better after *Earl Harrison*, emissary of *President Harry S. Truman*, visited the camps and delivered a truthful and very critical report to the president. The impact of the report was also felt by the American public. Soon after its publication, a special emissary of Jewish matters was appointed, and camps exclusively for Jews were set up.

Even though there were nations in Western Europe where some Jews had been saved, only about 10% of the Jewish population of Poland survived the Holocaust. In comparison: in Italy and France, about 75% of the Jews survived, whereas in the Netherlands, about 80% perished. In Slovakia, Hungary and Greece, most of the Jews were murdered, whereas in Bulgaria, about 75% survived.[278] As we understood earlier from Luna Kaufman's personal testimony, the Jews often were not welcome back to their former places of residence because the locals had taken over. Anti-Semitism was still very strong after the war. So, during the post-war pogroms in Poland, thousands more Jews perished. For this reason, the situation for the Jews was very difficult in post-war Europe. Immediately after the end of the war, refugees were gathered in camps in Germany, Austria and Italy, and by the end of 1946, there were still about 250,000 left in the camps. Italy was the final destination for many Jewish refugees, who believed that from there, it would be possible to travel by sea to what was then the British Palestine Mandate. The liberated Jews managed to organize in the refugee camps, despite the horrible experiences they had been through. They created a rich religious and cultural order, as well as a political organization through which they demanded free immigration, specifically to Palestine under the British Mandate.[279]

From the very beginning, it was clear that all Jews should fight against the immigration restrictions set by the British Mandate. The restrictions were laid out in the so-called *White Papers*, a political action plan in which decisions on Palestine were, generally, more pleasing to the Arab leaders than to the Jewish ones. The Jewish community of the Mandate sent their representatives to the camps to teach the refugees Hebrew and agriculture, but at the same time, they succeeded in importing them to Palestine in spite of the British blockade. It is estimated that about one-third of all homeless Jews later ended up in the Palestine Mandate – soon to be known as the State of Israel – in addition to the United States, Latin America, Canada and other countries. Between 1945 and 1948, about 70% of the refugees from Italy succeeded in coming to Palestine, and after 1948, to the State of Israel. Some of the refugees, those the British troops managed to stop before their ship arrived at the port or immediately after its arrival, were sent to Cyprus to internment camps set up by the British for this purpose.[280] About 1.5 million Jewish survivors are estimated to have settled in Israel. About one-third of the survivors stayed in Europe.[281]

From the 1916 *Sykes-Picot* Agreement through the Arab unrest of the 1920s, until the end of World War II, the leaders of the Yishuv in Palestine had waited for the establishment of their own state. The Sykes-Picot Agreement was a treaty made before the end of World War I, which mainly defined the French and British spheres of influence if they managed to overcome the Ottoman Empire. After the Ottoman Empire fell apart, the League of Nations allocated a certain territory as the British Mandate. This was the very area which was to become a national home for the Jews. The thought of and promise for a national home was presented in the Balfour Declaration, which was a letter dated November 2, 1917, from British

Secretary of State *Arthur Balfour* to Lord *Rothschild,* who was the President of the Zionist Federation of Great Britain and Ireland. The letter was also published in the press. However, Britain was afraid to fulfill its promises and repeatedly restricted Jewish immigration to the areas of the Mandate. The Balfour Declaration was verified in the *San Remo Agreement* in 1920, which was verified and ratified by the members of the League of Nations in 1922.

On November 29, 1947, Great Britain had to give up its Mandate when the United Nations made a decision to end the Mandate and divide the region into two parts. When the War of Independence broke out (immediately after the UN decision), many of those who had just been through the Holocaust had to go to the front lines in service of the young state. It is estimated that up to half of Israeli state fighters were Holocaust survivors. It can be said that their contribution was especially significant in the beginning stages of the new state. It has been estimated that about one-third of the victims of the War of Independence were survivors of the Holocaust.[282] Even though this seems sad in a way, many of the Holocaust witnesses have said to me that fighting for your own state, with all its risks, was a privilege that relieved the pain of the Holocaust. The young State of Israel, for which they now fought, was miraculously born in one day, as a result of the UN vote.

But was this sudden birth of a new state something new and unforeseeable?

The Prophet Isaiah lived around 740-700 BC. Again, his name is prophetic, as in Hebrew, *Yeshayahu* means *God is our salvation.* This prophet served four kings, and because his writing style was so graceful, it is assumed he was well educated and perhaps a relative to the kings; according to Jewish tradition, Isaiah was the nephew of King Amaziah. The book of Isaiah is one of the most interesting books in the Bible, for it is found exactly in the middle of the Bible and has 66 chapters, which is the number of all the books in the Bible. It is the only book found in the Caves of Qumran as a whole, and even though it contains both history (historical events that occurred during the prophet's lifetime) and prophecies of the future (historical events that occurred after the death of the prophet), it is clearly one entity. Although some disagree with this view, there was nothing in the discovered book to suggest that someone other than the prophet himself wrote it. Some researchers have commented on the uniform writing style of the book, even when there was a change in period and topic (although others say exactly the opposite). The book of Isaiah prophesies the future of the people of Israel and the future glory of Jerusalem, and is also clearly a Messianic book, which prophesies the coming of the Messiah. According to old Jewish tradition, Isaiah died a horrible death by being sawed in half. It may be that the writer of the letter to the Hebrews refers to him: *"...they were sawn in two..."*[283]

This prophet Isaiah clearly saw the rebirth of the Nation of Israel. This is an important piece of information for us. The metaphor "born in one day" is notably precise, as the Declaration of Independence of the State of Israel was finally given after the UN vote, which took place literally in a moment's time. *"Who has heard such a thing? Who has seen such things? Shall the earth be made to give birth in one day? Or shall a nation be born at once? For as soon as Zion was in labor, she gave birth to her children."*[284]

It is clear that as long as the Jewish State was only a dream, Jewish refugees had no home. Regardless of the fact that many refugees had family members in various parts of the Western world, most wanted to come to their own ancient homeland. We know this from the forms they had to fill out during their refugee period. In Italy's case, a large written interview was conducted concerning this issue in the refugee camps. Even though the refugees had no idea what was to come in 1948, the prophesies were fulfilled dramatically and at an astonishing speed in the eyes of a suspicious world. As described by Ezekiel, skeletal people, literally the dry bones, rose from their graves and were brought to their homeland. As described by Isaiah, the new state was born in a moment. If we think about this entire matter purely in terms of reason, we find it impossible, but in light of the Bible, it is a logical development.

It is notable that although research literature refers to the Jewish survivors of World War II as *homeless* or *refugees*, these words are not used in Hebrew. We use the term *Sh'erit HaPletah* in Hebrew, a Biblical term that refers to the *remnant*, as in Isaiah 37:32: *"For out of Jerusalem shall go forth a remnant, and those who escape from Mount Zion. The zeal of the Lord of hosts will do this."*[285] According to Biblical prophecies, only a remnant of the people is left behind, and this 1945 remnant was looking for a way to Palestine (and then to the State of Israel) from different European nations. According to the prophecies in the Bible, only a remnant returned; a remnant fought in the War of Independence, and an even smaller remnant survived and built an *old and new* state in their ancient homeland.

The First Years of the Jewish State

"Arise, shine; for your light has come! And the glory of the Lord is risen upon you. For behold, the darkness shall cover the earth, and deep darkness the people; but the Lord will arise over you, and His glory will be seen upon you. The Gentiles shall come to your light, and kings to the brightness of your rising. Lift up your eyes all around, and see: they all gather together, they come to you; your sons shall come from afar, and your daughters shall be

nursed at your side.... The sons of foreigners shall build up your walls, and their kings shall minister to you; for in My wrath I struck you, but in My favor I have had mercy on you."[286]

After the miracle had taken place, resistance was hard. As soon as the State of Israel made her Declaration of Independence, not even a full day passed before the armies of *Egypt, Jordan, Syria, Lebanon* and *Iraq* declared war on the young state. Immediately, the fledgling state was forced to defend herself and her sovereignty. The army of Israel is known by the name *Tzava Hagana LeIsrael*, Israeli Defense Forces (IDF), which at that time was hardly an army; not only was it ill-equipped and outnumbered in manpower, it was also incompetent and harassed by a superior opponent. War was waged for about fifteen months, during which about one percent of the Israeli citizens perished. At that time, the Israeli state population was only 650,000, compared to today's eight million, out of which six million are Jews.[287] How could the war ever be won? It was generally thought that the State of Israel would fall before it had properly begun, but this did not happen. Peace negotiations under the UN were conducted from the beginning of 1949, in such a way that each attacking army could make its claim to the Jewish state, except Iraq, which refused to negotiate with Israel at all. As the peace negotiations ended, Jerusalem was a divided city governed in part by Israel and in part by Jordan; Gaza was a region governed by Egypt; Judea and Samaria were under Jordanian rule.[288]

As long as the Jewish State was continually fighting for its existence and surrounded by its enemies, the sympathies of the world could somehow settle on its side and sympathize with the danger it faced. And, in a way, the existence of the Jewish State reconciled the sins of Europe, since it was developing along Western lines. It also offered a symbolic and perhaps also material atonement for the trauma of the Holocaust. But the truth was also that the hostile Arab armies were perceived as such a powerful threat that their assertion of pushing the Jewish State into the ocean was seen as a real possibility. Nothing was certain. The situation on the borders of Israel wavered and fluctuated. Since the end of the War of Independence, Arab terrorists had been making attacks across state borders, with hundreds of casualties. The attacks were still considered more of a regret than something that required fierce counterattacks. The President of Egypt, *Gamal Abdel Nasser* (1918-1970), took the situation to a new level when, in 1956, he decided to nationalize the Suez Canal. This attempt was followed by a war, after which Israel was given guarantees of using the channel for its transportation needs. One crisis was past. But, suddenly, one of the most miraculous events in modern history took place.

About 2000 years earlier, Jesus, speaking of the signs of the times, foretold that the situation in Jerusalem today would be one of the clearest signs: *"...Jerusalem will be trampled by Gentiles until the times of the Gentiles are fulfilled."*[289] Jesus said that it was important to read the signs of the times, for even though we do not know the exact moment of His return, we need to understand the day we live in.[290] What happened in 1967?

The Arab border attacks upon Israel from Egypt and Jordan continued unhindered for years. Also, Israeli border villages in northern Galilee near the Lebanese border were bombarded by artillery fire from Syria. Simultaneously, along with these continual hostilities, the massive military rearmament of the Arab world was taking place. This could mean only one thing: war was on the horizon. The development of this war culminated in May 1967 with two events: first, Egypt transferred a large number of troops into the Sinai Desert, and second, it ordered the UN Peacekeepers to leave the region, where they had operated as observers since 1957. As these procedures proved successful, Egypt formed a military alliance with Jordan and closed the Straits of Tiran. Israel was surrounded by hostile and well-equipped Arab armies on every side. It was apparent that a large-scale attack, which would threaten the very existence of the State of Israel, was prepared to begin at any given moment. In a situation like this, a state not only has the right but also the responsibility to act, in order to protect its citizens. Israel used this state-owned right to initiate a defensive strike on June 5, 1967, on three fronts: against Egypt in the south, against Jordan in the east, and against the troops of Syria on the Golan Heights in the north.

To the astonishment of the whole world, after only six days, as the battle was coming to an end, Israel was in possession of Judea and Samaria, Gaza and the Golan Heights. Judea and Samaria are the heartland of the Bible, as all the places such as Hebron, Tekoa, Bethlehem, Jericho and Shechem are located there. After thousands of years, Jerusalem once again was in the hands of the Jews, undivided. As we read the Scriptures, we understand the deep symbolism hidden in this. God created the world in six days and rested from all His work on the seventh day. Sabbath, the seventh day, is a sign of the Covenant. According to the rabbis, the history of mankind is also tied to the number seven, which is evident in many connections and prophecies. The return of Jerusalem to the Jews, as a result of the Six Day War, reaffirms the covenant to which Jerusalem is connected, and it marks the beginning of a ticking clock for all mankind.

Centuries earlier, *Rabbi Judah Ben-Samuel*, who lived in Regensburg, Germany, in 1150-1217, prophesied this state of affairs very precisely. Rabbi Ben-Samuel was also known as *Judah ha-Hasid* ("Judah the Pious"), and as this name indicates, he was considered to be especially obedient and righteous. According to the rabbi's study using Jewish *gematria arithmetic*, the Bible clearly states the number of Jubilee years (a 49 - 50 year period) Jerusalem would be in the hands of the Gentiles (Rabbi Ben-Samuel rightly assumed the last ones to be the Turks of the Ottoman Empire). The length of the Jubilee is, of course, defined in the Bible.[291] Only after the period indicated in the Bible would the Jews once again take possession of Jerusalem, and the end times or Last Days would begin from this point. When we examine history, we understand that even if the rabbi himself never saw the fulfillment of the prophecies, this is what truly happened: in 1967, the very year of which the rabbi prophesied, Israel returned to her ancient home city.[292] Many well-known rabbis have later come to the same conclusion concerning the end times. I believe that God Himself showed Rabbi Ben-Samuel His plans, for there is no other way we can explain his precise knowledge of the things to come, centuries before the actual events. The rabbi used all his time to study the Bible, and God rewards such reverence. It is quite another thing to believe the prophecies were fulfilled, now that we have seen it for ourselves.

Even though the Six Day War was followed by other wars, such as the 1973 *Yom Kippur War*, which Israel nearly lost, and the *First Lebanon War* in 1982, the short and triumphant Six Day War represents to the enemies of Israel all that they hate. The Yom Kippur War began, as the name suggests, on the *Day of Atonement,* October 6, 1973. On the Day of Atonement, the entire nation quiets down to fast and pray. No one listens to the news or knows what is happening outside their home during those twenty-five hours. For that reason and because of the general lack of preparedness, the joint attack of Egypt and Syria took the Israeli state leaders and army by total surprise. The

Bible continually promises that the Lord will fight for Israel, and there is no other way to explain this miracle either. In fact, the Biblical "the Lord of Hosts" would be the correct translation for *Adonai Tzevaot*. After a strenuous and difficult start, Israel could have conquered additional territory as a result of the war, had its political leadership not ended the conflict.

"But thus says the Lord: 'Even the captives of the mighty shall be taken away, and the prey of the terrible be delivered; for I will contend with him who contends with you, and I will save your children.'"[293]

The Lebanon War was preceded by the continued rocket fire of *Yasser Arafat's PLO (Palestinian Liberation Organization)* from Lebanon, as the UN Peacekeepers stood by watching. In June 1982, Israel attacked the PLO stations, which started the First Lebanon War. The Second Lebanon War occurred as a result of the attack by the terrorist organization Hezbollah in the summer of 2006.

To Christian churches, the birth of the State of Israel and the return of the Jews to their homeland has been a tough pill to swallow, as it completely silenced the talk which implied that Christians had replaced Israel in God's plans. If this shock to the churches had begun in 1948, then the events of 1967 were an even greater shock. All Bible interpretations now had to be re-examined. If and when the joy of the fulfillment of God's plans is not found in the churches, it only demonstrates how far from the clear revelation of the Bible they have wandered. If the fulfillment of prophecies is a grief and not a joy to a Christian, they have gone astray somewhere. Those who have doubts concerning the land of Israel and the fact that it belongs to the Jewish people would do well to remember that all the earth belongs to the Lord. This principle is presented for the first time in the first pages of the Bible: *"When the Most High divided their inheritance to the nations, when He separated the sons of Adam, He set the boundaries of the peoples..."* and in the New Testament, Paul says that God *"has determined their pre-appointed times and the boundaries of their dwellings."*[294] He has absolute sovereignty over all the earth, but He has delegated certain areas to certain peoples. There is, therefore, no doubt that He decides to whom the earth belongs.

In the case of Israel, of course, the matter is even clearer, as according to the Bible, the land of Israel is the only physical area where God dwells, and there, Jerusalem is the city God has marked for Himself. Therefore, the words of Jesus were fulfilled in 1967, and we know that, since that war, the countdown to eternity is closer to that goal than ever. Even though it is difficult for some to accept these facts, it is interesting that even the completely secularized Israeli journalists have suggested that it is the Christian Zionists who understand the destiny of Israel, and its past and future, better than anyone else.[295] Even if the Bible is completely ignored and the two-state solution is realized, it will by no means bring peace to the area. The truth is that Palestinians have more freedoms than their Arab brothers in the other nations of the region. Yet a true will for peace is not found among them, just as Israel's withdrawals from different areas have undisputedly shown thus far. Of course, I do not claim that all Palestinians would be against peace. I have worked for years with many Arabs, and I would never say a bad word about them. But to my sadness, I know that even the peaceful Arabs also fear the ironclad grip of their own terrorist organizations. Therefore, they will have no say as their own societies develop even further towards radical Islam.

10 Holocaust Denial

"Remember the days of old, consider the years of many generations. Ask your father, and he will show you; your elders, and they will tell you."[296]

I confess, I did not choose this passage of the Bible myself – the text chose its place. Deborah Lipstadt, a world-renowned historian, whom Holocaust denier David Irwing took to court (losing the case to Lipstadt in 2000), wrote this very sentence in the beginning of her book on Holocaust denial.

During one of my trips to the United States, I am in the state of New York as a guest of my friends Becky and Caren. Because they know my love for Barnes and Noble bookstores, where books can be browsed in a cozy café while considering a purchase, they decided to hold a business meeting in such a place before my speaking engagements. We look for a suitable table, and spot one further away. When we return to the table with our coffee, the expression on Becky's face conveys something strange has just happened.

On the table, there is a book facing down, showing only the black back cover with no text. Instinctively, I lift it up to see the title, but it almost immediately falls out of my hand, as I am surprised, even terrified. The book is Mein Kampf. *Of all the possible books, this very book of lies and curses is on that table, where we had chosen to sit only a moment before. We get a strange feeling, because in the upcoming days, we are to speak about the Holocaust. It was as if seeing the book had deepened our view on the power of evil. Why was the book on that very table...? We cannot prevent the sale of the book, but we think, in wonder, what kind of a person came before us to this wonderful café and browsed this book...*

In 2010 and 2011, I have the honor to be a speaker for Holocaust Education Week, an annual event organized by the Canadian government. The event is nationwide across Canada. During one week in November, hundreds of events related to the topic bring audiences to hear about the Holocaust and its many phases. The government of Canada is a forerunner in Holocaust remembrance, which it connects with the fight against anti-Semitism.

My main speaking engagement is at a large Anglican church in Toronto, where my topic is the Holocaust and Christianity. After I speak for a little less than an hour, the audience has an opportunity to ask questions. A university researcher wants to speak. He has never heard that Hitler was Catholic, and it is very difficult for him to accept this news. A young Englishman, in turn, says that his father does not believe the Holocaust ever happened, and therefore, he is uncertain about how much he can trust in historical material. It is not rare to hear the strangest comments about the Holocaust.

Holocaust survivors are still with us. We are free to visit the concentration camps and related museums. The incredible fact is that the denial, trivialization and distortion of the Holocaust are all part of our world.

In recent years, we have witnessed an attack on remembrance – it is difficult to put it any other way. Therefore, I see the denial of the Holocaust as a topic that needs to be discussed, as it touches an ever-growing part of our world. It is an attack on historical truth; therefore, we should be armed with facts and stand for the truth against lies. We know the truth because it was witnessed by all the Holocaust contemporaries, regardless of their personal opinions. The Holocaust was such an immense and extreme crisis for mankind that it has challenged us to reexamine human nature, to reexamine the roles of society and of individual responsibility. The Holocaust has become a topic for research in every place where great ethical and moral questions are pondered. Because the Holocaust was the world's largest genocide, it can be said that denying it is in many ways anti-Semitic, thereby continuing the genocide that the Allied troops witnessed.

General Dwight D. Eisenhower, Supreme Commander of the Allied Forces, witnessed the existence of the places of horror. He said: *"I visited every nook and cranny of the camp because I felt it my duty to be in a position from then on to testify at first-hand about these things in case there ever grew up at home the belief or the assumption that 'the stories of Nazi brutality were just propaganda.' ...I sent communications to both Washington and London, urging the two governments to send instantly to Germany a random group of newspaper editors... I felt that the evidence should be immediately placed before the American and British publics in a fashion to leave no room for cynical doubt."*[297]

Although the Allies reached a victory in the spring of 1945, support for Nazism and hatred of the Jews did not disappear from anywhere in Europe. On the contrary, hatred of the Jews was an extremely significant ideology in post-war Eastern Europe, Germany and Austria. We know, for example, from the stories of the Jewish refugees how difficult it was to be a Jew in these post-war societies. There, in that particular period, are the roots of the denial of the Holocaust. In Western Europe, anti-Semitism continued to live, hidden and shameful, but only as a phenomenon emerging from time to time, whereas in Eastern Europe, it never went out of fashion.

Scholar *Israel Charny* divides Holocaust denial into the following categories one might call "motivation-related":

- **Hypocritical Deniers** claim that we do not know enough about what happened, or that in any case, it is time to forget or to move on;
- **Scientific Deniers** believe the matter needs to be researched more;
- **Politicians** prefer not to speak about it;
- **Changers of the Past** forget certain facts because the present requires it;
- **Trivia Focusers** focus on trivial matters to make it possible not to speak about the actual questions.[298]

To the Holocaust witnesses, the ones who experienced it, the denial of their experience is just one more attack upon them, and it hurts all the more because it is a continuation of the Holocaust. The danger is that in time, when the contemporaries of the genocide are no longer with us, denial will become an accepted part of the historical discourse. It is for this purpose that the classic Holocaust deniers (those who started their activities only a few years after the end of World War II) have tried to call themselves revisionists. It should be noted that revisionism as such is a completely acceptable model of historical research, which uses certain means to review existing information and to add the results of new research. Of course, this is not the aim of the Holocaust deniers. They start from the idea that they already know the truth, and their purpose is not to add more information, but to deny the already existing information. The deniers call themselves by different names to blur their identities. It is easier to make people believe in claims that are presented under a scientific cloak. Often, the deniers do not directly vocalize their thought that the Holocaust never occurred, but they present a reasonable-sounding argument that the number of victims may have been wrong, or something to that effect.

"He who speaks truth declares righteousness, but a false witness, deceit... The truthful lip shall be established forever, but a lying tongue is but for a moment."[299]

The claims of the Holocaust deniers usually deny the following facts:
- that the Nazis had an **anti-Jew ideology**, which manifested itself as a murder policy against the Jews;
- that **millions of Jews** (the generally accepted figure is six million) **were murdered;**
- that **extermination camps** were established for this purpose;
- that **Jews were treated differently** from other citizens of occupied areas or enemy nations;
- that the **Holocaust is a lie** spread by the Jews.

Holocaust denial is one form of anti-Semitism. It is claimed that the Allies started to talk about the Holocaust only because they needed anti-German propaganda to overcome the war.

Many scholars in the field of Holocaust studies believe it better not to involve deniers in discussions, because answering them would give an impression that their claims were somewhat legitimate. We can hardly impact the Holocaust deniers who have already decided how history should be portrayed. On the other hand, we need to know the facts so we can influence those who simply do not know them. Therefore, I want to answer the most common claims in full. For those who need additional information, I would recommend my friend *Manfred Gerstenfeld's* book, *The Abuse of Holocaust*

Memory: Distortions and Responses, which addresses in more detail all the problems of the field, and also how we can oppose the denial of the Holocaust in our own societies.[300] Under no circumstances is it enough just to read about the topic; we must actively intervene in abuses.

First, the Holocaust, out of all the mass murders in history, is the most accurately documented. Not only do we have evidence left behind from its victims and speeches by the survivors, but we also have documents, lists and photographs from the Nazis, the perpetrators themselves. We have names of the victims, and we know the ways in which they were murdered. The Allied soldiers found a massive amount of evidence, such as unburied bodies of the victims, despite the Nazis' attempts to destroy them at the end of the war. Local resistance movements documented the Nazi operations. It can be accurately said that the Nazis themselves were the first to deny the Holocaust, for they were the ones who attempted to bury the evidence before the Allies arrived at the camps. Even at the end of the war, mass graves were opened in an attempt to quickly burn the corpses. Just inside the entrance to the historical museum of Yad Vashem, we see partially burned photos, identification cards, diaries and other personal papers. They are from the Klooga concentration camp in Estonia, where the Germans and local collaborators murdered 2,000 Jews in the camp just days before the Soviet troops arrived. However, they did not have enough time to destroy everything, which is the reason this evidence is in the museum today. It offers an example of how there was an attempt to destroy the memory of the Holocaust even during the war itself.

Denial often starts with belittling. Memories of the witnesses are belittled and used cynically for political purposes. The complicated historical process that modern Europe has gone through has caused a distancing from the Holocaust and, consequently, removal of guilt associated with colonialism concerning the Israelis and the Palestinians. European media, in most cases, maintains some sort of distinction between Israelis and local Jews, but this is an artificial distinction, and in no way would it provide security for the Jews of Europe in the event of a crisis related to Israel.[301] For example, the violent anti-Semitic actions in France in 2012 testify to the truth of this view. It is also evident that a sort of blurring of the boundaries has taken place when the worst acts of terror can be lightly replaced by the words "fight" or "freedom fight." The left-wing media in Europe is, therefore, aligned with the Islamic extremists, and this union cannot be easily explained. The Arabic media view, which does not distinguish between Israelis, Jews and Zionists, words it frequently uses interchangeably, is also shifting to the accepted European language.[302] In these days, an aide to the former President of Egypt, Mohamed Morsi, said that *"the myth of the Holocaust is an industry that America invented."*[303] The current President of the *Palestinian Authority, Mahmoud Abbas*, has questioned the figure of six million victims.[304] Holocaust denial is very common in the Arabic world, and this is even more so in such organizations as Hamas.[305] Using the Holocaust for political purposes is one form of its denial, as it uses inaccuracies to justify action against the Jewish people.

In 2006, the Iranian government hosted a conference for Holocaust deniers in Tehran, with 67 participants from 30 different nations. The actual purpose of the conference was not limited only to denying the historical occurrence of the Holocaust, but also included the abnegation of the right of the State of Israel to exist. According to the Iranian government's thinking, the Holocaust gave legitimacy to the State of Israel because the survivors of the catastrophe needed a homeland. If the catastrophe never took place, then the existence of the State could also be abolished. The objectives of the conference and the internationalization of its participants gave it a certain legitimacy, which made it all the more dangerous. Iran needs international support, but what was used to lure Western participants to the conference in Tehran? Different explanations have been given for this phenomenon. Of course, it is possible that Western Holocaust deniers are ignorant and believe in lies. But their motivation has little meaning in the end, whether it is ignorance or a political objective, for both are equally dangerous. Ignorance, too, is a choice. The fight is about the truth they deny, no matter what they themselves say.[306] While Iran was pressing for the legitimacy of its actions against Israel in the international arena, it was simultaneously threatening Israel with a nuclear weapon, which it might soon possess. In the light of all we have read, we understand that Iran's denial of the Holocaust is part of the preparation for genocide. At the same time, it attempts to prop up its position in the Arab world by appealing to the rights of the Palestinians.

On Holocaust Memorial Day, January 27, 2013, the *President of Switzerland, Ueli Maurer*, lauded the neutral wartime nations in his speech. However, he failed to mention that thousands of Jews would have been saved if they had not been turned away from the Swiss border when they came seeking asylum.[307] Here, I am immediately reminded of the Nazi gold and art treasures that lie in bank vaults to this day. Is this, too, about the denial of the Holocaust? Or, more precisely, is it the rewriting of history?

This also could be an attempt to steal the memory of the Holocaust from its actual victims. Allow me to explain this in more detail. Politicizing the memory of the Holocaust began in the Communist nations, where the identity of the Jews was denied. In other words, the Jews of the Ukraine are now considered Ukrainian victims of Nazism, which is problematic given the fact that the Ukrainian Jews were not murdered because of their background as

Ukrainians, but specifically because of their Jewish identity. In addition, the local people often participated in murders, sometimes more eagerly than the Nazis. In order to escape from the European, or in this case, Ukrainian guilt, the identity of the Jews as victims must be denied.

This line of thinking has led to an additional phenomenon in which Israelis are called Nazis and blamed for Nazi-like actions.[308] New denial of the Holocaust, therefore, does not deny the Holocaust as a historical event, but it belittles the role of the Jews as its main victims. Although this is a blatant lie, which is easy to point out as such, this kind of speech has unfortunately spread even to human rights organizations. Human Rights Watch, an internationally esteemed group working for human rights, had to expel a person who had previously worked in the UN and whose anti-Semitism was denounced by the UN Secretary-General. This person had gone on to spread these same lies in their human rights work. What is appalling is that the person was expelled only when another organization, UN Watch, issued a related complaint and organized a noisy campaign on the matter. Even the original founder of Human Rights Watch, *Robert L. Bernstein*, has criticized the growing anti-Semitism of the organization.[309]

Is there anything in the conflict between Israel and the Palestinians that would justify such claims? In my opinion, the question, in all its absurdity, does not require an answer. However, knowing the kind of false information under which many are forced to live, I want to answer this question. Let us forget for a moment the spiritual dimensions of the conflict and concentrate on the cold political and historical facts. We have already stated what the Holocaust was: an attempt to obliterate all Jews in Europe – which, according to the Wannsee Conference, totaled eleven million – by using the existing bureaucracy of the state machinery and a considerable military organization.

The entire political program of the Nazi Party – its racial doctrines, its fight against Communism and the decision to gain *Lebensraum* from the east – was ultimately aimed at the extermination of the Jewish people. All of this, on a practical level, lead to the murder of six million Jews. We should recognize here that nothing similar has happened at any point during the Middle East conflict.

The conflict between Israel and the Palestinians is national and political by nature, but because it involves land ownership, it is also a regional conflict. Throughout the conflict, various phases have taken place, such as terrorism, areal management and negotiations between the two parties in the presence of various mediators. The conflict is a tragic part of the lives of individuals on both sides. And yet, we must refrain from using inaccurate and perhaps very emotional terms in describing it. Inaccurate terms make the conflict seem even greater and more difficult, and they also make the facts more unclear. In addition, inaccuracies give birth to new murderous ideologies and organizations, which only exacerbates the situation.

The fight in this matter is a fight for the truth. Some Western governments have chosen to enact laws identifying Holocaust denial as a crime that must be penalized appropriately. The European Union tried to enact a law for the entire Union, but some of the Member States – at the time, mainly Great Britain and the Nordic countries – prevented the law from passing by appealing to the need to strike a balance between disavowal of racism, on the one hand, and freedom of expression on the other. According to current practice, EU Member States may choose to punish Holocaust deniers if they so wish. I find legislation against any speech difficult to accept, and in no way would I support it, but I know this is an issue that divides opinions. We know from history that freedom of speech is one of the first things taken away in a dictatorship. Because governments change, the definition of hate speech might be quite different in years to come; it may be best to stick with freedom of speech even though the price might mean listening to injustice. Anti-Semitism has since been defined by the EU, first by its agency EUMC, now known as FRA, Agency for Fundamental Rights.

Some of the points included in the EU definition are:

1. denying the Jewish people their **self-determination;**
2. insisting that the State of Israel, when defending itself, **has to act in a different way** than other nations;
3. the use of **classic anti-Semitic** symbols against the Jewish State;
4. comparing the **State of Israel** to Nazi Germany;
5. **holding all Jews responsible** for the politics of the Israeli State.

Naturally, the definition is not perfect, and it has been much criticized in almost all respects. There is a claim that the EU has recently given up this definition, but I was unable to confirm this one way or another.

"The righteous should choose his friends carefully,
For the way of the wicked leads them astray."[310]

This fight is a fight for the truth. You can learn from the Holocaust on religious and philosophical levels, but we need to remember that it took place on a human level. Therefore, Holocaust denial, with all its associated side effects, is our problem. It is a rapidly growing problem, thanks to new means of communication. Who will ensure that correct information is shared, and how will that take place? The fight against the truth through Holocaust denial is also a spiritual fight. If the truth of the Holocaust could be denied, all that I have written in this book would be a lie. The Word of God, however, is very clear: *"You desire truth in the inward parts, and in the hidden part You will make me to know wisdom."*[311] Jesus confirmed this old principle and the liberating effect of the truth when he said, *"And you shall know the truth, and the truth shall make you free."*[312]

When we become aware of something important, we are held responsible to speak about it. The need to warn about danger is a Biblical principle. Here is what the Lord says about it: *"For thus has the Lord said to me: 'Go, set a watchman, let him declare what he sees.'"*[313]

11 Nuclear Weapon Threat

"'No weapon formed against you shall prosper, and every tongue which rises against you in judgment you shall condemn. This is the heritage of the servants of the Lord, and their righteousness is from Me,' says the Lord."[314]

In the winter of 2008, I am in Brussels, in the European Parliament, at a true vantage point. With the help of various MEPs, I have the opportunity to organize many events, which makes it possible to bring out the truth. For example, we organize an educational event for the MEPs and their assistants on the Muslim Brotherhood, as well as a human rights inquiry on the abducted Israeli soldiers and many other important events.

But one situation that I will never forget has to do with Iran. The nuclear negotiator with a large Iranian delegation comes to visit the European Parliament's Foreign Affairs Committee. For days in advance, I had prepared a paper with questions I hoped the MEPs would ask the Iranian delegation. Because MEPs are very busy, it is common that they are given ready-made papers before meetings. I am there very early, as I understand the meeting is of utmost importance. As the MEPs arrive, I approach them, and most receive the paper gladly.

When everyone has settled down at the long tables, the Iranian delegation walks in. I do not know if anyone else feels the same way, but I sense a cold breeze drifting into the room, changing the temperature. Even though I was feeling fine a moment before, all of a sudden, I have terrible chills and my teeth begin to chatter. Because I am not prone to feeling such strong physical symptoms and have never before experienced anything like this, the moment has stuck very clearly in my mind.

Only later do I realize what happened in that moment. The delegation has no intention to answer truthfully to the questions posed, and they already know this upon entering. The room becomes cold right at the very moment that the first member steps inside.

The spirit of lies enters the room.

Iranian culture and art and the beauty of its people are world renowned. Many biographies[315] of people who have escaped from Iran testify of the old tradition that flourished and grew until 1979. Life was beautiful, traveling abroad was done freely and people were ahead of their time culturally. As an admirer of the Old Persian culture of Iran, I hesitated for quite some time as to whether I should include Iran in this book or not. I hesitated, but for two reasons, I felt I needed to include it: first, because Iran is quite a significant factor in the global Holocaust deniers' movement, which is one of the topics of this book, and second, because Iran threatens Israel with a nuclear weapon and thus with a complete genocide. Therefore, we must see how that beautiful country returned in 1979, in an inconceivable and sad way to the culture of the 7th century. At this point, it became an authoritarian theocracy whose dominant cultural, social and political power was absorbed into Islamic extremism. Even though there are a number of Islamic nations in which Islam is a cultural and social power, there are not as many where it is also a political power. The founder of the Islamic State, *Ayatollah Khomeini* (1902-1989), believed in the Islamist Caliphate, in which all Muslims would live under the religious sharia law, and the Islamic Revolution of 1979 in Iran was its first phase. The Islamic Revolution has been the most prominent export product of Iran. As a state, Iran began a journey into the events that made the

September 11 attacks possible. Years earlier, it had already taken terrorism outside its borders through the Revolutionary Guards and Hezbollah, and in our days, it has complicated the situation in Iraq by exporting terrorism through combatants, ideological activities and arms brokering.

The ideology produced by Iran deems all non-Islamic people as infidels, and that is why its anti-Israel speech is also full of hatred toward the Western world. Extremely anti-Semitic speeches are, therefore, full of anti-American views, as the United States is naturally seen as the leader of the Western world. In their propaganda, Jews are portrayed as controlling the world media and as playing a major role in all the crises seen as perpetrations against Islam. The Islamic aspect of this hatred is in how Islam sees non-Islamic people, called *kafir*. Islam can only coexist with non-Islamic people if they are under its authority, in which case they have a so-called *dhimmi*, a position subordinate to and guaranteed by Islam. According to this ideology, the existence of Israel in the otherwise Islamic Middle East is an absolute impossibility.

The former President of Iran, *Mahmoud Ahmadinejad*, managed to rally all the most old-fashioned elements of his society to support himself in the campaign against Israel, the anti-Semitic and anti-Holocaust elements of which have been reported widely by the world press.[316] Unfortunately, the support he has received is not only limited to his own country, as the UN also gave him the floor to publicly present his case against Israel. Iran is, of course, a UN Member State, but it goes against all the UN's principles by imposing genocide upon another Member State while feverishly attempting to acquire a nuclear weapon that would allow this to happen.[317] Of course, no one is able to estimate the price, in the form of the lives of its own citizens, Iran would be ready to pay in order to implement its intentions.[318]

Iran has thus publicly threatened Israel with a nuclear weapon. Hitler had also expressed his intentions, but instead of standing against him, Europe sacrificed Czechoslovakia to him. When this happened, the beginning of the end was in sight. Is not the case with Iran very similar? It has launched an extensive campaign against the legitimacy of Israel's existence, as I described earlier. Each genocide requires a certain kind of propaganda before action is taken, and it seems that Iran already began its campaign years ago, which has also extended to its allies. To the Iranian regime, and to its religious leaders, the denial of the Holocaust is central, as the government has adopted the destruction of Israel as a strategic objective. In other words, questioning the position of Israel is ideological preparation for genocide, as is accusing Zionism of a connection to the former Shah.

In a 2012 interview, Israeli Prime Minister Benyamin Netanyahu said: *"We are facing a government that threatens Israel with a complete destruction; it proposes a genocide and presents the worst anti-Semitic expressions we have heard in half a century; it threatens to subjugate the whole world. The whole world. Not just Middle East, Northern Africa or Europe, but the entire world. It is building a nuclear weapon for this purpose."*[319]

The former President of Iran *Ali Rafsanjani* confirmed the truth of this statement himself when speaking on *Al Quds* (or Jerusalem) Day in 2001: *"If one day, the Islamic world is also equipped with weapons like those that Israel possesses now, then the imperialists' strategy will reach a standstill because the use of even one nuclear bomb inside Israel will destroy everything."*[320] The Secretary General of the Hezbollah terrorist organization, *Hassan Nasrallah*, said that the gathering of Jews in one place, Israel, is more convenient for Hezbollah, saying, *"We would not have to go after them to different places around the world."*[321] Another leader of the main branch of Islam, the Sunni, has said that the gathering of the Jews to Israel is the will of Allah so that they can be annihilated there, which was also stated by *Mustafa Muslim*, a professor from the United Arab Emirates, in a TV interview.[322] Let us note that the number of Jews in the world is about 13.5 million, and that of Israel's over 9 million inhabitants, about 75% are Jews.

In its November 2011 report, *IAEA (International Atomic Energy Agency)* stated that Iran had never stopped working on a nuclear weapon, and at the time the report was written, it was already close to producing a nuclear weapon for *Shahab-3* missiles. According to IAEA, Iran already has enough uranium for nuclear warheads, and the world press published these estimates extensively. Yet the international community seems to suffer from some kind of apathy. In September 2012, many heads of state met in Tehran for a meeting with impartial countries. The mere fact that such a meeting was held in Iran, then under sanctions, tells us something about the state of affairs, since it did not seem to disturb anyone. When the supreme leader of Iran presented horrific, blood-chilling threats towards Israel, none of the world's leaders considered it appropriate to protest, and as the world media reported extensively, the UN Secretary-General at the time, *Ban Ki-moon*, offered a weak protest only afterwards. What does all of this tell us about the readiness of the world to face an Iran equipped with a nuclear weapon? It is apparent that time travels fast and nothing significant has been done to prevent the nuclear weapon from being made. According to the UN Genocide Resolution, incitement to genocide is a criminal offense. In spite of this, the former President of Iran visited the UN and other international forums. This kind of flattery can only lead to an increase in the self-confidence of the Iranian government. The threat of a nuclear weapon starts with Israel, but it will not end there.

It is no coincidence that Iran also supports Hamas. In the conflict of November 2012, Israel was careful not to hurt its own or Palestinian civilians, at the expense of its own army, whereas Hamas once again hid among civilians. *Richard Kemp*, former commander of the British troops in Afghanistan, said that he does not know any other army that would take care of civilians the way the IDF does.[323] Then Bulgarian Foreign Minister and former MEP *Nickolay Mladenov*, for his part, stated: *"Europeans tend to simplify things greatly, because war, conflict and terrorism are not a daily threat to many of them... many countries have lost their understanding of the security environment in which Israel is located."*[324]

Iran gives strong support to Hezbollah, and therefore, it is extremely important to understand the role Hezbollah has in the area's movement in a more dangerous direction. From the beginning, Iran's purpose was to take the Islamic revolution to other nations. It has gained a foothold, especially in Lebanon, through Hezbollah, which, in turn, through the support it receives from the Iranian government, has frightening capacities that many other terrorist organizations do not possess. As a result of the support from Iran, Hezbollah has great arsenals, terrorist training and intelligence services at its disposal. The annual budget of the organization is estimated to be around $100 million, which is possible only with government support. Therefore, Hezbollah is not a small group but a large military organization that can, if Iran so desires, quickly create a state of war on the northern border of Israel. Iran may, however, choose to deny everything by playing innocent. We should also remember that Hezbollah started the use of suicide bombings and is also a master of kidnapping. Even though Israel retreated from Lebanon in

2001, Hezbollah has a huge network there, and in 2006, it started a war against Israel. Every now and then, Hezbollah has shown its capacity even far away from Lebanon. An example of this is, of course, the July 1994 bombing of a Jewish community in Buenos Aires, Argentina, where the *AMIA* (*Asociación Mutual Israelita Argentina*) building was destroyed completely, and 85 lives were lost. It is believed that Hezbollah could, if it wished, carry out extremely devastating attacks, as it has in Europe.[325] Behind all this is its state sponsor, Iran. If and when Iran possesses a nuclear weapon, we can only imagine it being used by terrorist organizations.

Believing that the threat is against Israel alone would be a tragic miscalculation. Iran's threat is targeted at Israel, the Gulf States, Europe and ultimately the entire world. Even though part of the West believes that negotiations can lead to an appropriate outcome, the lessons of World War II are clear. To paraphrase Churchill from 1938: *"The choice was between war and dishonor. You chose dishonor. Therefore, you will have war."* I have often heard scholars say that, ultimately, the political leadership of Iran will behave in a rational way. But, concerning Israel and the United States, Iran has consistently shown its strong theological and nationalist, irrational side. This should make us wonder how far Iran would be willing to go in the destruction of its own citizens in order to destroy Israel. Presuming that the destruction of Israel is considered a divine order and taking into consideration the apocalyptic nature of the regime, we cannot just count on rationality when we are talking about a nuclear weapon. According to its political leadership, Iran could lose a large number of citizens in an Israeli counterattack and still consider itself a winner.

And thus says the Lord: *"The Lord also will roar from Zion, and utter His voice from Jerusalem; the heavens and earth will shake; but the Lord will be a shelter for His people, and the strength of the children of Israel."*[326] I check the Scripture in the original Hebrew and notice that the English does not do justice to the words of the prophet Joel. The prophet says the Lord will be a fortress for His people. He is thus both a shelter and a fortress. He is everything. You escape to a shelter, but you look down upon the enemies from a fortress.

It is appropriate at this point to say a few words about persecuted Christians. The human rights of the Iranian citizens have continually diminished, since attacks on women, the confiscating of passports and other interference have increased in recent years. In 2007, Iran executed almost as many people as China. Although it is true that the country's constitution offers the right to practice religion for both Jews and Christians, in practice, continuous interference, limiting work and study places and specifying religion on an identity card have greatly affected these minorities, as well as the persecuted Bahá'í minority. Beginning in May 1993, shops were marked to show customers if the owner is a non-Islamic believer. Not only have churches been closed, several pastors have also been tortured and murdered. The EU, for its part, has repeatedly mentioned human rights violations in the European Parliament resolutions, but they have been left on paper without concrete actions.

Iran treats Christians with extreme cruelty in its prisons, and for years, it has hunted Christians from the churches, which are illegal.[327] *Christian Solidarity Worldwide*, an international association in England for persecuted Christians, has for several years expressed their concern about the growing persecution of Christians in Iran. Frequently, detainees are questioned violently for long periods of time, some even for months. The purpose of this is for these Christians to abandon their faith, even though they would still have to go to trial. According to Iranian law, it is forbidden to evangelize Muslims, and the conversion of a Muslim to another religion, which is apostasy, is an act punishable by death.[328] We know that the Persian news agency Fars News, which is close to the Iranian security forces, has exposed the underground home churches – which were subsequently closed and their leaders arrested – and called them criminal.[329] For the most part, the West takes the threat of Iran, as well as its grim human rights situation, as a matter of no concern. Even worse: while Christians are suffering in Iran and elsewhere in the world, the majority of Christendom in the West is like a spoiled Sleeping Beauty.

I have heard many pastors speak about Iran and the threat it causes to the State of Israel. I have heard it said that Iran can only pursue its intentions if it is first able to remove God from His throne. God is Israel's security guarantee. This is without a doubt! The Bible is full of promises of how God will protect the apple of His eye from the attacking forces. But I also believe that the enemy forces need a true revelation of God, before it is too late. It is by no means intended that we happy-go-lucky Christians in the West would sleep like Sleeping Beauty while Christians are being persecuted around the world. I believe we all should do our part not only to be a witness but also to pray for the situation in Iran. The Bible seriously compels us to this.

"So I sought for a man among them who would make a wall, and stand in the gap before Me on behalf of the land, that I should not destroy it; but I found no one."[330]

In 2015, Iran agreed to be part of a long-term agreement between the world powers, including the United States. But by May 2019, Iran had suspended the commitments it made under the agreement. The IAEA now says that Iran has increased its production of enriched uranium.[331] By the beginning of 2020, an increasing number of EU Member States have joined the INSTEX mechanism, which allows them to trade with Iran, bypassing sanctions.[332]

Where is this leading us?

12 Jerusalem – The Glory Is Revealed

"Remember the former things of old, for I am God, and there is no other; I am God, and there is none like Me, declaring the end from the beginning, and from ancient times things that are not yet done, saying, 'My counsel shall stand, and I will do all My pleasure ... I bring My righteousness near, it shall not be far off; My salvation shall not linger, and I will place salvation in Zion, for Israel My glory.'"[333]

It is a typical Jerusalem morning. The morning is crisp and cool, for during the night, the wind has been blowing from the many hills that surround the city. The sun is not yet up in its full force, but rays of light caress the golden stone of the buildings around me. I sense a light perfume of cypress and rosemary in the early morning air.

As I start my car for my daily route to my office, I happen to look upwards. On a balcony above me, I see a man wearing a tallit, a prayer shawl. The man is praying. With a sudden wonderful clarity, I remember again that this is where I live: I live in Jerusalem. For thousands of years, prayer has been an unbreakable part of this city and its daily life. The tallit, the blue and white prayer shawl, too, has been a part of this city for many years. It is safe to live in this city – a city where God Himself lives among His people.

Later that day, I sit at my hairdressers. We speak about the city, where his family has lived for several generations. "My friend," I say to him, "always remember that it is easy to pray in this city, because this is God's home on earth." Later, he keeps repeating my simple words. Like so many secular Jews, in his heart he still understands the deep connection, the special relationship between God and His people. I can see that my words have made *a deep impression in his mind, since he cannot stop repeating them again and again.*

Afterwards, I go with a friend to the Kotel, The Western Wall. In the Jerusalem night, the wall reflects a strange white light – I can never approach the Wall without remembering where I am. White doves sit in the cracks and crevices of the wall. Suddenly, I have a thought: birds have made the Wall their home, which means that they live in the constant Presence of the Lord. I look at the woman praying next to me and suddenly feel like expressing what I just thought. "Those birds see God's face every day." She smiles at me; she does not deny the reality of what I have just said. Clearly, it is only here that I can say something like this aloud. It is only in Jerusalem that I can continuously speak about God without being considered a lunatic. I hardly know of another place in the whole wide world where people express their state of health by saying, "Baruch Ha-Shem," "Blessed is God." Nowhere else do people make plans with the qualifying sentence, "Be-Ezrat Ha-Shem," "With God's Help." This is the Land, and these are the People of God. Here God's Holy Name and His Word are a part of our everyday life.

This is Jerusalem, the City of the Great King.

"Lord, I have loved the habitation of Your house, And the place where Your glory dwells."[334]

God's word regarding His people is clear. Many Bible teachers have written about Israel and God; it is not my goal here to restate the case that has already been made throughout this book.[335] What is so clear is that the very foundation of God's expressed promises lies in His character as a faithful and trustworthy God. Should God cancel His promises or negate His covenants, His very character could be called into question. God Himself confirms His covenants with His people, for this is what He says about Himself: *"For I am the Lord, I do not change."*[336] Jesus confirmed this basic Biblical principle when He emphasized the validity of the Law and the Prophets:

"Do not think that I came to destroy the Law or the Prophets. I did not come to destroy but to fulfill. For assuredly, I say to you, till heaven and earth pass away, one jot or one title will by no means pass away from the law till all is fulfilled"[337]

If this is true, how is it possible that different interpreters of the Scriptures come to such different conclusions when analyzing the nature of the covenants? Why is there an attempt to deny the validity of God's covenants? Undoubtably, there is always a human factor present, which causes us to read things we would like to see written. In other words, the Bible becomes to us a book that confirms thoughts we already have. On the other hand, it is also possible that the spiritual climate of our times influences the way we read. As time goes by, it becomes more and more unpopular to declare the Bible as the sole truth. As accusations of narrow-mindedness and discrimination increase with regard to Biblical principles, it will be easier to give them up altogether.

The problem is that God's word is absolute. There is no justification in the Bible for changing any of its fundamental principles as times change. The Bible speaks about our day and time in a very clear and concise manner. In Scripture, we find a description of all the nations coming against Jerusalem and God standing up and fighting for His people. God fought for His people in 1948, 1967, 1973, 1991, 2006 and 2014, as well as on many occasions of terrorism. This will happen again in the future. We are the intended audience of God's word. We must stand on the right side of history.

"In that day the Lord will defend the inhabitants of Jerusalem; the one who is feeble among them in that day shall be like David, and the house of David shall be like God, like the Angel of the Lord before them. It shall be in that day that I will seek to destroy all the nations that come against Jerusalem."[338]

One of the prophets relevant to this issue is the prophet *Joel*. The name Joel means "The Lord is God" in Hebrew. We know very little about his background, and even the dates of his life are unknown to us. One of Joel's prophecies used the allegory of locusts to describe a fateful military attack. In agriculture, we know that locusts do indeed destroy all the crops as they move through an area.

Joel spoke about dividing the land of Israel. Dividing God's land would lead to judgment from the Lord Himself. He will judge the nations of the world according to how they have dealt with His Land – His property. When considering land in general, we all understand that we cannot build on any land without an agreement confirming our rights as landowners. It was exactly in this way that God chose a piece of land for Himself – He designated this Land for the people of Israel. We saw earlier that God divided the whole earth into different nations, each receiving their own portion. *"...He set the boundaries of the peoples according to the number of the children of Israel."*[339] This is confirmed in the New Testament: *"And He has made from one blood every nation of men to dwell on all the face of the earth, and has determined their pre-appointed times and the boundaries of their dwellings..."*[340]

According to Joel, nations will be taken into the Valley of Jehoshaphat – the Valley of Judgment – because they have violated the principles of land ownership. Joel is literally speaking about the Valley of Judgment here, for the Hebrew word *Jehoshaphat* means "God Judges." Jesus made the same case when speaking to His disciples about the judgment of the nations: *"All the nations will be gathered before Him, and He will separate them one from another, as a shepherd divides his sheep from the goats..."*[341]

The most important thing we need to understand is the reason for God's judgment of the nations. Why does God judge the nations? Joel describes it clearly as being connected to the division of His Land:

"For behold, in those days and at that time, when I bring back the captives of Judah and Jerusalem, I will also gather all nations, and bring them down to the Valley of Jehoshaphat; and I will enter into judgment with them there on account of My people, My heritage Israel, whom they have scattered among the nations; they have also divided up My land."[342]

If indeed there exists a spirit of our times, what kind of a spirit is it in relation to Israel? How do we recognize it? Can we say that it is not just a spirit against the State of Israel, but also an anti-Jewish spirit? Immediately, a specific event comes to mind that gives an accurate expression to the spirit of our days. The United Nations has designated January 27 as International Holocaust Memorial Day for its Member States, recognizing that January 27, 1945, was the day when Auschwitz-Birkenau was liberated by the Soviet troops. It has indeed become a global day of remembrance. On that very date in 2013, *The Sunday Times*, a highly rated British publication, allowed a picture to be posted, a caricature drawn by the famous artist *Gerald Scarfe*. In the picture, the Israeli Prime Minister, Benyamin Netanyahu, was portrayed building a wall. Instead of building with bricks and cement, he was building using the blood and bodies of Palestinians. Many people from around the globe protested the appearance of such a picture, especially on such a date. However, according to the initial reaction by *The Sunday Times*, there was simply no connection between the publication of the image and Holocaust Memorial Day. The President of the European Jewish Congress, Moshe Kantor, said: *"Amazingly ... this cartoon was published days after the only democracy in the Middle East, Israel, underwent fully democratic elections."*[343] Indeed, the caricature is a surprising key to understanding the Jew-hatred that targets the Jewish State right now. Examples are many.

One of the key characteristics of the modern anti-Israel hatred is how it sees itself. Very often, it is claimed that anti-Israel attitudes or excessive criticism of (real or perceived) Israeli actions are not anti-Jewish, but just anti-Israel. This is very difficult to believe when the accusations used against the only Jewish State in the world are the very same accusations that have always been made against the Jews. The symbolism that is employed against the Jewish State comes from classical anti-Semitism and is easily recognizable as such. The caricature by Scarfe, while by no means unique, serves as an example of many such caricatures with a traditional anti-Jewish motif.

As was explained earlier in this book, one of the oldest and most enduring false accusations against the Jews is what is known as the Blood Libel. The Blood Libel claims that Jews kidnap Christians, preferably children, and use their blood for their sinister religious purposes. Scarfe's picture would be clearly understandable to an illiterate person from the

Middle Ages – these people would obviously not recognize the face of the Israeli Prime Minister, but they would identify the man as a Jew. The picture would also work well in Nazi anti-Jewish propaganda. If this is the case, who are the media serving by their anti-Israel writings and drawings? Who are they working for when they use their talents in this manner? There are sadly many examples in the Western media today.

"Woe to those who call evil good, and good evil; who put darkness for light, and light for darkness…"[344]

Toward the end of 2013, the European Union published a report based on an inquiry undertaken by its office FRA (Agency for Fundamental Rights) around the Member States of the European Union. According to this report, there are European Jews who have already considered moving to Israel because of anti-Semitism; the anti-Semitic cases vary from little-publicized verbal comments to arson, murder and well-publicized cases of terrorism. All of this has happened because anti-Jewish attitudes are encouraged and fueled by different sectors of the European society. According to this research by the EU, about 40% of Europeans believe that Israelis murder Palestinians; at the same time, there is talk in various Member States about banning the kosher slaughter of meat, as well as ritual circumcision. Radical Islam is obviously bringing in a completely new pressure.[345] The world-famous anti-Semitism expert and professor at the Hebrew University of Jerusalem, *Robert Wistrich*, before his untimely death, urged European Jews to leave Europe.[346]

In remembering that most of Europe's Jews are descendants of Holocaust victims or survivors, one cannot but shudder at the ramifications of such statements. Does this mean that European Jews are indeed now confronting the same choices their great-grandparents had to make? Is this only the situation in Europe, or does it mean that in other Western nations, including the United States, Jews will have to face the same pressures and choices? Will this new reality have to be faced very soon?

According to the December 2018 FRA report on anti-Semitism – which covered 12 Member States of the European Union and included the staggering number of 16,500 individuals – there are three trends to take into account:

1) Anti-Semitism **undermines Jews' feelings of safety and security**, as Jews become targets of harassment and attacks;
2) **Harassment** has become normalized;
3) **Discrimination** in key areas of life remains invisible;
4) Anti-Semitism is deep-rooted and **increasingly normalized.**

As more than seventy years have passed since the end of World War II in 1945, we can clearly identify a historic Golden Age, a period of unprecedented peace, tolerance and prosperity that followed the war. The European Union put forth an effort of rebuilding and reconstruction born from the ashes of the war, bringing in its wake a new tolerance for the European Jewish communities. In the United States, the period of peace and prosperity has been much longer, giving unprecedented rights to minorities, including to its well-integrated Jewish community. Now, more than seventy years later, we can identify troubling trends and signs of a change. The suspicion and hatred that now targets the Jewish State is only one of these signs. Even churches and entire congregations have come under the spell of hatred that targets the Jewish State.

Don Finto, a well-known Bible teacher, expressed it well in drawing attention to what Jesus said about the days of Noah. There were many in the days of Noah who remained ignorant of what was happening, but many knew and understood.[347] In other words, if we look back in history, we can see the possibilities and dangers of our own time.

One thing that is clearly identifiable in our world today is the breakdown of Judeo-Christian values. This development has taken place all over the Western world, even in countries that share these same values and have based our culture on them. This wider cultural trend can easily enter churches and communities – and if it is allowed, it means that, as Christians, we are aiding and facilitating the fight against our own values, not for them. Popular culture, media and new legislation can all be identified as factors that serve to weaken Judeo-Christian values, and these phenomena do not happen in a vacuum. The breakdown in Judeo-Christian values is related to the pressure the Jewish State finds itself under. The attitudes of many churches toward Israel are a result of absorbing the spirit of our times and allowing it to shape our views.

So, how is our attitude toward the Bible related to all of this? It is possible that churches, in increasing numbers, will reject the values of the Bible as they become more and more uncomfortable with them at this time in history. If this should be the case, Israel will certainly be one issue in which this rejection of the Bible will be seen. Supporting Israel is becoming more and more difficult as the world's political situation develops in a critical direction. It is by no means a coincidence that the very churches that teach Replacement Theology are also openly anti-Israel.[348] Just as in the Medieval world, where anti-Jewish theology became a social law, anti-Israel theology is now becoming a political practice. If this is done so that churches can be acceptable to the wider community, then this is a huge mistake and extremely short-sighted. The very same groups that campaign against Israel are also campaigning against Bible-believing Christians, so it will be impossible to please them. The cultural fight marginalizes Bible-believing Christians because of their views, but also because of the support these Christians are willing to extend to the Jewish State. It goes without saying that the Biblically based worldview includes support for the Jewish State. What is so interesting is that the pressure to conform no longer comes solely from outside churches, but increasingly from within them.

This situation can be examined in light of the actions of the liberators during World War II. Why did the liberators agree to go to Europe to fight, sometimes in situations in which their death was assured? Why would anyone come and fight in other people's wars? The answer is actually very simple. The liberators came to war-torn Europe in the first place because they knew what they were fighting for. But, having said that, we clearly understand that just arriving in Europe was not enough. The liberators would never have won the war had they not been able to identify their enemy. Fraternizing with the enemy would also have brought a sure loss.

There is a clear meaning in all of this. In the Hebrew language, we have such concepts as *yirat Elohim*, meaning "Fear of God," and from the Talmud, *yirat shamayim*, meaning "Fear of the Heavens." Both concepts relate to the respect we should feel toward God. According to ancient Jewish wisdom, having this kind of awe and fear toward God is the deepest expression of our love for Him. The practical expression of this awe is how we treat God's Word. The key to knowing God's will is through His Word. The Word has to be in the most respected position in our lives. As Christians living in these challenging times, we need to treat God's Word with awe and respect that knows no bounds.

"Even the stork in the heavens knows her appointed times; and the turtledove, the swift, and the swallow observe the time of their coming. But My people do not know the judgment of the Lord. How can you say, 'We are wise, and the law of the Lord is with us'? Look, the false pen of the scribe certainly works falsehood. The wise men are ashamed, they are dismayed and taken. Behold, they have rejected the word of the Lord; so what wisdom do they have?"[349]

"The statutes of the Lord are right, rejoicing the heart; the commandment of the Lord is pure, enlightening the eyes; the fear of the Lord is clean, enduring forever; the judgments of the Lord are true and righteous altogether. More to be desired are they than gold…"[350]

As we understand the fact that traditional anti-Jewish attitudes and accusations are increasingly expressed with regard to the Jewish State, we also realize that, in terms of this issue, many churches have decided to go with the flow rather than swimming against the tide. This is extremely disturbing because of the nature of the hatred that targets the Jewish State –in many ways, it is a hostility that actually targets God's word. It is related not to political issues, but to God's purposes for this time. As the church, we share a responsibility, not just in terms of our immediate community, but also in upholding God's truth for the wider society to see.

It is not that I do not know what the critics of Israel have to say. In their thinking, Israel does not represent the Jews, and you can therefore hate Israel without hating the Jews – this way, you are not an anti-Semite no matter what you say. This argument is empty and void of content because it is so easily refuted. The fates of the Nation State of Israel and of the Jews in the Diaspora are tied together. Even Israeli schoolchildren, who have never experienced the Holocaust nor any kind of Diaspora, identify Holocaust Studies as something related to Judaism and their Jewish identity. When I speak in churches, I tend to emphasize the universal, moral teaching of the Holocaust, while for Israeli youth, the lessons are first and foremost Jewish. Research proves that the Holocaust is the ultimate experience of Diaspora helplessness, and it has become a central feature of their Israeli identity. Each Jewish person has to identify with the Holocaust and its victims even if they never experienced it.[351] In so many ways, Israel today represents everything that is Jewish. It is thus impossible to uphold the artificial separation between the Jewish communities around the world and the State of Israel. This means that, in many cases, criticism of Israel spills over to the area of ancient hostility: anti-Semitism. Needless to say, the Bible does not make a distinction between God's people whether they live in the Diaspora or in the Land of Israel.

Israel is naturally a geographical entity, a real piece of land, which God gave to His people. Jerusalem is the heart and soul of that area. God, according to His Word, dwells in Jerusalem. The word *yerushalaiym* has many meanings, all of which are important for our understanding of the future. Jerusalem is a City of *shalom*, Peace; a city that is *shalem*, whole, and *mushlam*, perfect. It is also God's heritage. It can be said, then, that Jerusalem is a very real and physical capital of the modern State of Israel, but it is also the City of God. It is where I live today, but it is also the City of God as a Messianic vision. In that context, as written throughout the Bible, Jerusalem is called by its Hebrew name *Tzion*, Zion. The Hebrew word "tzion" literally means to mark or to sign; this really is the geographical place God marked for Himself, for His eternal possession.

"Afterward he brought me to the gate, the gate that faces toward the east. And behold, the glory of the God of Israel came from the way of the east. His voice was like the sound of many waters; and the earth shone with His glory... And the glory of the Lord came into the temple by way of the gate which faces toward the east. The Spirit lifted me up and brought me into the inner court; and behold, the glory of the Lord filled the temple. Then I heard Him speaking to me from the temple, while a man stood beside me. And He said to me, 'Son of man, this is the place of My throne and the place of the soles of My feet, where I will dwell in the midst of the children of Israel forever.'"[352]

The God of heaven and earth, to whom belongs everything He created, marked one place for Himself, one city, which is called Yerushalaiym, Jerusalem. This City of God is the heritage of peace. It is a perfect city. It is a city which is whole. It is God's heritage forever and ever. So it shall be.

Endnotes

The endnotes have been used primarily when presenting a direct quotation. There are many poems, songs and such in the book; these all have either been referenced in the text or have an endnote.

For information that comes from a museum or an exhibition, the name of the relevant institution is given either in the text or as an endnote.

For items that are very much known or accepted, endnotes have generally not been used. If the information could be contested or many and varied views exist, an endnote is given. If readers can find the information by a simple Google search, sources have usually not been given.

When more information on a story or person is available and may interest readers, I have tried to give that reference even if my information is generally accepted and not controversial.

All of the Bible quotations are referenced and come from the NKJV.

---

1. Genesis 1:26-27. Scripture taken from the New King James Version. 1982 by Thomas Nelson, Inc. Used by permission. All rights reserved.
2. Genesis 3:1
3. Genesis 2:17.
4. Genesis 3:3.
5. Genesis 3:6.
6. Genesis 3:9.
7. Yaakov Meir, Ha'aretz Magazine, September 4, 2013.
8. Isaiah 55:7.
9. Genesis 4:7.
10. Genesis 20:6.

11 Genesis 4:9.
12 Genesis 4:9.
13 Genesis 22:2.
14 See Numbers 22-24.
15 Numbers 23:8,20.
16 Jeremiah 27:6.
17 Ezra 1:2.
18 Nehemiah 2:8.
19 Exodus 17:16.
20 See, 1. Samuel 15.
21 Esther 9:13.
22 Exodus 20:2.
23 Irving Greenberg, The Jewish Way: Living The Holidays (Northvale, NJ, and Jerusalem: Jason Aronson, 1998), p. 2.
24 Isaiah 43:1.
25 Genesis 35:16-19.
26 Genesis 12:2-3.
27 Genesis 14.
28 Psalm 110:4.
29 Genesis 15:11-12.
30 Genesis 15:17.
31 Genesis 23.
32 Genesis 13:18.
33 Genesis 18:1-19.
34 Isaiah 41:8.
35 Genesis 26:24-25.
36 Genesis 28:13-14.
37 Genesis 37-46.
38 Genesis 45:5.
39 See, for example, Alex Woolf, A Short History of the World: The Story of Mankind from Prehistory to the Modern   Day (New York: Metro Books, 2008).
40 Exodus 2:24-25.
41 Exodus 2:5-6.
42 Acts 7:21-22.
43 Exodus 6:6-7.
44 Numbers 13:30.
45 Numbers 14:24.
46 www.bibleplaces.com
47 2 Samuel 2:1, 5:4-7, 10.
48 Ruth 4:11.
49 History of Jerusalem: Myth and Reality of King David's Jerusalem by Daniel Gavron, www.jewishvirtuallibrary.org
50 1 Kings 2:10.
51 1 Kings 15:11.
52 1 Kings 16:25.
53 1 Kings 15:4-5.
54 1 Kings 18.
55 2 Kings 10:32.
56 Miller p. 48.
57 Jeremiah 18:8.
58 Daniel 5: 9 – 12.
59 Ezra 1:3.
60 Nehemiah 4:16-17.
61 Woolf p. 64.
62 Daniel 11.
63 1 John 2:18.
64 Acts 3:2-6.
65 Paul's letter to the Philippians 4:22.
66 Talmud, Ta'anit 2a.

67 http://timetracts.com/wordpress/wordpress/tracts/church/ten_major-persecutions-of-the-early-church/
http://individual.utoronto.ca/hayes/earlychurch/lecture1.htm
68 http://www.allaboutreligion.org/history-of-christianity-in-rome-faq.htm
69 Jacob R. Marcus, The Jew in the Medieval World: A Source Book, 315-1791 (Cincinnati: Sinai Press, 1983), pp. 3-4.
70 Karen Spector, "God on the Gallows: Reading the Holocaust through Narratives of Redemption," Research in the Teaching of English, Vol. 42, No. 1 (August 2007), pp. 7-55.
71 1 John 1:5.
72 Carol Rittner, Stephen David Smith, and Irene Steinfeldt, (eds.), The Holocaust and the Christian World: Reflections on the Past, Challenges for the Future (London: Continuum, 2000), p. 174.
73 Derek Prince, The Destiny of Israel and the Church: Understanding the Middle East Through Biblical Prophecy (Charlotte: Derek Prince Ministries, 1992), p. 23.
74 The Gospel of Matthew 26:54, 56.
75 The Gospel of Matthew 20:19.
76 See for example, Merrill Bolender, When the Cross became a Sword: The Origin and Consequences of Replacement Theology (self-published, 2011).
77 https://www.jewishvirtuallibrary.org/blood-libel
78 https://www.jewishvirtuallibrary.org/john-chrysostom-x00b0;
http://www.catholic.org/saints/saint.php?saint_id=64
79 Saint John Chrysostom, On the Incomprehensible Nature of God, trans. Paul W. Harkins (Washington, DC: The Catholic University of America Press, 2010), p. 163.
80 These utterances are found in slightly varied translations in John Chrysostom's Eight Homilies against the Jews.
81 John Chrysostom, Homily I, VI 7.
82 St. Augustine, Contra Judaeos.
83 Paul's letter to the Romans 11:25-26, 29.
84 http://www.luther.de/en/kontext/juden.html
85 http://www.jewishvirtuallibrary.org/jsource/anti-semitism/Luther_on_Jews.html
86 http://www.ushmm.org/propaganda/themes/writing-the-news/ http://www.zionism-israel.com/his/judeophobia7b.htm
87 Quoted in Randy Weiss, The Passion Conspiracy: Did the Jews Kill Christ or was Jesus the Victim of Identity Theft? (Cedar Hill, TX: EICB, 2004). Dr. Weiss quotes the original sources.
88 The Gospel of John 4:22.
89 The Gospel of John 7:10, 14.
90 The Gospel of John 7:37-38.
91 Isaiah 12:3.
92 The Gospel of John 10:22-23.
93 The Gospel of John 10:22-42.
94 The Gospel of Matthew 26:17-29; The Gospel of Mark 14:12-15 and the Gospel of Luke 22:14-20.
95 http://www.haaretz.com/jewish-world/the-day-chabad-came-to-the-last-supper-1.425442
96 The Letter of James 3:10.
97 Prince, p. 15.
98 Jeremiah 31:37.
99 Jeremiah 33:23-26.
100 Paul's Letter to the Romans 11:20-21.
101 Genesis 1; The Gospel of John 1.
102 Isaiah 59:8.
103 Woolf, pp. 126-127.
104 For an easy yet profound explanation of this theme, see https://www.history.com/topics/middle-ages/crusades or https://www.bbc.co.uk/bitesize/guides/zjbj6sg/revision/4
105 Woolf, pp. 114-115.
106 Daniel 3:17-18.
107 See, for instance, https://www.myjewishlearning.com/article/from-golden-to-grim-jewish-life-in-muslim-spain/; https://www.thejc.com/comment/comment/so-what-did-the-muslims-do-for-the-jews-1.33597 I also recommend, Vivian B. Mann, Thomas F. Glick, and Jerrilynn D. Dodds, eds., Convivencia: Jews, Muslims, and Christians in Medieval Spain (New York: George Braziller Inc., 2007).
108 More information on the theme for instance in the Jewish Encyclopedia.
109 For more basic information on the Spanish Inquisition, see https://www.newworldencyclopedia.org/entry/Spanish_Inquisition or

       https://www.history.com/topics/religion/inquisition.
110 Genesis 2:2.
111 Jacob Keegstra, God's Prophetic Feasts: The Joy and Importance of Seasonal Celebrations (Jerusalem: Tsur Tsina Publications, 2012), p. 20.
112 This English translation of the poem can be found at
       http://www.jewishmag.com/128mag/spanish_forced_conversion/spanish_forced_conversion.htm
113 Luis Roniger, Antisemitism, Real or Imagined? Chávez, Iran, Israel, and the Jews (Jerusalem: The Hebrew University of Jerusalem, 2009).
114 http://www.angelfire.com/ct/halevi/halevi-poem4.html
115 Ecclesiastes 3:1-2,8.
116 For basic information on the Age of Enlightenment, see for instance,
       https://plato.stanford.edu/entries/enlightenment/.
117 See www.voltaire.ox.ac.uk
118 See https://www.jewishvirtuallibrary.org/alfred-dreyfus-and-ldquo-the-affair-rdquo
119 I recommend visiting the Herzl Museum in Jerusalem for more information on this story.
120 For an explanation of racial hygiene, see https://encyclopedia.ushmm.org/content/en/article/the-biological-state-nazi-racial-hygiene-1933-1939
121 Bolender, pp. 47-48; Norbert Kampe (ed.), The Wannsee Conference and the Genocide of the European Jews (Berlin: House of the Wannsee Conference, 2009), p. 32.
122 Brauhaus, Tivoli, Berlin, 1892, The Wannsee Conference, p. 31.
123 The Wannsee Conference, p. 32.
124 Rink, The Wannsee Conference, p. 37.
125 Paul's First Letter to the Thessalonians 5:4-6.
126 Amos Elon, The Pity of It All: A Portrait of the German-Jewish Epoch, 1743-1933 (New York: Picador, 2002).
127 Rink, The Wannsee Conference, p. 23.
128 Bärbel Schrader and Jurgen Schebera, The Golden Twenties: Art and Literature in the Weimar Republic, trans. Katherine Vanovitch (New Haven: Yale University Press, 1990); Rink, The Wannsee Conference, p. 23.
129 See more about this in www.holocaustexplained.org
130 Adolf Hitler to Adolf Gemlich, September 6, 1919, in The Wannsee Conference, p. 39.
131 More information on the aftermath of WWI and the rise of Nazi party, see, www.holocaustexplained.org
132 https://www.facinghistory.org/topics/holocaust/weimar-republic
133 Rink, The Wannsee Conference, p. 71.
134 Erwin W. Lutzer, When a Nation forgets God: 7 Lessons We Must Learn From Nazi Germany (Chicago: Moody Publishers, 2010), pp. 41-42.
135 Daniel 8:24-25.
136 Hitler's rise to power is explained easily and clearly at
       https://www.bbc.co.uk/bitesize/guides/z3bp82p/revision/1, https://www.britannica.com/biography/Adolf-Hitler/Rise-to-power or https://www.history.com/topics/world-war-ii/adolf-hitler-1
137 Hermann Göring to Reich minister of Interior Wilhelm Frick, January 24, 1939, in, The Wannsee Conference, p. 86.
138 The Wannsee Conference, p. 81.
139 Bella Gutterman and Avner Shalev, eds., To Bear Witness: Holocaust Remembrance at Yad Vashem (Jerusalem: Yad Vashem, 2005), p. 98.
140 Michael Berenbaum in The Holocaust and the Christian World, p. 71.
141 http://www.ushmm.org/wlc/en/article.php?ModuleId=10005200
142 Quoted in Leah Goldstein,"Justice on Trial," Yad Vashem Magazine, Volume 44, Winter 2007: 7.
143 Ibid.
144 http://www.ushmm.org/outreach/en/article.php?ModuleId=10007698
145 Israel Gutman, ed., The Righteous of Austria: Heroes of the Holocaust (Vienna: Austrian Federal Ministry for Foreign Affairs, 2006), pp. 16-17.
146 Gutman p. 180.
147 Miller p. 184.
148 The Wannsee Conference, p. 86.
149 Daniel 10:7-9, 14.
150 Oxford English Dictionary, "Genocide," quoting the Sunday Times, October 21, 1945; see also Raphael Lemkin, "Genocide," American Scholar, Volume 15, no. 2 (April 1946), pp. 227-230.

151 United Nations General Assembly Resolution 96 (I), https://undocs.org/en/A/RES/96(I)
152 Norman L. Friedman, "Teaching about the Holocaust," Teaching Sociology, Vol. 12, No. 4 (1985): pp. 449-461.
153 Eckahrdt Alice L. and Roy, The Holocaust and the Enigma of Uniqueness: A Philosophical Effort at Practical Clarification, The Annals of the American Academy, 450, July 1980, pp. 165-178.
154 Safira Rapoport, ed., Yesterdays and then Tomorrows: Holocaust Anthology of Testimonies and Readings for Holocaust Study Through Literature, Excursions to Poland, and Holocaust Memorial Ceremonies (Jerusalem: Yad Vashem, 2002), pp. 44-46.
155 This classic Holocaust poem can be found at the Yad Vashem Museum in the section on Warsaw Ghetto.
156 Janus Korczak, Ghetto Diary (New York: Holocaust Library, 1978).
157 The Gospel of John 15:13.
158 Peter Klein in The Wannsee Conference, p. 137.
159 The full text of this speech can be read at https://www.nationalchurchillmuseum.org/blood-toil-tears-and-sweat.html
160 Lars, Westerlund, Suomalaiset SS-vapaaehtoiset ja väkivaltaisuudet 1941-1943 (Helsinki: Kansallisarkisto, 2019).
161 Army orders, Erich von Manstein, 11. Commander-in-chief, November 20, 1941, in The Wannsee Conference, p. 110.
162 Westerlund, p. 288. Reference is made to Verbrechen der Wehrmacht: Dimensionen der Vernichtungskrieges 1941-1944 (Hamburg, 2002).
163 Kurt Werner of Special Commando Unit 4a of task squads, quoted in Irena Steinfeldt, How Was It Humanly Possible? A Study of Perpetrators and Bystanders during the Holocaust (Jerusalem: Yad Vashem, 2002), p. 64.
164 Statement of Schröder, of Police Battalion 322, quoted in Steinfeldt, p. 65.
165 Steinfelt, p. 118.
166 Reinhardt Heydrich's invitation sent on November 29, 1941, to the Wannasee Conference, published in The Wannsee Conference, pp. 158-159.
167 Governor Hans Frank in Krakow, December 16, 1941. The Work Diary of Germany's Governor to Poland 1939-1945, published in The Wannsee Conference, p. 163.
168 Marcus Gryglewski in The Wannsee Conference, pp. 253-257.
169 Here I rely on information from Yad Vashem. At the Yad Vashem Museum, it is possible to see models of these camps as well as the figures.
170 Christa Schikorra in The Wannsee Conference, pp. 306-307.
171 This poem is shown at the Yad Vashem Museum.
172 Lamentations 2:13.
173 Kampe, The Wannsee Conference, pp. 173-175.
174 Quoted in The Wannsee Conference, p. 361.
175 Corrie ten Boom, Elizabeth Sherrill, and John Sherrill, The Hiding Place: The Triumphant True Story of Corrie ten Boom (Grand Rapids, MI: Chosen Books, 1971).
176 Obadiah 11-12, 15.
177 Daniel Schatz and Ruth Deech, "Ghosts of the Past," August 27, 2012, https://www.ynetnews.com/articles/0,7340,L-4273450,00.html
178 The writer was present in a special ceremony at Yad Vashem for the handing over of these valuable documents.
179 Quoted in Steinfeldt, p. 7.
180 For more information, see, Auschwitz from A to Z. An Illustrated History of the Camp. Oswiecim: Auschwitz Birkenau State Museum, 2013.
181 This quotation appears at the Yad Vashem Museum by the Hall of Remembrance,
182 Translation by Sarah Honig https://sarahhonig.com/2014/05/28/a-small-tragedy/
183 The entire event is documented in the movie Eagles Over Auschwitz, Ephraim and Stephanie Kaye, Jerusalem, 2005. Translated from the Hebrew.
184 The Gospel of Matthew 25:45.
185 See www.hebrewsongs.com
186 Deuteronomy 30:19.
187 The story has been covered in numerous books, films and such. Yad Vashem's web site has resources as well as an exhibition on the topic.
188 See, for example: https://plato.stanford.edu/entries/adorno/
189 A classic is Browning, Christopher, Ordinary Men: Reserve Police Battalion 101 and the Final Solution in Poland (Harper Perennial, 2017).
190 Steinfeldt, pp. 130-135.

191 In addition to the film documentary, Bauer's thoughts were documented in the National Post, June 4, 2005.
192 Walter Stier, in charge of the timetable planning of the German railway in Eastern Europe, Dusseldorf, 1946, published in Steinfeldt, p. 111.
193 Hans Pitsch, station master Bialystok, Puola, Dusseldorf, 1946, published in Steinfeldt, p. 111.
194 Egon Weber, railroad engineer who drove the train from Bialystok to Treblinka, Dusseldorf, 1946, published in Steinfeldt, p. 111.
195 Echoes and Reflections: A Multimedia Curriculum of the Holocaust (Anti-Defamation League, Survivors of the Shoah Visual History Foundation and Yad Vashem, 2005), p. 23
196 Thoughts of Elie Wiesel are, for example, in Carol Rittner and Sondra Myers, eds., The Courage to Care: Rescuers of Jews during the Holocaust (New York: NYU Press, 1986). Wiesel lectured all around the world, and his own fictional and autobiographical production includes plenty of thoughts on these themes.
197 Elie Wiesel, in Our Living Legacy (Jerusalem: Yad Vashem, 2003).
198 Zvi Gill in Our Living Legacy.
199 Yad Vashem Stands by Pius Text, 19.10.2008, www.israelnationalnews.com
200 Franklin H. Littell in The Holocaust and the Christian World, p. 45. Doris L. Bergen in The Holocaust and the Christian World, p. 52.
201 The Holocaust and the Christian World, pp. 49 and 62.
202 http://www.ynetnews.com/articles/0,7340,L-3288687,00.html
203 One of the most known researchers of this topic is Susannah Heschel, who lectured at Yad Vashem in 2012.
204 Lutzer, pp. 43-44.
205 Lutzer, pp. 15-16. Lutzer is the pastor emeritus of Moody Church in Chicago and a known author on Holocaust-related topics.
206 Paul's letter to the Romans 13:1-2, 7.
207 Bergen in The Holocaust and the Christian World, p. 49.
208 The Gospel of Matthew 22:21.
209 Quoted in The Holocaust and the Christian World, p. 48.
210 Lutzer, p. 62, 67.
211 John K. Roth and Carol Rittner in The Holocaust and the Christian World, p. 39.
212 Bergen cites Helen Fein in The Holocaust and the Christian World, p. 54.
213 Ernst Christian Helmreich, The German Churches under Hitler: Background, Struggle, and Epilogue (Detroit: Wayne State University Press, 1979), p. 329.
214 Bergen in The Holocaust and the Christian World, p. 49; The Holocaust and the Christian World, p. 63.
215 Ger van Roon, Ger in The Holocaust and the Christian World, p. 93.
216 The quotation is displayed at the Yad Vashem Museum in the section on Righteous Among the Nations.
217 Irena Stenfeldt, "Paying the Ultimate Price," Jerusalem Post, April 8, 2009
       https://www.jpost.com/Opinion/Columnists/Essay-Paying-the-ultimate-price
218 Quoted in Rittner and Meyers, Courage to Care, p. 2. Elie Wiesel's famous description can also be found on Yad Vashem's website: https://www.yadvashem.org/righteous/about-the-program.html
219 Mordecai Paldiel, the former director of the Righteous Among the Nations Department at Yad Vashem, has analyzed this in more detail. His article is found at https://www.yadvashem.org/righteous/resources/the-face-of-the-other-reflections-on-the-motivations-of-rescuers.html
220 Gutman, p. 38.
221 The full story can be found on Yad Vashem's website.
222 Eva Fogelman, Conscience and Courage: Rescuers of Jews during the Holocaust (New York: Anchor Books), 1994.
223 Stephen D. Smith quoting Karski in The Holocaust and the Christian World, p. 236.
224 The full story of Aristides de Sousa Mendes can be found on Yad Vashem's website:
       https://www.yadvashem.org/yv/en/exhibitions/righteous/mendes.asp
225 The whole story is as told on the Yad Vashem web site under the section of Righteous Among the Nations.
226 This famous, often-quoted sentence is found with the full story on Yad Vashem's website (https://www.yadvashem.org/yv/en/exhibitions/righteous/mendes.asp) as well as in many books on the Holocaust.
227 Exodus 2:5-6.
228 Joshua 2:3-4.
229 2.Chronicles 22:10-11.
230 Esther 2:10.
231 All the stories of the helpers are on Yad Vashem's website. For Schindler's story, see the movie Schindler's List (1993).

232 The story has been documented in countless articles, books and films. For understanding his thoughts, I recommend his own books, which are still available too.
233 Eric Metaxas, Bonhoeffer: Pastor, Martyr, Prophet, Spy (Nashville: Thomas Nelson, 2010), pp. 105-110.
234 Ralf Retter, Theological-Political Resistance: The role of Dietrich Bonhoeffer and Hans-Bernd von Haeften in the German Resistance against Hitler (Berlin: Logos Verlag Berlin, 2008), pp. 34-35.
235 Edwin Robertson, The Shame and the Sacrifice, p. 89.
236 Romans 13:1-2. See Dietrich Bonhoeffer, Selected Writings, ed. Edwin Robertson (London: Fount, 1995), pp. 45-47.
237 Robertson, pp. 84-85, 92-93; Metaxas, p. 222.
238 Metaxas, pp. 197-198; Dietrich Bonhoeffer, The Cost of Discipleship (New York: Collier Books, 1963), originally published in 1937 in Germany under the title Nachfolge.
239 Metaxas, p. 302.
240 Metaxas, p. 316.
241 The direct quotation is from the book of Matthew 26:52.
242 Retter, p. 46 and 48.
243 Retter, p. 44.
244 Metaxas, p. 380.
245 Metaxas, p. 480. I recommend the following webpage:
http://www.jewishvirtuallibrary.org/jsource/biography/Stauffenberg.html
246 Metaxas, p. 352.
247 Dietrich Bonhoeffer, The Cost of Discipleship (New York: Simon and Schuster, 1995), pp. 43-45.
248 Bonhoeffer, The Cost of Discipleship, p. 45.
249 The poem has been translated in slightly different variations by various translators.
250 Isaiah 45:3.
251 Henry R. Huttenbach, "Locating the Holocaust on the Genocide Spectrum: Towards a Methodology of Definition and Categorization," Holocaust and Genocide Studies Vol. 3, No. 3 (1988): pp. 289-303.
252 The role of the Jews and the unique position of the Holocaust in world history is discussed, for example, in Gavriel D. Rosenfeld, "The Politics of Uniqueness: Reflections on the Recent Polemical Turn in Holocaust and Genocide Scholarship," Holocaust and Genocide Studies Vol. 13, No. 1 (Spring 1999): pp. 28-61.
253 A clear presentation of these ideas can be found, for example, in Gunnar Heinsohn, "What Makes the Holocaust a Uniquely Unique Genocide?" Journal of Genocide Research Vol 2, No. 3 (2000): 411-430.
254 Samuel Bak's art is displayed all around the world, as well as in the Yad Vashem Museum of Holocaust Art. I also recommend Danna Nolan Fewell, Gary A. Phillips and Yvonne Sherwood, eds., Representing the Irreparable: The Shoah, the Bible, and the Art of Samuel Bak (Boston: Pucker Art Publications), 2008.
255 Emil L. Fackenheim, "The Holocaust and Philosophy," The Journal of Philosophy Vol. 82, No. 10 (October 1985): 505-514.
256 Ibid.
257 Jacob Neusner, "The Implications of the Holocaust," The Journal of Religion,Vol. 53 (July 1973), pp. 293-308, at p. 293.
258 The Gospel of John 4:24.
259 Michael McGarry in The Holocaust and the Christian World, p. 3.
260 Jobst Bittner, Breaking the Veil of Silence (Tuebingen: TOS Publishing, 2013), pp. 133-135.
261 Haynes in The Holocaust and the Christian World, pp. 174-176.
262 The Holocaust and the Christian World, p. 257.
263 Peggy Obbrecht in The Holocaust and the Christian World, p. 174-176.
264 Aumann, Moshe. The Protestant Churches and Israel, Jerusalem, 2008, p.8-9.
265 Reinhold Niebuhr, "Anger and Forgiveness," in Discerning the Signs of the Times: Sermons for Today and Tomorrow (New York: Charles Scribner's Sons, 1946), pp. 21-38.
266 Genesis 6:6.
267 Job 5:8-9.
268 Spector, p. 30.
269 For academic processing of the subject, see, for example, Walter Brueggemann, "Theodicy in a Social Dimension," Journal for the Study of the Old Testament Vol. 33 (1985): pp. 3-25. A more personal approach to the subject can be seen in, for example, Rabbi Harold Kushner, When Bad Things Happen to Good People (New York: Random House, 1981).
270 Henry Abramson, "The Esh Kodesh of Rabbi Kalonimus Kalmish Shapiro: A Hassidic Treatise on Communal Trauma from the Holocaust," Transcultural Psychiatry Vol. 37, No. 3 (September 2000): 321-335.
271 Robert Eisen, "A. J. Heschel's Rabbinic Theology as a Response to the Holocaust," Modern Judaism Vol. 23, No.

3 (2003): 211-225. See Abraham J. Heschel, God in Search of Man: A Philosophy of Judaism (New York: Farrar, Straus and Giroux, 1976 [reissue]).

272 Ibid.
273 Job 42:12.
274 Jacob Neusner, "The Implications of the Holocaust,", Vol. 53, No. 3 (1973): 293-308.
275 The Gospel of Luke 21:29-31.
276 Interview with the author in New York, August 21, 2013. The whole life story of Luna Kaufman is found in her autobiography, Luna's Life: A Journey of Forgiveness and Triumph (Margate, NJ: ComteQ Publishing, 2009).
277 Ezekiel 37:1-14.
278 Numbers are from Yad Vashem's sources.
279 See this writer's doctoral thesis on Jewish Refugees in Post-War Italy, 1945-1951 (Hebrew University of Jerusalem, 2004).
280 Ibid.
281 Ibid.
282 This information is from different sources including Yad Vashem.
283 Letter to Hebrews 11:37.
284 Isaiah 66:8.
285 Isaiah 37:32.
286 Isaiah 60:1-4, 10.
287 The figures are from the Jerusalem Post "Breaking the Barrier" appendix, August 2013.
288 The stages of the War of Independence can be found in various sources. See, for example, the Israeli Ministry of Foreign Affairs section on history at https://mfa.gov.il/mfa/aboutisrael/history/Pages/default.aspx
289 Gospel of Luke 21:24.
290 Gospel of Matthew 16:3; Paul's first letter to the Thessalonians 5:4.
291 Leviticus 25.
292 Ludwig Schneider, a well-known Messianic Bible teacher, commented in Israel Today, January 2013.
293 Isaiah 49:25.
294 Deuteronomy 32:8; Acts 17:26.
295 Ben Menahem in Maariv, March 2012.
296 Deuteronomy 32:7.
297 Dwight D. Eisenhower, Crusade in Europe (New York: Doubleday, 1948), 409. More on the US Army and liberation can be found, for instance, at https://www.jewishvirtuallibrary.org/u-s-army-and-the-holocaust
298 Israel Charny, interview, in Jerusalem Post Christian Edition, August 2012. See also www.ldeajournal.com July 17, 2011.
299 Proverbs 12: 17, 19.
300 Manfred Gerstenfeld, The Abuse of Holocaust Memory: Distortions and Responses (Jerusalem: Jerusalem Center for Public Affairs / Anti-Defamation League, 2009).
301 See for instance Colin Shindler, "The European Left and Its Trouble With Jews," New York Times, October 27, 2012 https://www.nytimes.com/2012/10/28/opinion/sunday/europes-trouble-with-jews.html
302 See Gerstenfeld's research.
303 https://www.ynetnews.com/articles/0,7340,L-4338799,00.html (January 30, 2013).
304 Israel Today, December 2012.
305 Israel Today, December 2012.
306 The conference was reported on by all Western media. See https://www.nytimes.com/2006/12/12/world/middleeast/12holocaust.html (December 12, 2006)..
307 https://www.ynetnews.com/articles/0,7340,L-4338215,00.html (January 29, 2013).
308 Alice L. Eckardt and A Roy Eckardt, "The Holocaust and the Enigma of Uniqueness: A Philosophical Effort at Practical Clarification," Annals of the American Academy of Political and Social Science Vol. 450 (July 1980), pp. 165-178.
309 Reported for instance, at https://jewishjournal.com/news/world/111312/
310 Proverbs 12:26.
311 Psalm 51:6.
312 The Gospel of John 8:32.
313 Isaiah 21:6.
314 Isaiah 54:17.
315 See, for example, Azar Nafisi, Reading Lolita in Tehran: A Memoir in Books (New York and Toronto: Random House), 2003; Mahbod Seraji, Rooftops of Tehran (New York: Berkley, 2009).
316 www.reuters.com September 18, 2009; www.npr.com September 25, 2009.

317 www.cnn.com August 30, 2009.
318 Chuck Freilich, "The United States, Israel, and Iran: Defusing an 'Existential' Threat," Arms Control Association, November 5, 2008.
319 Interview of Prime Minister Netanyahu by Herb Keinon, Jerusalem Post Christian Edition, November 2012.
320 Jerusalem Post Christian Edition, November 2012.
321 Ibid.
322 Ibid.
323 Israel Today, December 2012.
324 Jerusalem Post Christian Edition, November 2012.
325 The data is compiled from various sources. For potential attacks, see https://www.ynetnews.com/articles/0,7340,L-4338862,00.html (January 30, 2013).
326 Joel 3:16.
327 Jerusalem Post Christian Edition, November 2012.
328 https://www.csw.org.uk/2014/04/17/feature/2137/article.htm
329 Jerusalem Post Christian Edition, November 2012.
330 Ezekiel 22:30.
331 https://www.bbc.com/news/world-middle-east-48587347
332 See, for instance,https://www.euractiv.com/section/global-europe/news/six-european-countries-join-eu-iran-financial-trading-mechanism-instex/ (November 29, 2019).
333 Isaiah 46:9-10; 13.
334 Psalm 26:8.
335 See, for instance, David Pawson, Defending Christian Zionism (Ashford, UK: Anchor Recordings, 2008); Malcolm Hedding, Biblical Zionism series (ICEJ USA, 2004).
336 Malachi 3:6.
337 Matthew 5: 17-18.
338 Zechariah 12: 8-9.
339 Deuteronomy 32:8.
340 Acts 17:26.
341 Matthew 25:32.
342 Joel 3: 1-2.
343 The caricature is available online with key words, such as Gerald-Scarfe-Netanyahu-caricature.
344 Isaiah 5:20.
345 Michael Gurfinkel,You only Live Twice, Mosaic Magazine, August 2013.
346 Ibid.
347 Finto, p. 35.
348 Lecture by David Parsons, Spokesman, ICEJ, March 2013.
349 Jeremiah 8:7-9.
350 Psalm 19:8-10.
351 Yair Auron, Jack Katzenell, and David Silberklang, "The Holocaust and the Israeli Teacher," Holocaust and Genocide Studies Vol. 8, No. 2 (Fall 1994): 225-257.
352 Ezekiel 43:1-2; 4-7.